ISBN 978-1-331-11547-2
PIBN 10146875

1 MONTH OF
FREE
READING

at

www.ForgottenBooks.com

By purchasing this book you are eligible for one month membership to ForgottenBooks.com, giving you unlimited access to our entire collection of over 700,000 titles via our web site and mobile apps.

To claim your free month visit:
www.forgottenbooks.com/free146875

Similar Books Are Available from
www.forgottenbooks.com

A Syllabus of Modern European History, 1500-1919
by Herbert Darling Foster

Revolutionary Europe, 1789-1815
by H. Morse Stephens

An Account of Denmark
As It Was in the Year 1692, by Robert Molesworth

The Emperor William and His Reign, Vol. 1 of 2
by Edouard Simon

The Royal Marriage Market of Europe
by Princess Catherine Radziwill

History of the Netherlands
Holland and Belguim, by Alexander Young

France Under Louis XV, Vol. 1 of 2
by James Breck Perkins

The Cabinet of History
History of Switzerland, by Dionysius Lardner

History of the House of Austria
From the Accession of Francis I. to the Revolution of 1848, by Archdeacon Coxe

Balkan Problems and European Peace
by Noel Buxton

Norway and the Union With Sweden
by Fridtjof Nansen

The French Revolution and First Empire
An Historical Sketch, by William O'Connor Morris

Germany in the Nineteenth Century
Five Lectures, by J. H. Rose

The Great Condé and the Period of the Fronde, Vol. 1
A Historical Sketch, by Walter Fitz Patrick

The Historical Development of Modern Europe
From the Congress of Vienna to the Present Time, by Charles M. Andrews

Modern France, 1789-1895
by André Lebon

The Evolution of Prussia the Making of an Empire
by J. A. R. Marriott

Modern Spain, 1788-1898
by Martin Andrew Sharp Hume

Since Waterloo
A Short History of Europe and of the British Empire, 1815-1919, by Robert Jones

Italy
From 1494 to 1790, by Mrs. H. M. Vernon

THE SECRET TREATIES OF AUSTRIA–HUNGARY
VOLUME II

NEGOTIATIONS LEADING TO THE TREATIES OF THE TRIPLE ALLIANCE

WITH DOCUMENTARY APPENDICES

TRANSLATED BY

J. G. D'ARCY PAUL
AND
DENYS P. MYERS

17082

27.4.

CAMBRIDGE
HARVARD UNIVERSITY PRESS
LONDON: HUMPHREY MILFORD
OXFORD UNIVERSITY PRESS
1921

PREFACE BY THE AMERICAN EDITOR

THIS second volume of the Secret Treaties of Austria-Hungary offers to the English reading public the story of the negotiations of the five successive treaties of the Triple Alliance, and corresponds in the main to the second half of Professor Pribram's first German volume. In addition it contains in the appendices three hitherto unprinted agreements between Austria and Russia, which Professor Pribram has copied from the Vienna archives, namely the convention of Schönbrunn of 1873, the pact of Reichstadt of 1876, and the treaty of Budapest of 1877. The existence of these agreements has long been known, and the texts were consulted by the Hungarian writer, Wertheimer, in his biography of Count Andrássy, but they are now made public for the first time.

It has also seemed worth while, in a volume like this devoted to the history of the treaties of the Triple Alliance, to reproduce for convenience in reference and comparison some of the chief and not commonly accessible documents of the great rival league, the Dual Alliance between France and Russia. These were first given out to the world by the French Government in a Yellow Book after the fall of the Russian Empire, one of the signatories. Likewise the recently published exchanges of notes between the French and Italian governments in 1900 and in 1902 are relevant to the subject of the Triple Alliance, especially in connection with the third treaty, the one concluded in 1902. The essential passages of this correspondence are therefore reproduced here.

CONTENTS

NEGOTIATIONS LEADING TO THE TREATIES OF THE TRIPLE ALLIANCE

50

CHAPTER I

THE FIRST TREATY OF THE TRIPLE ALLIANCE[1]
MAY 20, 1882

In the councils of the statesmen of Germany and Austria-Hungary, following the conclusion of the alliance of October 7, 1879, the question of the attitude to be assumed by the Central Powers towards Italy took preëminent place.[2] Neither Bismarck nor Haymerle had any faith in the trustworthiness of the Italians, nor had they any too exalted an opinion of Italy's military strength. Their views diverged only in one particular. The Imperial Chancellor held the reëstablishment of friendly relations with Russia to be the all-important objective now that the alliance with Austria-Hungary was an accomplished fact, and emphasized the urgency of a speedy adjustment of the differences between Austria and Russia and of giving a subordinate position to Italy's relations with the Central Powers.[3] Haymerle, on the

---

[1] Bismarck's attempts in the first decade after the establishment of the German Empire to bring about a permanent alliance of the Three Empires and Italy directed against republican France will be dealt with at length in the introduction to the treaty between Austria-Hungary, Germany, and Russia in Volume III of this work, together with the circumstances which led him to conclude the close alliance of October 7, 1879, between Austria-Hungary and Germany after his first plan had been defeated by the insurmountable opposition of interests of Russia and Italy on the one hand, and of Austria-Hungary on the other. To Eduard von Wertheimer, author of *Graf Julius Andrássy: sein Leben und seine Zeit* (1910–13, 3 vols.), we owe the most exhaustive and authoritative account which has yet been given of this portentous epoch of European history. A. C. Coolidge's clear exposition, *The Origins of the Triple Alliance* (New York, 1917), is intended for a wider audience, its purpose being introductory. Hermann Oncken, in his comprehensive book, *Das alte und das neue Mitteleuropa* (1917), treats the various problems in a broad way. A useful compilation of the most significant events is to be found in Arthur Singer's *Geschichte des Dreibundes* (1914).

[2] [For an Italian view of one aspect of the question, see Domenico di Rubba, *Bismarck e la questione romana nella formazione della Triplice* (1917). A.C. C.]

[3] [For the interesting negotiations going on at this period between Germany and Russia, see the articles of J. Y. Simpson on "Russo-German Relations and the Sabouroff Memoirs" in the *Nineteenth Century* for December, 1917, and January, 1918. A. C. C.]

other hand, being still firmly convinced that Russia's isolation was to the best interests of the Monarchy, regarded Italy as an important piece in the game, and wished for this reason to avoid any step that would drive her into the arms of France. He therefore gave a clear-cut refusal to Germany's suggestion that preparations be made against the Irredentist movement, which had been flourishing more vigorously than ever since the defeat of the Italian policies at the Congress of Berlin. In February, 1880, Count Kálnoky, who was on the eve of assuming his post as ambassador to Russia, received orders to consult with Bismarck in Berlin regarding the Italian question. In the instructions given Kálnoky at the time, Haymerle expressed his conviction that, although he had no confidence in Cairoli, the Italian premier, he nevertheless believed it to be neither necessary nor advantageous to bring the difficulties with Italy to a head at that particular moment. "Just now," he declared, "the situation in Italy is less menacing to us than to the Italian government. The internal difficulties, the revolutionary and particularist tendencies of the extreme Left, as well as the positive opposition of the Right, are on the increase. It is our interest to let them come to a head. If it is to be feared that the Italian government will seek a diversion in action directed abroad, then we should be playing into its hands if we were now formally to raise the question of the Irredenta in any form. We are taking measures against surprise attacks and attempts to bring about a *coup*, but we wish carefully to avoid identifying the Italian government with the *comitati*. . . . In general, we ought not to divide our political resources or to allow our eyes to be diverted from the chief goal, the permanent blocking of Russia; these are sufficient further reasons for keeping any difference with Italy from the docket as long as possible."

Moreover, Haymerle felt that the results even of a victorious campaign against Italy would not justify the trouble and expense involved. The Monarchy, he said, coveted no Italian territory; and, to use his own words, "Italy is not yet ripe for partition into provincial republics." Great indemnities were not to be thought of, while, on the other hand, a conflict with Italy would engage considerable portions of the Austro-Hungarian army for a long

time. If Russia, in the meanwhile, were to begin war, the Monarchy would be confronted by a grave peril. Supported only by Germany, she would have to battle against the united forces of Russia, France, and Italy. In this connection Haymerle reverted to an idea which had played a decisive rôle in the political calculations of his predecessor, Count Andrássy, and which Haymerle had adopted as his own: the induction of England into the political councils of the Central Powers. He emphasized the similarity of interests of Austria-Hungary and England. "Russia is our arch-enemy, Italy only a secondary consideration," he declared. "Our policy is thus wholly in harmony with that of England." He then alluded to the fact that, with Bismarck's approval, he had imparted to the British government as early as the autumn of 1879 the fundamental idea of the German-Austrian alliance, and requested Kálnoky to put before Bismarck the question "whether, and to what extent, we should further enlighten Beaconsfield and Salisbury in order to obtain promises or declarations pledging England, in case of a conflict with Russia or an indirect collision with her which might threaten our position in the Orient, to use her influence, her direct pressure, or, should occasion arise, a naval demonstration to prevent Italy from attacking us and to safeguard the Adriatic for us." No matter how strong England's aversion to far-reaching alliances might be, in this particular case, where such great advantages accrued from such insignificant obligations, the inducements offered her were bound to prove irresistible. It could also be assumed with all probability that a word spoken by England with the necessary firmness would suffice to keep Italy neutral. Haymerle was quite aware that it would be no easy task to win Germany over to a sort of 'Triple Alliance' directed against Russia. He believed that Emperor William would not give such a project his assent. He therefore declared his willingness, in case Bismarck should approve and hold out hopes of his support, to enlist England's aid merely "pro domo nostra." [4]

Bismarck did not agree with Haymerle's views as laid before him by Kálnoky. It was true, he told the latter, that he did not

[4] Instruction to Count Kálnoky, February 7, 1880.

desire war between Austria-Hungary and Italy, and had not the least intention of stirring up trouble. He insisted, however, that the cabinet of Vienna should make very energetic representations at Rome. His judgment regarding Italian policy at that time was exceedingly severe: "a jackal policy," he called it.[5] "Insatiable Italy, with furtive glance, roves restlessly hither and thither, instinctively drawn on by the odor of corruption and calamity — always ready to attack anybody from the rear and make off with a bit of plunder. It is outrageous that these Italians, still unsatisfied, should continue to make preparations and to conspire in every direction. On the one hand the Irredenta, on the other machinations in Albania, Montenegro, and the Balkan territories; republican propaganda at home; and, finally, conspiracies with the Internationale in London." He — Bismarck — would like to administer to them a thoroughgoing reprimand and humiliation, for such behavior should not be allowed to go unpunished. In view of the internal condition of the country, it would not be difficult to give the Italians a good fright; threats would suffice to intimidate them. "For example," said Bismarck, "you could tell them that your boundaries do not satisfy you and that they must extend once more to the Mincio — or that you are convinced that the sovereignty of the Pope is necessary to the independence of the head of the Catholic church; or let them know that the Bourbons must be reëstablished at Naples," etc. In appraising these words of Bismarck's, one must not forget to whom they were spoken, and at what time. Bismarck was a realist in politics; he adapted his words as well as his actions to changing circumstances, and they can be properly understood only by continually bearing in mind the purpose which they served.[6] He wished to stir the temperate, cautious Haymerle to strenuous action; hence the extravagance of his denunciation of the Italian politicians and

[5] According to Moritz Busch (*Bismarck*, ii, p. 233), Bismarck about this same time compared the Italians to carrion crows on the battlefield, that let others provide their food.

[6] In his *Zur Vorgeschichte des Weltkrieges* (1918), p. 18, Otto Hammann very truly remarks: "Injustice has been done to many a written or spoken word of Prince Bismarck by detaching it from the time and circumstances under which he employed it, and regarding it as a general, permanently applicable truth."

of the measures recommended by him for attaining the desired end.

Kálnoky's suggestion for securing England's coöperation did not meet with Bismarck's favor. He declared that this was neither advisable nor necessary. Should there be a conflict between the Central Powers and Russia, England, he believed, would in any case hold Italy in check. In support of this view, Bismarck said he knew positively that in August, 1879, Cairoli had had Beaconsfield sounded as to the attitude the British cabinet would take in case Italy should conclude an alliance with Russia. To this Beaconsfield immediately replied, "with the impudence which he alone possesses," that England would regard this as a casus belli. Bismarck did not deem it advisable to afford still further securities to England, "arrogant enough already." Moreover, as Haymerle had foreseen, he was afraid of giving Russia fresh ground for alarm through the bugbear of a coalition, and of nullifying the efforts of those Russian statesmen who wished for peace with the Central Powers.[7] This, above all, Bismarck was anxious to avoid, for he still considered the reconciliation of the cabinets of Vienna and St. Petersburg, and the cultivation of friendly feelings at the Russian court, to be the chief goal, first and last.

Haymerle, impressed by these utterances of the German Imperial Chancellor, avoided for the time being any further discussion of the Italian question; and since the opening of negotiations in the course of 1880 with the Russian government made the danger of war with the mighty neighbor in the East appear increasingly remote, there seemed to him no necessity for returning to it. In the meanwhile, however, Italy's need to attach herself to the Central Powers had grown more pressing. The disturbances within the kingdom and the headlong advance of the French in Tunis threatened the overthrow of the dynasty. King Humbert and his statesmen longed with increasing anxiety to secure a guaranty of Italian possessions, as well as protection against French expansion in North Africa and against republican propaganda in Italy, through the support of the Central Powers. It was felt that the time was not yet ripe for an official declaration; but indirect

[7] Despatch from Kálnoky to Haymerle, February 17, 1880.

inquiries were made at Berlin and at Vienna. In Germany the intermediaries met with a refusal; they were told that the road to Berlin lay through Vienna.[8] In the Austrian capital a willingness was expressed to listen to the wishes of the Italians, whereupon the Secretary-General of Foreign Affairs in the Cairoli cabinet, Count Maffei, transmitted to the government of Austria the draft of a treaty of neutrality "as a first step towards more intimate relations." This took place at the beginning of 1881, before King Humbert's first visit to Vienna in February of the same year.

"Respect for the status quo in the Orient as established by the provisions of the Treaty of Berlin" was to serve as a basis for this agreement.[9] Maffei dwelt especially on the fact that the Italian council of ministers, and Cairoli in particular, had given their sanction to this idea.[10]   At the same time he announced, in order to make his offer seem the more tempting, that France was eagerly

[8] No information is to be had in the Vienna Archives regarding the mission to Berlin, which was undertaken by one Grunert-Görke. In Wimpffen's dispatch, dated December 23, 1880, it is stated that Grunert-Görke was brusquely repulsed by Bismarck. According to Crispi (*Memoirs*, ii, pp. 118 ff.), the Secretary-General of the Ministry of Foreign Affairs, Count Maffei, had, by authorization of Cairoli, officially sounded Berlin "regarding the possibility of giving a character of greater intimacy to the relations existing between Italy and Germany, and of working toward an actual alliance." Bismarck, it is reported, replied to this that "the way to Berlin lay through Vienna, and that Italy must above all cultivate the best of relations there if she wished to renew the ties of her old friendship with Germany." In the Vienna Archives nothing is to be found regarding Maffei's mission in Berlin. It is probable, however, that Görke was merely Maffei's intermediary in Berlin, as was later Hirling in Vienna.

[9] Crispi deals in detail with these negotiations (*Memoirs*, ii, pp. 119 ff.). These *Memoirs* of Crispi (translated by Mary Prichard-Agnetti: New York and London, 1912-14, 3 vols.) are in part a translation of the work published by Tommaso Palamenghi-Crispi, *Francesco Crispi: Politica estera. Memorie e documenti* (Milan, 1912). The citations given here are from the English edition. According to Crispi, the German ambassador in Rome, Keudell, was in the confidence of both governments, and worked energetically for a secret agreement between Austria-Hungary and Italy, in which both parties should pledge themselves to maintain peace. This agreement was to have been renewed from year to year. As soon as this treaty had been concluded, Germany was to communicate to Italy proposals regarding the bases of an alliance for the reciprocal protection of common interests. Maffei was said to have begun negotiations to this end with Vienna.

[10] According to Crispi's *Memoirs*, ii, pp. 101, 119, Cairoli was at that time opposed to an alliance with Austria-Hungary and only yielded gradually to Maffei's importunities to enter into unofficial negotiations with Vienna.

seeking Italy's friendship. A French statesman, he said, had declared a short time before that the Tunisian controversy could be settled by giving Tunisia to France, Tripolitania to Italy: "pour le reste, nous nous entendrons." The Austrian government replied to the unofficial offer with a suitable counter-communication drawn up by Baron von Teschenberg, then a member of the Foreign Office, in which the idea of a reciprocal assurance of neutrality in the event of attacks by foreign powers was eagerly welcomed. It was most decidedly emphasized, however, that "as regards respect for the status quo in the Orient as established by the provisions of the Treaty of Berlin, which Austria wished to safeguard, there must be no discussion of Bosnia and Herzegovina." On the other hand the Dual Monarchy would be willing to pledge itself to undertake no campaigns of conquest in the direction of Albania or Salonica provided Italy made a similar declaration. The Austrian government would also be inclined to recognize in friendly fashion Italy's legitimate interests as a great power and a sea power. It would therefore not oppose an extension of the Italian sphere of influence in the Mediterranean if Italy, for her part, adhered strictly to the status quo in the Adriatic and made no attempts to convert it into an Italian sea. In conformity with these sentiments, Austria-Hungary, far from placing any obstacle in the way of a settlement of the Tunisian question to Italy's advantage and the possible acquisition of Tripoli by Italy, would regard such a step benevolently.[11] Further negotiations, however, did not follow at that time. Maffei's proposal, if it was meant at all seriously,[12] was not renewed by the Italian statesmen in spite of Austria's friendly answer. As for the Austrian cabinet, it had no reason to press the matter. The conclusion of the agreement with Russia on June 18, 1881,[13] had depreciated for the Central Powers the value of an agreement with Italy. In Vienna, as in

[11] Teschenberg's note of January 2, 1881, and the communication from Hirling, who conducted the negotiations with Maffei in Rome, dated February 16, 1881 (copy). Cf. also Crispi, *Memoirs*, ii, pp. 122 ff.

[12] The Austro-Hungarian ambassador at Rome, Count Wimpffen, was later of the opinion that this proposal had no serious basis. Despatch of December 23, 1880.

[13] Cf. Vol. I, pp. 36–49. Detailed information with regard to the negotiations leading to the conclusion of this agreement will be given in a subsequent portion of this work.

Berlin, it was believed that Italy in her weakness must seek union with the Allies, not they with her.

As a matter of fact, time worked to the advantage of the Central Powers. The French, anticipating the Italians, forced the Bey of Tunis to recognize the supremacy of France in the treaty of the Bardo (May, 1881). The excitement caused among the Italians by this coup was tremendous. Unmindful of their debt of thanks to French soldiers and diplomats for their far-reaching support of the Italian struggles for unity, public opinion throughout Italy clamored for a breach with France and revenge for the slight that had been inflicted. Sonnino, the same man who, thirty-four years later, shattered the Triple Alliance, wrote at that time that Italy must strive towards the double goal of friendship with England and a close alliance with Germany and Austria-Hungary. "No conflicts of interest," he declared, "separate us from Germany, while many common interests unite us; primarily, the preservation of peace and the curbing of France's lust for power. As soon as we have removed the causes of the distrust existing towards us in Austria, the accomplishment of an alliance with Germany will meet with no obstacle. Our diplomacy must accordingly remove every suspicion that our policy might be disadvantageous to the former power, in order to win for us her friendship . . . [14] Austria's friendship is a prerequisite to our successful political effort. Isolation means annihilation."

In many circles of the Italian nation the chief responsibility for the checkmate in Tunisia was attributed to the king and his counsellors. Cairoli paid for the disaster with his fall; the anti-monarchical movement gained strength; and King Humbert considered it imperative to enlist the support of the Central Powers against the aggressiveness of the French Republic. After surmounting a long line of difficulties — among them the passivity of the new Minister of Foreign Affairs, Pasquale Mancini, the opposition of the new Premier, Depretis, and the untiring efforts of the French statesmen,[15] — the partisans of a rapprochement with the Central

[14] Luigi Chiala, *La triplice e la duplice alleanza (1881-1897)* (2d ed., 1898), pp. 23 ff.

[15] Robilant, the Italian ambassador in Vienna, also favored an attitude of reserve

Powers, among whom Secretary-General Blanc, a conservative politician of the Cavour school, was particularly zealous, succeeded by dint of great effort in arranging a personal conference between King Humbert and Emperor Francis Joseph I.[16] This took place in Vienna towards the end of October, 1881. Nothing was said at the time regarding the conclusion of a treaty, though, according to Blanc, the Italian ministers who accompanied King Humbert to Vienna, not altogether with his approval, would have been ready to proceed at once with the conclusion of a treaty of guaranty.[17] No move was made in this direction on the part of the Austro-Hungarian government, while the Italians kept silence, not wishing to face a refusal; nevertheless, the warm reception accorded the royal Italian couple in Vienna, and the friendly sentiments exchanged there between the sovereigns and the leading statesmen, opened up an auspicious outlook for the future.[18]

The Italians saw fit at this time to try again for Bismarck's mediation in Vienna;[19] but he showed not the slightest inclina-

on the part of the Italian government, as Haymerle, in a conversation with him in September, 1881, declared that although he considered the establishment of close relations between Vienna and Rome desirable, he recommended that the negotiations be deferred, lest it should appear they were directed against France. Cf. Fraknói, *Kritische Studien zur Geschichte des Dreibundes* (1917), p. 20.

[16] In regard to the negotiations which preceded this meeting, the correspondence of the Austro-Hungarian ambassador in Rome with the Department of Foreign Affairs furnishes interesting details. Cf. also Chiala, *La triplice e la duplice alleanza (1881-1897)*, 2d ed., pp. 78 ff.

[17] Wimpffen's despatch of December 9, 1881.

[18] The reports, published shortly after by the Hungarian press, of unfriendly utterances by Andrássy and Kállay in the committee meeting of the Hungarian Delegation produced a disagreeable sensation in Italy. These statements were corrected in the session of the Delegation of November 8, 1881. On November 14, Robilant wrote to Rome that the incident had turned out favorably for Italy, "for had it not occurred, the value of our friendship would not have been realized in Vienna; nor should we have received a declaration which could not be improved on for clearness." Cf. Fraknói, p. 22.

[19] Wimpffen to Kálnoky, December 9, 1881. The strictures made by Bismarck against Italy at that time created a particularly painful impression in those circles which favored the rapprochement with the Central Powers. Keudell, the German ambassador in Rome, said that "for his part, he believed that Prince Bismarck underestimated the weight which Italy could throw into the scale in the event of a great European complication." Bismarck thereupon attempted, through assurances of his friendly intentions toward Italy, to set Mancini's mind at rest, but the latter

tion, even now, to take this office upon himself. Once more he referred Launay, the Italian ambassador, to the Austro-Hungarian government, and gave him clearly to understand that Italy, as the weaker power, must make the advances to the allies. At the same time he instructed the German ambassador in Vienna, Prince Reuss, to acquaint Kálnoky with Italy's wishes, and to declare in his — Bismarck's — name, that any agreement with Italy, whatever its form might be, "would in reality be always a one-sided affair, to Italy's advantage: all the more so because the unsettled and untrustworthy character of the Italian policy could easily embroil Italy's friends in difficulties." His advice was not merely to decline any proposition which might serve to strengthen the position of the king of Italy: "your answer should first of all express a wish for the establishment of a modus vivendi which would be agreeable to the Pope; if matters should get as far as serious negotiations, the assumption of obligations by Austria and Germany should be made dependent on the duration of the present relations (of these two states) with Russia." [20]

The leisureliness of the Central Powers did not accord with the wishes of the Italian Court. King Humbert was convinced that a speedy decision must be reached, and he did not allow himself to be diverted from this view by the objections raised by many Italian politicians.[21] Disregarding all Gambetta's efforts to keep Italy out of further negotiations with the Central Powers, and thinking only of the dangers besetting the kingdom from the republicans within its confines and from France, he resolved, toward the end of 1881, to take another step — a radical one. He instructed his ambassadors in Vienna and in Berlin to inform the

continued to be apprehensive lest Bismarck should instigate a modification of the law of guaranty. Wimpffen to Kálnoky, December 23, 1881.

[20] Telegram from Bismarck to Reuss, December 28, 1881. Transmitted by Reuss to Count Kálnoky.

[21] Wimpffen's despatches of December, 1881, contain many interesting particulars regarding the differences of opinion in the Italian government. Cf. also A. Singer, *Geschichte des Dreibundes*, p. 65. Sonnino belonged at that time to the most ardent advocates of the new order; he urged the government to take no half-way measures, but to make every effort to obtain a strong and positive alliance. Cf. Fraknói, *Kritische Studien zur Geschichte des Dreibundes* (1917), p. 22; Chiala, *op. cit.*, pp. 234 ff.

governments to which they were accredited that, "without regard to certain questions," he wished to join hands with Germany and Austria-Hungary,[22] and was ready to reach an understanding with the Central Powers even in case the obligations they had assumed toward other powers — by this Russia was evidently meant — stood in the way of concluding an alliance with Italy.[23] Shortly after this the Italian ambassadors in Berlin and Vienna received instructions to begin negotiations.

On January 19, 1882, there took place the first conference between Count Kálnoky, who had been guiding Austro-Hungarian foreign policy since November 21, 1881, and the Italian ambassador, Count Robilant. It was conducted with the greatest wariness on both sides. Robilant was anxious to avoid giving the impression that Italy was approaching the Dual Monarchy as a suppliant for aid. The Italian cabinet, he stated, actuated by its conviction that the interests of Italy were identical with those of Germany and Austria-Hungary, was ready to ally itself with these conservative powers and "to make this alliance the basis of its policy." In reaching this decision, he said, the Italian government had been influenced by no momentary consideration of either foreign or domestic conditions. Its aim was to strengthen "par des engagements d'une nature plus précise" the existing good relations, but without haste and without insistence on an immediate decision. Robilant made no formal proposal to conclude a treaty; he also avoided indicating, in the course of the parleys, whether a treaty of guaranty or of neutrality would best correspond to Italy's wishes.

The generalizing tone of these utterances, which Robilant himself characterized as "not of a binding nature," allowed Count Kálnoky to reply in a manner no more binding. He emphasized the favorable impression produced throughout Austria-Hungary by King Humbert's visit to Vienna, and laid stress on the inclina-

[22] Wimpffen's telegram of December 30, 1881, and his despatch dated January 6, 1882.

[23] Wimpffen's despatch of January 6, 1882. Wimpffen declared that these resolutions had been backed up by the council of ministers as a whole, and therefore by Premier Depretis as well; "but they are primarily to be regarded as an expression of the personal wishes of the king and queen."

tion of Emperor Francis Joseph and of the Austro-Hungarian government to support the royal house of Italy. As for the idea of a close rapprochement between Italy and the Central Powers, Kálnoky declared that Robilant knew as well as he "that such written agreements no longer harmonize with the diplomatic usage of our times; and, as far as secret treaties are concerned, I shall not conceal from you that in these parliamentary days I personally regard them with a certain distrust." If, however, matters should get as far as the point of negotiations, the question of determining precisely the purpose, the tendencies, and the form of such a treaty could then be taken up. Kálnoky further declared that he would get in touch with Prince Bismarck; he did not forget, however, to express doubt as to the seriousness of the intentions of Depretis, the Italian premier. Robilant admitted that there might be ground for this doubt, but insisted that the decision taken by the Italian council of ministers bound Depretis as well.[24]

In a conversation with Bismarck on February 1, 1882, to which the latter had consented only after long hesitation that caused apprehension and displeasure in Italy,[25] Count Launay went further than Robilant. According to the information imparted by Reuss to Kálnoky at Bismarck's instruction, Launay had begun by declaring that the Italian government had made the irrevocable resolution "to identify itself with the conservative and peaceful policy of the two empires. Italy stood ready to give practical proof of this resolution, which was independent of foreign influences, by the conclusion of binding agreements." Launay had then made the direct request that Bismarck draft a treaty of alli-

---

[24] Notes of a conversation between Kálnoky and Robilant, January 19, 1882, and a private communication from Kálnoky to Wimpffen, January 20, 1882 (copy).

[25] Wimpffen to Kálnoky, February 3, 1882. On January 21, 1882, Széchényi informed Kálnoky in detail of an interview with Launay, in the course of which the latter made the following utterance: "Comme nous ne voulons rien de plus que le respect des traités et le simple maintien de la paix, tout en renonçant même à une idée quelconque d'accroissement de notre influence du côté de la Méditerranée, il nous semble que le bon vouloir de ceux aux quels nous nous ouvririons à cet égard ne saurait nous manquer, et cela d'autant moins qu'une ligue pacifique qui s'étendrait depuis Palerme jusqu'à Koenigsberg serait la garantie la plus certaine de la tranquillité et du repos de toute l'Europe."

ance between the Central Powers and Italy.[26] Bismarck categorically rejected this request, emphasizing more strongly than Kálnoky the difficulties of drawing up secret treaties between states
with parliamentary governments.[27] Moreover, he declared himself to be "incapable of finding a wording which would satisfy all ✓
the various claims and prove acceptable to all parties." Germany
and Italy had no points of friction, but between Austria-Hungary
and Italy such points existed in the Mediterranean and in the
Adriatic. Furthermore, there was the Irredenta. For these reasons, Italy must first win over Austria-Hungary to the idea of a
treaty. "The key of the door which leads to us is to be found in
Vienna," concluded Bismarck. "Whatever agreement you reach
with the government there will be acceptable to us, and will receive the most favorable reception at our hands." [28]

Bismarck's flat refusal to assume the rôle of intermediary between Vienna and Rome forced the Italian government to proceed with the negotiations begun in January, 1882, with the
Austro-Hungarian government. On February 20 Robilant again
had an interview with Kálnoky [29] and imparted to him, in the
name of his government, a project for the conclusion of a treaty of
guaranty. Kálnoky declined this with the greatest firmness. A
secret treaty guaranteeing to the Great Powers the integrity of
their possessions would, he said, lay upon the respective governments such portentous obligations that "no parliamentary minister could lightly assume responsibility for the consequences
arising therefrom." How, for instance, could an Italian statesman

[26] Outline of a conversation with Prince Reuss on February 9, 1882. In this summary mention was made of the three empires. Launay had, as a matter of fact,
spoken several times of an agreement between the three empires and Italy: Bismarck,
however, had not approved of this "new version."

[27] "In a country," said Bismarck, "where the king goes about in civilian clothes,
his dominant position cannot be counted upon." Ibid.

[28] Ibid. Prince Bismarck at that time advised Vienna in favor of an oral agreement, and believed that this would satisfy the Italians.

[29] At that time considerable tension existed between Robilant and Mancini.
Robilant's recall was spoken of in Rome. Private communication from Wimpffen to
Kálnoky, February 21, 1882. Cf. also Chiala, pp. 256 ff. Kálnoky came vigorously
to the defence of Robilant, characterizing him as the person best fitted to carry on
the treaty negotiations. Kálnoky to Wimpffen, February 28, 1882.

persuade the Italian people that they must fight for Austria against Russia, in case the former were attacked in Bukowina ? The same would be true of Austria in case of a conflict between Italy and France. Besides, Kálnoky concluded, it would be over-venturesome for Italy to assume a guaranty for such extensive territories as those of Germany and Austria-Hungary.

Robilant, nothing daunted, stuck to his point. Again and again he emphasized the fact that only in a treaty of guaranty would full account be taken of the wishes of the Italian people; and he declined Kálnoky's proposal to conclude a treaty of neutrality, on the ground that no profit could be discerned in it for Italy. With remarkable frankness, but all to no purpose, Kálnoky pointed out in his reply that it would mean a great deal to Italy to be pro-tected by such a treaty of neutrality against Austro-Hungarian attacks on Venetia in the event of a Franco-Italian war. The par-ley closed with a question from Robilant (expressly characterized as unofficial) regarding the advisability of reaching an agreement providing for joint action in matters affecting the common in-terest, but guaranteeing reciprocal support *per compensationem* "in cases where only one state had a predominant interest." Kál-noky declared his readiness to negotiate on this basis, and re-quested proposals from the Italian government.[30]

In a private letter to Count Wimpffen, the Austro-Hungarian ambassador in Rome, Kálnoky gave in detail the circumstances which led him to sink his fundamental objection to a secret treaty with Italy, and described the spirit in which he carried on his ne-gotiations with Robilant. From this we learn that the unquestion-able advantage of being sure of Italy's position in case the Dual Monarchy were to become involved in war with another power, together with the desire "to satisfy, as far as possible, in the in-terests of the monarchical principle, the eagerness of King Hum-bert and his government to join the peaceful and conservative German-Austrian alliance, and to check defections to the side of his opponents," had induced him to disregard his deep-rooted mis-givings and enter into secret negotiations "with such untrust-

[30] Outline of the conversation between Kálnoky and Robilant, on February 20, 1882. Original notes by Kálnoky.

worthy persons as Depretis and Mancini." To Wimpffen Kálnoky also expressed his belief — which he had been careful not to
reveal to Robilant by a single word — that the anxiety of the
Italian government to have Rome safeguarded by the Central
Powers was the chief reason for Robilant's insistence on a treaty
of guaranty. "The idea of a secret treaty," wrote Kálnoky, "regarded in the light of the reasons brought forward by Robilant
during our parley, is, in my opinion, not acceptable; but I will not
deny that the craftiness of the Italians in thinking that they
could thus quietly smuggle in the guaranty of their capital would
in itself be a reason for not acceding to it. I shall not examine the
merits of the Roman question here; if, however, we should guarantee their capital to the Italians, they must certainly pay a fitting price for a concession which means so much to them." [31]

Kálnoky's firm refusal to accept the Italian project for a treaty
of guaranty was received with bitterness in Italy. Blanc, one of
the most ardent advocates of a rapprochement with the Central
Powers, expressed to Wimpffen his great concern over Kálnoky's
unfavorable attitude, and pointed out the portentous results
which might follow a breaking off of the negotiations already
under way. When, however, it was borne in upon him by Wimpffen's attitude and Robilant's despatches that no advances could
be hoped for on the part of the Austrian government, he yielded.
In a conversation with Wimpffen on February 24, Blanc insisted
that "the question of Rome had no bearing on the positive agreement which the Italian government wished to conclude with
Austria-Hungary. What his government was really working for
was an alliance similar to that existing between Austria-Hungary
and Germany, which would go hand in hand [32] with an Italian
policy of conciliation and friendship toward France." But the
purpose of this utterance was clear. It was intended to dispel any
suspicion that the Italian government wished to make use of an
alliance with the Central Powers to guarantee the integrity of its
present possessions, and possibly to take the initiative, with their
support, in a hostile move against France.[33]

---

[31] Letter from Kálnoky to Wimpffen, March 3, 1882.
[32] Wimpffen to Kálnoky, February 25, 1882.   [33] Ibid.

Kálnoky had in the meanwhile kept Bismarck posted as to the course his negotiations with Robilant were taking, and had requested suggestions from him. As regards the question of guaranty, the chancellor supported Kálnoky's views without reserve. He strongly advised him to stand firm in this matter, and "as long as possible, to turn a deaf ear to everything concerning the Pope." Nevertheless the general situation, which had assumed a more threatening aspect, especially in Egypt, caused him to feel inclined to enter into a written agreement [34] with Italy which would bind her to the Central Powers for some length of time. This, he realized, could not be done without concessions. He therefore advised Kálnoky not to stand too firmly for a treaty of neutrality. There was no probability, said he, that Mancini would be satisfied with such a treaty, which would only gain for Italy an assurance that Austria-Hungary and Germany would not interfere with her in a war with France — and for this she had no need of a treaty. If Italy were left alone, however, she might be strongly tempted to enter into an 'active alliance' with France and offer herself to that country in return for the guaranty of Rome. "To forestall this, to hold Italian policy to its present lines, and to protect the Italian monarchy from the dangers which must inevitably arise from an alliance by treaty with France and from the reciprocal support of the radical elements of France and Italy, it might after all be advisable to consider whether the Teutonic powers would not be doing well to give Italy hopes of their assistance in case of an unprovoked attack on the part of France." Consideration for Italian self-respect and for the interests of Austria-Hungary and Germany would make it seem desirable to base such an offer on reciprocity. Bismarck made no secret of his opinion that Italy, by reason of her military weakness and her limited capacity for action outside her own borders, was undoubtedly getting the best of the bargain; nevertheless, he realized the importance to the Central Powers of being assured against attacks from the south in the event of a war on two fronts.[35]

[34] Bismarck had previously spoken of an "oral agreement." Cf. p. 15, note 28.

[35] Instruction from the Foreign Office in Berlin to Reuss (copy), February 28, 1882.

While views were thus being exchanged between the German and Austro-Hungarian cabinets, the eagerness of the Italian government for a union with the Central Powers increased with the growing tension of Franco-Italian relations. Blanc and his fellow-partisans pressed still harder for the quickest possible closing of the pending negotiations. It was an excellent omen for the success of their efforts when Keudell, the German ambassador in Rome, doubtless acting under Bismarck's instructions, began to work in the same direction. Through him and Launay the Italian government may have learned that Bismarck was ready to make certain concessions,[36] to which he was also attempting to gain the accession of the Austrian government. This was one of the factors which contributed to the final triumph of those Italian politicians who favored union with the Central Powers.[37]

On March 3 Wimpffen informed his government that in view of the blunt rejection of a treaty of guaranty in Berlin and Vienna, the Italians had discarded the plan of an offensive and defensive alliance which should also include an express guaranty of the territorial integrity of the respective parties, and had decided to lay before the Central Powers a project for "a secret agreement, drawn up in general terms and based on the observance of existing treaties and the maintenance of the peace, with a supplementary agreement to the effect that the several parties, in the event of a common peril, should come to a closer understanding, and, in case of necessity, take such measures as might be necessary for furnishing one another assistance. These declarations were to be reciprocal, but only verbal; their substance would simply be embodied in aide-mémoires which were not to be signed." Robilant and Launay were shortly to receive instructions to this effect.[38] Blanc declared that the chief reason for the general nature of this

[36] Launay's despatches from Berlin were undoubtedly more encouraging at the beginning of March than in January and early February. On January 18 he had written: "I do not believe that the people here or in Vienna intend at present to enter into negotiations with us. They wish to put us to the test and make sure whether we are going to stick to our resolve." On March 12, however: "Bismarck is wholly satisfied with Italy's attitude. It would greatly please him if an agreement were first reached between Austria and Italy." Cf. Fraknói, pp. 22 ff.

[37] Despatch from Wimpffen to Kálnoky, March 3, 1882.

[38] Ibid.

projected agreement lay in the hope of winning the sanction of Premier Depretis, who was still opposing an agreement with the Central Powers. The next two weeks were taken up with the spirited battling of the Italian politicians. Depretis's opposition on principle was overcome by the fact that the friends of a rapprochement could now point to the fact that Italy was already bound by the declarations made by King Humbert [39] toward the end of 1881. Now, however, Depretis insisted that an agreement couched in such general terms was not in harmony with Italian interests, and recommended the conclusion of a defensive treaty of neutrality which "should be limited to envisaging a war with France." [40]

The struggles of the two parties ended in a compromise. In the middle of March Wimpffen notified Vienna that the instructions for Robilant and Launay had been completed.[41] From information which had reached him, he believed he was justified in assuming that Mancini would make the following propositions: "The chief purpose of the agreement between the three powers should be the maintenance of peace and of the existing territorial integrity of the three states. In the event of war between Germany and Austria-Hungary on one side and France on the other, Italy would immediately take offensive and defensive action. In a war of the Central Powers against Russia, Italy would observe a benevolent armed neutrality, but would actively participate if France were to align herself with Russia." Wimpffen said nothing about the counter-demands of Italy. As regards the form of the agreement, he believed that Mancini wished it to be "as positive as possible, but that he would be" satisfied "if it were oral, since it is believed that the agreements on which our (Austro-Hungarian) alliance with Germany are based depend only on oral engagements, guaranteed by the word of the two monarchs." The task of composing an eventual written agreement was to be left to Kálnoky and Robilant.[42]

<hr>

[39] Cf. p. 13.   [40] Wimpffen's telegram of March 13, 1882.

[41] Wimpffen to Kálnoky, March 17, 1882.

[42] On March 19, Wimpffen telegraphed that the instructions had been despatched on the 18th and "répondent assez exactement aux indications contenues dans ma lettre particulière d'avant-hier."

It was plain that these proposals of Mancini could not be acceptable to Count Kálnoky. We know that, in view of the Roman question, he did not wish to assume the obligation of guaranteeing Italy's existing territorial integrity. It was equally distasteful to him to hear Mancini speak of an Austro-Hungarian and German war against France in which Italy should take an active part. Following out Andrássy's tradition, he firmly opposed involving the Dual Monarchy in any obligations toward the West or concluding any agreements pledging it to participate in a war between Germany and France. He decided to wait and see whether Robilant's proposals would correspond with Wimpffen's predictions; in the meanwhile, however, in order to force the Italians to come out into the open and learn to what lengths they would go, he drew up the draft of a treaty reading as follows:

"ARTICLE 1. The signatory parties reciprocally promise one another peace and friendly relations. No one of them will go to war with the others, or enter into an alliance against them.

"ARTICLE 2. Reciprocal support in certain questions of a political and economic nature.

"ARTICLE 3. Should one of the signatory parties be drawn into war with a power not belonging to this alliance, the two others are pledged to observe a benevolent neutrality toward the signatory power which is at war.

"ARTICLE 4. Should one of the signatory parties be attacked without provocation, for whatsoever cause, by a power not belonging to this alliance, the two other parties are bound to furnish help and assistance with all their strength to the party attacked.[43]

"ARTICLE 5. Should, however, one of the signatory parties become involved in a war with two or more powers not belonging to this alliance, or should two of the signatory parties become involved at the same time in a war each with one or more [44] powers

[43] Kálnoky subsequently struck out this article and gave it another wording. Cf. the details given on p. 27.

[44] The words "each with one or" were later eliminated by Kálnoky. Cf. the details on p. 30. This draft, written in German in his own hand, was marked as "Draft no. 1, made before conversation with Count Robilant on March 20." The consultation with Robilant, however, took place on March 22.

not belonging to this alliance, the *casus foederis* shall simultane
ously be established for all parties."

The duration of the treaty, and the provisions for denunciation,
which were to have formed Article 6, are not indicated.

Kálnoky's project can hardly be called a success. In judging it,
however, we should remember that it was merely a 'first draft,'
which he did not intend to lay before Robilant.

The first article needs no comment. Its wording is similar to
that of many earlier treaties destined to serve the same purpose.
The second article is only briefly sketched, and, by virtue of its
general, vague wording, noncommittal. What was to be understood by "certain questions of a political and economic nature "?
One could include or exclude anything here.

In Articles 3 and 5 one is struck by the fact that the explicitly
defensive character which gave the Triple Alliance its peculiar
quality was absent from this first draft. According to Article 3, in
the event of a war between one of the allies and a state not belonging to the alliance, whether it was a great power or not, the
two remaining allies were pledged to observe a benevolent neutrality. It made no difference whether the allied state was attacked or attacking. In drawing up Article 5, as little attention
was paid by Kálnoky to the question of attack or defence as to the
strength of the adversary. The *casus foederis* was to be considered
as established by any war in which one or two of the allies were to
become involved with two or more powers. Here again it made no
difference whether these were Great Powers or not. It is particularly noteworthy that Kálnoky stipulated the obligation of all the
signatory powers to participate even in the event that the allies
should become separately involved in war, each with a single
power not belonging to the alliance. According to this, for example, the *casus foederis* would have been established for Italy if
Austria had invaded Russia and Germany at the same time had
invaded France. In Article 4 of his draft Kálnoky only contemplated the unprovoked attack of an adversary; but from its wording an obligation might have been construed on the part of
Austria-Hungary to give armed assistance, not only to Italy, but

to Germany, in case of an unprovoked attack by France. This he wished to avoid under all circumstances.

On March 22 Robilant was received by Kálnoky. His proposals did not altogether coincide with Wimpffen's forecast. The latter had either been deliberately misled by the Italians, or — what is more probable — the instructions destined for Robilant had, under the influence of German representations, undergone substantial eleventh-hour changes. Robilant harked back to the interview which he had had with Kálnoky on February 20, and again brought up the matter of a treaty of guaranty, expressing his regret that this was looked on with disfavor by Kálnoky. 'Mancini,' he said, 'had really believed he would be meeting Austro-Hungarian wishes in such a treaty, not only because there could be no more conservative basis than the guaranty of territorial integrity, but because, as he thought, he was thus also offering us security against all possible subversive tendencies directed against our frontier possessions.' As Kálnoky remained firm in his refusal, Robilant turned to a discussion of the treaty of neutrality mentioned by Austria-Hungary in February. Mancini, he declared, considered such a treaty insufficient. Italy was bound by the positive declaration of the Italian cabinet, made in Berlin and Vienna, that it intended in future to identify itself with the policy of the two empires; neutrality, in the case of such friendly relations, was to be taken for granted. 'For Italy, more was at stake than this. She had, to be sure, only one dangerous neighbor — dangerous, however, in a double sense. France was a menace, not only as a military power, but to the monarchical interests and to the social order of Italy as well. Now that Italy had taken her stand at the side of the two conservative empires, she also hoped to receive protection and help at their hands against possible peril from France.'

Robilant, carrying out further this line of thought, now unfolded the outlines of a secret treaty, the contents of which were to be substantially as follows: "In the event that France, under no matter what pretext, should attack Italy without provocation, the two other powers shall pledge themselves to furnish help and

assistance to the attacked party with all their strength. The same obligation falls upon Italy in the event of an unprovoked attack by France upon Germany." This project coincided with that presented to the Austro-Hungarian government by Bismarck towards the end of February, with the terms of which he had meanwhile presumably acquainted the Italian statesmen. Robilant's further proposals read: "In case of a war between the two empires and Russia, Italy shall observe a benevolent, possibly an armed, neutrality; but the *casus foederis* shall immediately be established for her should France enter into action. Should one or more of the signatory powers become otherwise involved in war, the others shall under all circumstances observe a benevolent neutrality, and, should occasion arise, shall reach an agreement with regard to furnishing aid." The treaty was to remain in force for a definite number of years and contain a clause of prolongation.

The proposals made by Robilant were clear and were meant to serve a particular purpose. Italy wished to secure the assistance of Germany and Austria-Hungary against an unprovoked attack by France. By way of compensation, she promised Germany similar assistance in a war between France and Germany determined by the same circumstances. In a war of the Central Powers against Russia alone, she would observe a benevolent neutrality, and, in case France came to the aid of Russia, she would participate actively on the side of the Central Powers. Robilant said nothing about a war between Austria-Hungary and Russia alone. This, it is assumed, was due to the fact that Italy knew nothing of the contents of the German-Austro-Hungarian alliance of October, 1879, and was acting under the false supposition that in any Austro-Russian war Germany would fight at the side of her ally, even if the latter were the attacking party.

Kálnoky's reception of these proposals of Robilant was extremely reserved. He replied that he agreed in general with Robilant's ideas; that he would lay the matter before his sovereign, communicate with Bismarck, and then attempt to outline the draft of a treaty *à trois*. To a suggestion made by Robilant during the course of the conversation, that the treaty might begin, if not with a guaranty, at least with "a sort of confirmation of territo-

rial integrity," Kálnoky did not give his assent. "In any case," he wrote to Wimpffen shortly after, "I should like to keep such a disguised recognition from being smuggled in." He also expressed himself to his friend regarding the impression made upon him by Robilant's proposals. He liked above all the provision that Austria-Hungary should not be pledged to participate in a Franco-German war. "From the draft outlined above," he wrote Wimpffen, "Your Excellency will doubtless have noticed that the *casus foederis* is not established for us if France becomes involved in war with Germany. No such obligation would exist for us even if Italy came to the help of Germany — provided Russia kept out of the war; in the same way Italy would not be pledged to take action in the event of a war involving both, or one of the empires and Russia, provided France did not participate."[45] The unanimity of Kálnoky and Robilant on this point had a decisive influence on the further course of the negotiations.

Kálnoky, as we know, had given the following wording to Article 4 of the first draft, which he had composed for his own guidance and had not imparted to Robilant: "Should one of the signatory parties be attacked without provocation, for whatsoever cause, by a power not belonging to this alliance, the two other parties are bound to furnish help and assistance with all their strength to the party attacked." According to this, Italy would have been pledged to fight at the side of Austria-Hungary in case of an unprovoked attack by Russia on the latter; Austria-Hungary, on the other hand, would have been bound to participate, not only in a Franco-Italian war brought on by a French attack, but in a Franco-German war as well. The last danger was now obviated through Robilant's project; for the Italian statesman, in his interview with Kálnoky, had not uttered generalities concerning unprovoked attacks of a power outside the alliance against a signatory power, but had specifically mentioned an unprovoked French attack upon Italy or Germany, and had claimed Austria-Hungary's assistance only in the former instance. This, from his point of view, was quite comprehensible. Italy at that time foresaw a menace from France alone. On that side only did she need

---

[45] Kálnoky to Wimpffen, April 1, 1882 (original).

to protect herself. This would be most adequately done if Austria-Hungary and Germany promised to align themselves with Italy, in the event of her being attacked without provocation by France.

It was the business of Italy's cosignatories to look out for the compensating counter-services. Germany had already announced her wishes in Rome, and Robilant had taken account of these in the plans he laid before Kálnoky, since he had provided for Italy's participation in a Franco-German war brought about by French aggression. But what about Austria-Hungary? Could he hope that the concessions which he was empowered to make in Vienna would satisfy Kálnoky? The benevolent, or possibly armed neutrality promised by Italy in the event of an Austro-Russian war was no equivalent for the active participation which was demanded of Austro-Hungary in case Italy were invaded by France without provocation. He must have expected that Kálnoky would point out the discrepancy between demand and counter-service. Remarkably enough, however, this was not done. Kálnoky did not ask for Italian help in the event of an unprovoked attack by Russia on the Danubian Monarchy.

Not a word is to be found among Kálnoky's notes of the period to explain the motives prompting him to take this extraordinary attitude — an attitude which brought down on him the censure of his successors in office. Even in his private correspondence with his friend Wimpffen this subject, for some strange reason, was not touched on.[46] He merely closed his description of the negotiations with Robilant with the words: "The outline of the secret agreement with Italy which I have given above corresponds, on the whole, very closely to my wishes, and I believe that the scheme will go through. We are favorably disposed toward it; so is the German Imperial Chancellor. And when we consider the dangerous internal conditions in Russia and the terrible disorder of her whole political organization, we must take care in good season to win friends and allies on all sides for the Monarchy in view of the dangers threatening from the East. Thus, it is to be hoped, we shall make sure of peace."[47]

---

[46] For the reasons which may have determined Kálnoky's conduct, cf. pp. 42 f., infra. [47] Kálnoky to Wimpffen, April 1, 1882.

As a result of his interview with Robilant, Kálnoky changed Article 4 of his first draft and gave it a wording which took into account the wishes expressed by all parties. "In case Italy" (so it ran now), "without direct provocation on her part, should be attacked by France for any reason whatsoever, the two other contracting parties shall be bound to furnish help and assistance with all their forces to the party attacked. This same obligation shall devolve upon Italy in case of an aggression without direct provocation by France against Germany."[48] Shortly after this he began negotiations with Prince Reuss, the German ambassador in Vienna, communicating to him orally [49] the draft of the treaty and explaining the several articles. He gave particular emphasis to the reasons which had led him to make no provision for the support of Germany by Austria-Hungary in the event of an unprovoked attack by France upon Germany. "I have maintained this position in my conversations with Prince Reuss," he wrote to Wimpffen, "chiefly making use, among other arguments, of the fact that we have no common boundaries with France and are therefore in a different position from that of the powers which stand in direct contact with her. Our geographic position with regard to France is similar to that of Italy regarding Russia. If Italy is to be able to keep neutral in the event of a war in the East, we must also be free to make similar reserves in the West." At the same time he informed Bismarck that he was considering establishing the duration of the treaty at five years and adding a clause governing prolongation.

Kálnoky's proposals seem, in general, to have met with approval in Berlin. It does not appear from the documents at our disposal — the record is somewhat incomplete, to be sure — that Bismarck took umbrage at Kálnoky's refusal to promise Austro-Hungarian participation in a war between France and Germany. All the other stipulations governing the relations of the allies in case of war were assented to by him.[50] Bismarck thoroughly ap-

---

[48] Compare the French text, p. 30, note 54. On this occasion Kálnoky undertook a renumbering of his first treaty draft.

[49] Kálnoky here made the note in his own handwriting: "Communicated orally to Reuss."

[50] As Kálnoky informed Wimpffen, on April 1, he had transmitted to Berlin,

proved of Kálnoky's silence regarding the "recognition of territorial integrity." On the other hand, he considered it hazardous to express in such general terms the obligation to furnish "reciprocal support in certain questions of a political and economic nature," since the Central Powers would thus be "pledging themselves to back all the Italian aspirations in Egypt." He proposed instead a limitation of the obligations to be assumed through the insertion of the words "in proportion to their own interests." Bismarck also expressed himself cautiously, but unambiguously, against mentioning Russia by name as an adversary in the treaty. No such mention is to be found in Kálnoky's draft, but it existed in the proposals made by Robilant in his conversation with Kálnoky. "Such actual bearing as the treaty may have on Russia "— so Bismarck informed Vienna —"should preferably be expressed in a paraphrase, not mentioned directly. The former, *rebus sic stantibus*, I find preferable." As for the secret nature of the treaty, and its duration of five years, Bismarck gave his approval and repeated that "Austria-Hungary's assent was a prerequisite to that of Germany." [51]

Kálnoky lost no time in satisfying the Imperial Chancellor's few wishes. On April 11 he drew up a second draft, this time in French, which he communicated to the German and Italian governments. The introduction contained a solemn dedication to peace and to the monarchical system of government.

"The emperor of Austria-Hungary, the German emperor, and the king of Italy," it read, "animated by the desire to increase the guaranties of the general peace, to fortify the monarchical prin-

through Reuss, 'observations' regarding the topics of his talk with Robilant. Prince Reuss's reports are not at our disposal, and we can only guess at their contents from the summary of a despatch from Under Secretary of State Busch to Reuss, which the latter communicated to Kálnoky on April 3. In this we find a passage which for the present we are unable to explain: "The other wording of Article 3 desired by Count Kálnoky would, he [Bismarck] fears, be too fine-drawn to permit of the establishment of the *casus foederis* from it. If Italy is honorable and mistress of her own destinies, she will realize that it is to her own interest to prevent a French victory. We scarcely need anything more than a benevolent neutrality: Italy's resources would perhaps permit no more than this. Bismarck considers that our purpose is rather to save Austria's fighting forces than to gain Italy's."

[51] Extract from a despatch from Busch to Reuss, April 3, 1882.

ciple, and thereby to assure the unimpaired maintenance of the social and political order in their respective states, have agreed to conclude a treaty which, by its essentially conservative and defensive nature, pursues only the aim of forestalling the dangers which might threaten the peace of their states and of Europe." So far, Kálnoky could count on the assent of the Italian and German statesmen; in fact, no serious objection to the wording of this introduction was raised from any quarter during the course of the negotiations.[52]

The first article of the new draft combined the provisions of Articles 1 and 2 of the original draft. The tenor remained substantially the same, though account was taken of Bismarck's wish, the pledge of the allies "to guarantee reciprocal support in questions of a political and economic nature," as it was expressed in general terms in Kálnoky's first draft, being limited by the insertion of the clause "dans la limite de leurs intérêts."[53]

[52] On April 27, on the occasion of the deliberations over Kálnoky's third draft, Robilant requested, by instruction of his Government, that in the passage specifying that the treaty should guarantee its signatories against those dangers which might threaten "le repos de leurs états et de l'Europe," another phrase, "la sécurité de leurs états et le repos de l'Europe" should be substituted. Kálnoky accepted the wording proposed by Robilant, which as à matter of fact expressed more exactly the purposes of the alliance, and Bismarck gave his assent.

[53] The text is as follows: "Article I. Les parties contractantes se promettent mutuellement paix et amitié, et n'entreront dans aucune alliance ni engagement dirigé contre l'un de leurs états.

"Les parties contractantes se promettent en outre leur appui mutuel dans la limite de leurs propres intérêts pour les questions politiques et économiques qui pourraient se présenter."

Fraknói, in his analysis of this article (*Kritische Studien zur Geschichte des Dreibundes*, p. 31), has pointed to the fact that "consistency in the use of the most important expression is lacking." In this connection he notes that in the case of equal obligations expressions not identical in meaning, such as "se promettent, s'engagent," etc., are used interchangeably throughout. Fraknói's observation is correct, but it should not be forgotten that in many earlier and contemporary treaties the words chosen by Kálnoky were employed in the same connection and regarded by the diplomats as equivalent. A thorough critical investigation of the texts of international treaties would be an extremely profitable work, which would doubtless lead to the conclusion that most treaties are lacking in the necessary clearness and precision of expression. The use of forms, which played so great a part in the documents of the Middle Ages, has had a decisive influence on the wording of later treaties. Again and again, single words, whole phrases, and even entire articles have been

Article 2 of the new draft — assistance for Italy from both her allies in case of an unprovoked attack by France, and a corresponding counter-service on the part of Italy alone in the event that France should attack Germany without provocation — corresponds entirely to Kálnoky's first draft.[54]

Article 3 — establishment of the *casus foederis* in case one or two of the signatory parties should become involved in war with two or more Great Powers not belonging to the alliance — is more briefly worded than the corresponding Article 5 of the first draft, and does not contain the provision for the establishment of the *casus foederis* if two of the signatory parties become involved "in a war each with a single power not belonging to this alliance." [55]

Article 4 — benevolent neutrality on the part of two of the allies in case the third becomes involved in war with a single power not belonging to the alliance — is in complete harmony with the tenor of Article 4 of the first draft; however, especial attention is called to the fact that here, in contradistinction to Article 2, a war is meant in which the ally has become involved "sans être provoquée." [56]

passed on from one treaty to another, even when they were ill suited to the new situation. In discussing the question of the ambiguity of so many treaty stipulations, one should also not forget that they are for the most part the results of lengthy negotiations, and represent a compromise between divergent views. The treaties of the Triple Alliance bear convincing testimony to this. Last but not least, one must recall that the obscurity and ambiguity were often deliberately intended by the signatory parties, in order to serve as a pretext for future protests or claims. Cf. also L. Bittner, *Göttinger gelehrte Anzeigen*, 1914, pp. 458 ff.

[54] "Dans le cas où l'Italie sans provocation serait attaquée par la France pour quelque motif que ce soit, les deux autres parties contractantes seront tenues à prêter à la partie attaquée secours et assistance avec toutes les forces. Cette même obligation incombera à l'Italie dans le cas d'une agression non provoquée de la France contre l'Allemagne."

[55] In Kálnoky's second draft this article reads as follows: "Si une ou deux des parties contractantes sont engagées dans une guerre avec deux ou plusieurs grandes puissances non signataires du présent traité, le casus foederis se présente simultanément pour toutes les parties contractantes." For the wording of Article 5 of the first draft, see p. 21.

[56] Article IV. "Dans le cas où l'une des parties contractantes, sans être provoquée, serait engagée dans une guerre avec une puissance non signataire du présent traité, les deux autres s'obligent à observer une neutralité bienveillante à l'égard de celle des parties contractantes qui se trouve en guerre." For the later negotiations regarding this article, cf. pages 32 ff.

Article 5 rounded out the preceding provisions by stipulating that the signatory parties, as soon as the peace of one of them was menaced, should come to an agreement in due season concerning the military measures which might have to be taken in view of a possible coöperation. The substance of this article was new.[57] Articles 6 and 7, too, were not found in the earlier draft. They contained (6) the reciprocal promises to keep secret the fact that a treaty had been concluded, as well as the contents of that treaty, and (7) the establishment of the duration of the treaty at five years.[58] These two articles were incorporated into the final text in the form given them by Kálnoky.

On April 12 there took place the first consultation between Kálnoky and Robilant with regard to the draft of the treaty. The Italian received a copy of the document and promised to express himself in detail after receiving the instructions of his government. The first reading pleased him well; he had little fault to find with Kálnoky's draft, and his objections for the most part concerned the form rather than the substance of the various articles. The improvements suggested by him had to do with Articles 1 and 4; these met with Kálnoky's approval.[59]

[57] Article V. "Si la paix de l'une des parties contractantes venait à être menacée dans les circonstances prévues par les articles précédents, les parties contractantes se concerteront en temps utile sur les mesures militaires à prendre en vue d'une coopération éventuelle."

[58] See Vol. I, p. 69.

[59] Kálnoky's wording of the second paragraph of Article 1 read as follows: "Les parties contractantes se promettent en outre leur appui mutuel dans la limite de leurs propres intérêts pour les questions politiques et économiques qui pourraient se présenter." Robilant proposed instead of this: "elles s'engagent à procéder à un échange d'idées sur les questions politiques et économiques d'une nature générale qui pourraient se présenter et se promettent en outre leur appui mutuel dans la limite de leurs propres intérêts." It was probably Robilant's intention, in inserting the words "elles s'engagent à procéder à un échange d'idées," to lay upon the Central Powers the obligation to undertake, at Italy's request, the safeguarding of the Italian position in the Mediterranean. In 1887, when Crispi voiced his complaints of the neglect of Italy by the Central Powers, he pointed out that this article of the treaty of 1882 had not been sufficiently taken into consideration by the Central Powers. Robilant asked for two other changes in the wording of Article 4. In Kálnoky's draft the benevolent neutrality of two of the allies was stipulated in case the third power, "sans être provoquée, serait engagé dans une guerre avec une puissance non signataire." Robilant wished this provision to be more precisely stated, and suggested

Keeping Robilant's wishes before him, Kálnoky drew up on April 12 a third draft, which he transmitted to Robilant the same day, and on the day after to Prince Reuss. [60]   By April 18, it was learned from Berlin that Bismarck had accepted Kálnoky's new draft of the treaty without alteration, and had instructed the Secretary of State to submit it to Emperor William for his approval. [61]

The reply from Rome was slower in coming and did not altogether meet Kálnoky's hopes. The Italian government brought forward a new draft which differed in many points — some of them essential ones — from that prepared by Kálnoky. The Italians also let it be plainly seen that they did not wholly trust the Central Powers, and that they were most anxious to secure the assistance of both Germany and Austria-Hungary in the event of an unprovoked French attack upon Italy, without offering a corresponding counter-service to Austria-Hungary. [62]   Particularly characteristic were the changes proposed by Mancini and his counsellors in Article 4 of Kálnoky's draft. The wording in the original draft had run: "Should one of the signatory powers become involved in a war with a power not belonging to the alliance, both the others are pledged to observe a benevolent neutrality towards the signatory party which is at war." In order to make the sense of this provision perfectly clear, Kálnoky had inserted the words "sans être provoquée" in his second draft. No possible

the phrase "sans provocation directe se verrait forcée de faire la guerre à une puissance non signataire." Moreover, it was to be expressly emphasized at the end of this article that the allies should be free to abandon their benevolent neutrality and furnish armed assistance to their consignatory, if this should be found desirable. The wording given to this provision by Robilant is as follows: "sauf à intervenir avec les armes en faveur de leurs alliés si elles le jugeraient à propos." He doubtless wished to make it possible for Italy to participate in an Austro-Russian war in case her ally was winning and a suitable portion of the spoils of victory was to be expected. All these wishes of Robilant's were respected by Kálnoky in the third draft, which he prepared forthwith on April 12.

[60] "Draft No. 3, amended after a conversation with Count Robilant on April 12. Copy handed to Count Robilant April 12, and to Prince Reuss on April 13."

[61] Kálnoky to Wimpffen, April 18. Telegram. In a private note to Kálnoky, Széchényi had as early as April 15 predicted the early conclusion of the treaty, and had congratulated Kálnoky on his success with the words "much has been gained for us thereby."

[62] "Draft No. 4, with the Italian amendments. Transmitted by Robilant on April 27, 1882. Copy given to Prince Reuss on the 28th."

doubt could therefore exist that benevolent neutrality was to be observed under all circumstances; this covered the case where one of the allies, without being provoked, should enter into war with a power outside the alliance, Austria-Hungary, for example, could count on Italy's benevolent neutrality in case she were to become involved, without provocation by her adversary, in a war with Russia or any other state — one of the small Balkan nations, perhaps. Robilant had opposed this wording in his statement of April 11, and had succeeded, as we already know,[63] in getting Kálnoky to substitute for the phrase "sans être provoquée" another wording providing for the observation of benevolent neutrality in the event that the ally "sans provocation directe se verrait forcée de faire la guerre." This version was hardly fortunate, since doubt might arise as to what was meant by "direct provocation." Was it on the part of the ally or on that of the adversary? Kálnoky, as it would appear from the words "sans être provoquée" in the second draft, doubtless had the latter in mind.

The text, however, was also open to the interpretation that benevolent neutrality was to be observed by two of the allies toward the third only if the latter should find itself forced to declare war on a power outside the alliance, without having directly provoked its adversary. But it had been stipulated that, under all circumstances, benevolent neutrality was to be observed if an ally were to become involved in offensive as well as defensive warfare. Now, in the treaty draft which Robilant submitted on April 27 to Vienna, by instructions of the Italian government, it was expressly stated that benevolent neutrality should be observed by two of the allies toward the third ally if the latter were to be "attacked without provocation by a Great Power outside the Alliance." [64] Here was no longer a question of an offensive war on the part of one of the allies, but only of a defensive war — and, at that, not a defensive war with any adversary whatsoever, but only with a great power. If one considers that Italy was at that

[63] Cf. p. 31, note 59.

[64] "Dans le cas où l'une des H.P.C. sans provocation directe de sa part venait à être attaquée par une grande puissance," etc. As to what was meant by "attack," Hermann Rehm, writing in the *Frankfurter Zeitung* of June 20, 1915, has discussed in detail the articles of the treaty of the Triple Alliance known at that time.

time menaced by France alone and had made sure of the help of Germany and Austria-Hungary, by the terms of Article 2, in the event of an attack by that power, while Austria-Hungary could not count on corresponding aid from Italy in an Austro-Russian war, one can understand that Kálnoky must have been deeply chagrined when Italy showed her unwillingness to promise even a benevolent neutrality in case Austria-Hungary should find herself compelled, by force of circumstances, to go to war with Russia or with another state, even if the latter were not a great power.

It is unfortunate that we have no information concerning the course of the conversation held between Kálnoky and Robilant in this matter. We may assume that Robilant, by way of justifying the Italian version, pointed to the purely defensive character of the draft, which corresponded to the wishes expressed with such clearness in the preamble by all the signatories. Indeed, it cannot be denied that the Italian government was consistent in this regard. In the wording of Articles 2 and 3 it had proposed changes which made it plain that the establishment of the *casus foederis* should in all cases depend on the fact that the ally had been attacked and that this attack had not been superinduced by direct provocation on its part.[65]

[65] Article 2. The Italians proposed that "In the provisions regarding support to be furnished to Italy or Germany in the case of a French attack, the words 'sans provocation' were to be changed to ' sans provocation directe,' and 'd'une agression non provoquée' to 'd'une agression non directement provoquée." Kálnoky noted in his own handwriting here: "No objection, if Germany approves." As a matter of fact, Austria-Hungary had no particular interest in this matter. Possibly this proposal was prompted by the fear of the Italians that in case the words "sans provocation" alone were used, Austrian or German participation in a Franco-Italian war on Italy's side might be declined under the pretext that there had been provocation on the part of Italy, even if it were not "direct." This danger was doubtless averted by the insertion of the word "directe" after "provocation." Reciprocity demanded that a similar change in the treaty text should be made in Germany's favor.

Article 3. Robilant proposed that the stipulation governing the establishment of the *casus foederis* in the case of a war between one or two of the signatory parties and two or more great powers should not be expressed by the phrase "si une ou deux parties contractantes sont engagées dans une guerre," but by the words "Si une ou deux des hautes parties contractantes, sans provocation directe le leur part, viennent à être attaquées et à se trouver par ce fait engagées," etc. Kálnoky noted here in his own handwriting: "accepted *ad referendum*, in order to reach an agreement with Berlin concerning the change. Said to Prince Reuss that I found the words

Kálnoky accepted Robilant's proposals, in so far as they related to Articles 2 and 3, for further consideration; those bearing on Article 4, however, he firmly declined, insisting on the restoration of the wording as chosen by him in the third draft.[66] To certain other changes in the text of the Preamble [67] and in Article 4,[68] which he considered unessential, he immediately gave his assent. As for the proposal made by Robilant to extend the scope of Article 5 regarding possible preparations for joint action in case of war, by inserting a provision according to which the allies would pledge themselves, in a common war, to conclude an armistice, peace, or treaty only after reaching an agreement among themselves, he made his assent conditional on a previous agreement with Bismarck.[69]

As we have seen, however, the Italian demands were not limited to far-reaching plans for alterations in the treaty text. On the same day that Robilant presented to Kálnoky the new Italian

'attaquées et à se trouver par ce fait' superfluous, and that these had better be eliminated." Rehm, in the article cited in note 64, has concluded from the wording "venaient à être attaquées et à se trouver engagées dans une guerre" that only a menace, not an actual attack, was necessary on the part of the adversary: "A beginning of hostilities following a challenge is, according to the sense of the treaty, to be regarded as defence." It may be doubted, however, whether this was Robilant's intention.

[66] Kálnoky's note, in his own handwriting, reads: "Refused change, since it alters the sense, and insisted on restoration of text according to Draft no. 3, 'se verrait forcée de faire la guerre à une.' No objection to 'grande puissance.'"

[67] Toward the close of the preamble, Robilant insisted on the words "le *repos* de leurs états et de l'Europe" being replaced by "la *sécurité* de leurs états et le *repos* de l'Europe." Kálnoky noted here, "No objection." Cf. p. 29, note 52.

[68] In addition to the minutely discussed change in the text relating to the question of benevolent neutrality (pp. 30 ff., *supra*), Robilant proposed that the final sentence in Kálnoky's third draft, "sauf à intervenir avec les armes en faveur de leur allié si elles le jugeaient à propos," which had been adopted at his request, should be replaced by the phrase "en se réservant chacune la faculté de prendre part à la guerre, si elles le jugeaient à propos pour faire cause commune avec leur allié." Kálnoky noted here: "No particular objection to the altered wording."

[69] The Italian draft read: "Elles s'engagent dès à présent dans tous les cas de participation commune à une guerre à ne conclure ni paix, ni armistice, ni aucune espèce de traité que d'un commun accord entr' elles." Kálnoky notes here: "This paragraph accepted *ad referendum* for the purpose of reaching an understanding with Prince Bismarck. Said to Prince Reuss that I see no objection to accepting this, with the omission, however, of the words 'ni aucune espèce de traité.'"

draft of the treaty of the Triple Alliance, he also gave him the outline of a 'supplementary protocol,' the acceptance of which he
urgently recommended. This supplementary protocol, which was
to be signed simultaneously with the main treaty, affirmed that
the latter contained no offensive tendencies of any nature whatsoever against England — that, on the contrary, the signatory
powers would "accept England's accession to this treaty—or even
to a mere pact of neutrality. They reserve for themselves, however, the right to establish, by means of an agreement to be
reached among themselves, the time and the substance of every
communication which might possibly be made to the British cabinet to this end." [70] This proposal did not surprise Kálnoky. As
early as April 15, Wimpffen had reported from Rome that the
Italian government had not agreed to the wording of Article 3,
governing the establishment of the *casus foederis* in the event of
one or two of the allies becoming involved in a war with two or
more Great Powers. "It is feared," said Wimpffen, "that this
general wording might possibly draw Italy into war with England,
and that, if not France, some other nation — Russia, for example
— might be England's ally. The Italians wish to avoid every
semblance of suspicion of England, for they feel that she could
completely paralyze any military action that they might take." [71]

The reasons cited by the Italians to justify their especial con
sideration for England were not happily chosen; their point of
view, however, was well founded. England was at that time dealing with the Egyptian question in common with France. No one
could predict what further course their undertaking might assume; no one could guess what the future combinations of the
European Great Powers might be. Italy, whose chagrin over the

[70] The wording of the Italian draft for a protocol is as follows: "Les plénipotentiaires soussignés, dûment autorisés par leurs gouvernements, déclarent que les stipulations du traité conclu et signé ce même jour entre l'Allemagne, l'Autriche-Hongrie
et l'Italie dans l'intention défensive et préalablement exprimée des parties contractantes ne visent aucune offensive contre l'Angleterre; et qu'au contraire les dites
hautes parties contractantes accepteront l'accession de l'Angleterre au dit traité
d'alliance ou même seulement au pacte de neutralité, mais en se reservant de déterminer d'un commun accord entre les trois alliés le temps et la forme de toute communication qui devrait eventuellement être adressé dans ce but au cabinet Anglais."
[71] Wimpffen to Kálnoky, April 15, 1882. Private letter.

occupation of Tunisia by the French had drawn her closer to the Central Powers, was on the verge of concluding with them a treaty safeguarding her against a swift victory of the French army, which was far superior to her own. Neither Germany nor Austria-Hungary, however, was in a position to protect the Italian coasts against raids by the French fleet. England alone was able to do this. "As a friend and ally of England," Crispi declared later, "we have nothing to fear at sea; if the opposite were the case, we should never be masters of our own coasts." [72] And to whom, if not to England, was Italy to look for furtherance of those colonial plans to which she adhered with the utmost determination, never for a moment losing them from sight? In the course of the negotiations the Central Powers had shown no inclination to identify themselves with Italy's special interests in the Mediterranean.[73] Here, too, only a friendly understanding with England could open up more favorable prospects for the future; and Mancini's desire for a declaration becomes all the more comprehensible — a declaration which not only could serve, if the need should arise, to let the English government know that Italy had never thought of war against England, but also contemplated the entrance of England into the Triple Alliance.

Mancini could count with certainty on Kálnoky's assent to this project. Austria-Hungary was at that time still on the best of terms with England; her chief statesmen wished this state of affairs to continue, and would undoubtedly have welcomed Britain's admittance to the Triple Alliance with eagerness. Bismarck, too, could make no objections to a provision which expressed the peaceful intentions of the Triple Alliance in special relation to England. He understood Italy's need to stand on good terms with England. "As a result of the proximity of Italy's extensive coast line to the French harbors and arsenals on the Mediterranean," he said on a certain occasion,[74] "together with Italy's lack of

---

[72] Cited by E. von Reventlow, *Deutschland's auswärtige Politik, 1888 bis 1913*, p. 11.

[73] In 1886 Robilant wrote: "En 1882 nous avons eu l'air de mendier l'alliance plutôt que de la négocier, et, en la concluant, nous nous sommes exposés à une guerre continentale sans prendre nos suretés contre une guerre maritime." Cf. Tardieu, *La France et les alliances*, pp. 163 ff.

[74] Cf. H. Hofmann, *Fürst Bismarck, 1890-1898*, i, p. 257.

coast defences, the latter, as England's ally, is completely protected against France by the British fleet; while without England,
Italy's position is exposed indeed." Quite different, however, was
his attitude toward the project for the prospective inclusion of
England in the Triple Alliance. He was primarily prejudiced
against this by regard for Russia, whose more intimate association
with the Central Powers he had at heart now, as before. He knew,
too, that he could never persuade his aged sovereign to take a
step which could only be interpreted at the Russian court as a
challenge. Moreover, Bismarck was not inclined to smooth the
way for the policy of expansion which was even then being vigorously pushed by English statesmen; and he was convinced that
the English cabinet could conclude no secret agreements on account of Parliament.

We unfortunately have no information concerning the negotiations carried on between the German and Austro-Hungarian governments toward the end of April and the beginning of May with
regard to this question and the new Italian project for a treaty;
we only know the results to which they led. Robilant's project for
a protocol contemplating the inclusion of England in the Triple
Alliance was rejected by the Central Powers — at Bismarck's
wish, without doubt. Italy's suggestion, however, was successful
to the extent that it was decided to state expressly that the provisions of the Triple Alliance were not directed against England.[75]
This was done by means of similarly worded ministerial declarations of the three governments, signed on the same day as the
main treaty and annexed thereto. Bismarck proved to be very
accommodating as regards the changes suggested by the Italians
in the main treaty. In the case of most of the articles he accepted
the wording of the Italian draft, and persuaded Kálnoky to drop
his objections. Only in the case of Article 4, regarding the benevolent neutrality to be observed by two of the allies toward the
third, did he fail to overcome Kálnoky's opposition; but a solution was finally found which satisfied Kálnoky and took account
at the same time of Italy's wishes. According to the new version,
it was no longer a question of observing neutrality only when the

[75] Cf. the text, Vol. I, p. 68.

ally was attacked, without provocation on its part, by a great power not belonging to the Alliance. The wording now ran: "In case a great power nonsignatory to the present treaty should threaten the security of the states of one of the high contracting parties, and the threatened party should find itself forced on that account to make war against it, the two others bind themselves to observe towards their ally a benevolent neutrality." [76]

When this question had been settled, no obstacle stood in the way of the signing of the Treaty and its supplementary Protocol. This was done at Vienna, on May 20, 1882, by Kálnoky, Reuss, and Robilant. On the 30th of the same month the exchange of ratifications was consummated. [77]

The purposes of the treaty of May 20, 1882, were explicitly defensive_in every respect. It was intended to secure the allied sovereigns and their states against any disturbance of the peace from without or within. In the latter regard, one should not' underestimate the significance attributed to the treaty by the allied sovereigns and their chief statesmen as a safeguard of the monarchical principle and a protection against 'destructive' social movements. If the desire for strengthening the monarchical power had been one of the chief reasons for the rapprochement between Italy and the two empires, then the conclusion of the Triple Alliance must be regarded as the triumph of this idea — a triumph, primarily, of the house of Savoy, which had not yet been firmly established in Italy. [78] The reason why this purpose finds expression only in the preamble to the treaty lies in the peculiar nature of international agreements. In other respects the arrangement was profitable to all three signatories — to Italy, without doubt, in the greatest measure. This is a noteworthy fact, since Italy, as the suppliant, should have had to pay the highest price for the realization of the alliance.

[76] See Vol. I, p. 67.   [77] See Vol. I, p. 68, note.
[78] The anonymous author of the article "La France, l'Italie, et la Triple Alliance" (*Revue des deux mondes*, xciv, p. 279), expresses this idea correctly: "c'était peut-être davantage le désir de se rapprocher de l'Europe conservatrice, de se donner une sorte de consécration vis-à-vis des cours et de garantie vis-à-vis de la révolution. . . . A vrai dire, la triple alliance a été moins l'oeuvre d'un ministère ou d'un parti, que de la dynastie."

No guaranty of Italian territory, including Rome, was undertaken by the Central Powers; in this respect Italy had failed to obtain the satisfaction of her demands. However, the words in the preamble stating that the allies pledged themselves to the "unimpaired maintenance of the social and political order in their respective states" could be interpreted by the Italian government as containing a safeguard against the restoration of the temporal power of the Pope. Indeed, Italy must have realized with considerable complacency that she, the state which had been humiliated at the Congress of Berlin, treated with scorn and contempt as the least of the nations of Europe,[79] now, freed from her perilous isolation, was taking her stand as a great power, with equal rights, beside the two Central Empires. Italy's greatest political advantage, however, lay in the fact that she was guaranteed against any attack by the Austro-Hungarian monarchy, and had won the additional assurance of being supported by the full strength of both her allies in case she were attacked by France, the only country whose menace was immediate.

The obligations assumed by her in return for these considerable advantages were insignificant. Participation at the side of mighty Germany in a war against isolated France that had been brought on by French aggression against Germany would entail but little danger; while, in the event of a victorious conclusion, inviting prospects of territorial acquisitions along the northwestern frontiers would be opened up. In case of a combined attack by France and Russia — the allies were threatened by no other great power at that time — the remoteness of Italy from the probable scene of action gave her little ground for fear. The Italians were not pledged to support the Austro-Hungarian monarchy in a war with Russia alone. They merely promised in this event to observe a benevolent neutrality, reserving the right to participate in the war in case their interests so demanded — in other words, if the success of their ally was certain — and thus share in the spoils of victory.

[79] Chiala, *Pagine di storia contemporanea*, ii, p. 17: "Umiliati a Berlino come l'ultimo popolo d'Europa ne tornammo colle beffe et collo scorno."

Germany derived a double advantage from the alliance. First of all, she was now sure that Italy would not be fighting on the side of her adversaries in a war which she might have to wage alone against France, or jointly with Austria against the combined armies of France and Russia. This was what Bismarck had in view when he remarked that he would be satisfied if "one Italian corporal with the Italian flag and a drummer at his side should take the field on the Western front (against France) and not on the Eastern front (against Austria)."[80] Then, too, there was the hope that Italy might after all participate actively on the side of Germany in a war begun by France. In this way the new ally would have filled the gaps left open in Bismarck's system of defence by Kálnoky's adherence to Andrássy's policy, which precluded the idea of coöperation on the part of Austria-Hungary in a Franco-German conflict.[81] Military circles in Berlin, to be sure, cherished no illusions as to the real value of the Italian army. They believed, however, that an Italian advance against southeastern France might have a value for their strategic plans which was not to be ignored; and the Italian fleet, at that time considered the third strongest in Europe, might also render the German army certain services.

As for Austria-Hungary, the chief advantage accruing to her from the Triple Alliance lay in the neutralization of the danger which had heretofore existed of an attack on her southern borders by Italy while she was involved in a war with Russia. Protected on this side, the Dual Monarchy could concentrate its entire strength against its eastern neighbor if the attitude of the latter

---

[80] Cf. Bülow, *Deutsche Politik* (1916), p. 72. Bismarck expressed himself to an American journalist (cf. Poschinger, *Also sprach Bismarck*, iii, p. 151) as follows: "Though Italy should reduce her army by two, three, or even four army corps, the chief point is that the entire Austrian army would be left free, through Italian friendliness, for action on the Eastern frontier."

[81] It is therefore incorrect that — as has been repeatedly asserted by French authors (recently by Antonin Debidour, *Histoire politique de l'Europe*, iii, p. 51) — Austria-Hungary had pledged herself to participate in a war against France, in the event that the latter alone were the adversary of the allies. On the contrary, Austria-Hungary had absolutely declined this obligation. In the event of an offensive war of France against Germany, she was only pledged to participate in case Russia aligned herself with France.

should make it necessary to assume the offensive. No provision was made in the treaty pledging Italy to furnish armed assistance to Austria in case she should be attacked by Russia alone without provocation. Later Austro-Hungarian statesmen have censured Count Kálnoky for this, and have declared that he allowed himself to be outwitted by the Italians, since he promised them the full military asistance of Austria-Hungary in case France assumed the offensive against Italy without demanding similar aid from them in the event of a Russian attack on the Dual Monarchy. There can now be no doubt that such a pledge on the part of the Italians would in itself have been desirable, even if Kálnoky, like Prince Bismarck, did not value the fighting strength of the Italians very highly, and considered the Dual Monarchy strong enough to carry out a successful war with Russia by the side of Germany, whose assistance in the event of attack by Russia was assured by the treaty of October, 1879.

There were certain reasons, however, for Kálnoky's attitude. Years later he admitted that he had renounced Italian aid in warding off a Russian attack on Austria because he wished to afford his greedy neighbor no opportunity to stretch out a hand toward the Balkan countries and turn the Adriatic into an Italian sea.[82] And there was still another reason. Kálnoky held firmly to

[82] It may have been this consideration which determined Kálnoky not to demand Italy's support of Austria-Hungary in a conflict with one or more Balkan states. Fraknói (*Kritische Studien zur Geschichte des Dreibundes*, p. 336), says: "Austria-Hungary was exposed to the danger of attack by ambitious small states whose races were represented within the Dual Monarchy (Serbia, Montenegro, Rumania). In the event of such an attack — even if it were undertaken by these small states in cooperation with a single great power — Austria-Hungary could not demand the assistance of her allies in protecting her imperilled integrity by virtue of Article III. The possibility and probability that this dangerous situation might arise escaped the attention of those Austro-Hungarian diplomats who concluded the treaty and repeatedly renewed it." It should nevertheless be observed that Kálnoky wished under all circumstances to avoid Italian meddling in the Balkan questions. In 1882 he succeeded in doing this, but not in 1887. Cf. pp. 72 ff., *infra*. Kálnoky characterized this in 1887 as a very heavy sacrifice which Austria had made for the great cause. Moreover, Serbia was completely bound to the Dual Monarchy by the treaty of June 28, 1881, and had pledged herself to support Austria-Hungary in a conflict with the surrounding Balkan nations. Hostilities were no longer to be feared from the Rumanian sovereign. The sudden change which resulted in 1883 in the alliance of Rumania with the powers of the Triple Alliance was in preparation as early as 1882.

the principle which had governed Andrássy at the time of the conclusion of the Austro-German treaty: he wished under no circumstances to bind Austria to take part in a war between France and
Germany. He was delighted that Bismarck had made no demand
of this nature during the course of the negotiations leading up to
the Triple Alliance, and was anxious to avoid everything which
might induce him to put forward such a proposal. This danger
would have been imminent indeed if Austria had stipulated in the
treaty for the support of both her allies in the case of an attack by
one great power — namely Russia — while herself refusing to
lend aid to Germany in the similar event of an attack by France.
Italy retained her specially favored position, but the cause of it
lay in her military weakness. This may have been the reason why
Kálnoky renounced a corresponding counter-service in return for
the armed assistance which had been pledged the Italians if attacked by France, and contented himself with their promise to
fight at the side of Austria-Hungary and Germany in case these
powers should be forced to meet an attack launched without provocation by France and Russia together.

CHAPTER II

THE SECOND TREATY OF THE TRIPLE ALLIANCE
FEBRUARY 20, 1887

It was hoped that the Treaty of the Triple Alliance of May 20, 1882, would form the basis of really friendly relations between Italy and Austria-Hungary. This hope, however, was not fulfilled. The two governments, to be sure, adhered strictly to their obligations, and their leading statesmen neglected no opportunity to speak of the excellent relations existing between the two countries, and the cordial sentiments of their sovereigns. They also showed their readiness to smooth over nascent difficulties in the most accommodating spirit. The Italian press, however, echoed the reckless talk of certain members of the Chamber, and kept urging the Italian people to unfriendly utterances and deeds against Austria-Hungary, thus arousing a retaliatory spirit on the other side. The difficulties preventing Francis Joseph's return visit to Rome [83] were not given due consideration by the Italian press and people, and every alternative proposed by Vienna was stigmatized as an insult to the national honor and brusquely rejected. The Irredentist movement spread and increased in strength. Prince Bismarck, to whom the Austro-Hungarian statesmen had expressed their concern over these developments, made repeated attempts to influence the Italian press, only to be forced to admit the failure of his efforts. When the heir to the Austrian throne, Crown Prince Rudolph, spoke to the Imperial Chancellor in February, 1883, concerning the hostile attitude of the press and the people of Italy toward the Austro-Hungarian Monarchy, Bismarck said that unfortunately one could not depend much on the friendly assurances of the Italian government. Even if good will

[83] This question gave rise to repeated discussions between Kálnoky and the Italian statesmen, regarding which the Vienna State Archives contain valuable material. Cf. Crispi, *Memoirs*, ii, pp. 156 f.

were present, strength would be lacking. King Humbert might easily find himself so placed that he would have to choose between "taking his place as leader of a popular movement against the allies and holding fast, in open opposition to the wishes of his nation, to the obligations he had assumed toward them." It was impossible, Bismarck declared, to count with full confidence on Italy if war were to break out with France or Russia.[84]

At first, however, there appeared to be no reason for disturbing the existing relationship, especially as the chief Italian statesmen kept referring most cordially to the Triple Alliance and its beneficial results for Italy, and promised it their unswerving allegiance. It was the colonial plans of Italy, developed in 1885 in emulation of the Western powers, which first caused serious concern to the two empires. The military occupation of the Egyptian port of Massowah on the Red Sea, without previous notification to Vienna or Berlin, seemed to the statesmen of Germany and Austria-Hungary not altogether in accord with the provisions of the treaty of the Triple Alliance. In April, 1885, Count Kálnoky submitted to the Imperial Chancellor the question whether Italy's attention should be called to this, but abstained for the moment from following the matter up, since Bismarck, though sharply condemning the step taken by Italy, decided it would be better "to give the Italians time to reform."[85] But this hoped-for 'reformation' did not materialize. The lack of confidence shared by Bismarck and Kálnoky in the trustworthiness of Italian policy persisted even after Count Robilant, a sincere friend of the Triple Alliance, had assumed control of the Foreign Office in June, 1885. On the occasion of an interview which took place in August of this same year between Bismarck and Kálnoky, the two statesmen agreed that Italy "could not be regarded as a significant factor in any possible combination." They were also of the opinion, however, that the treaty of the Triple Alliance should be renewed if Italy so requested, since it bound her at least morally to the Central Powers. It is significant that this time it was Bismarck who

[84] Report of Crown Prince Rudolph regarding his interview with Prince Bismarck, March 1, 1883.
[85] Copy of a letter from Bismarck to Reuss, April 17, 1885.

recommended that a close watch be kept on Italy's advances in the Red Sea. "We must see to it," he said, "that there is no chance of Italy through her pranks involving us — perhaps deliberately — in a conflict with France." [86]

No further discussion of this and other questions, however, was undertaken for the time being, since Italy had not yet requested the prolongation of the alliance.[87]   This she first did in July, 1886,[88] when certain fundamental changes in the general political conditions of Europe gave the Italians reason to believe that they could now enter into negotiations under more favorable circumstances. The Bulgarian affair, with the annexation of Eastern Rumelia to Bulgaria in September, 1885, had destroyed the passable relations which, thanks to the mediatory policy of Bismarck, had existed up to that time between the governments of Vienna and St. Petersburg. The events following this — the Serbo-Bulgarian war, Austria's intervention in favor of the vanquished Serbian king, and the firm stand taken by the government of Vienna against that predominance of Russian influence in the Balkans which had manifested itself in the enforced abdication of Alexander of Battenberg — aggravated the struggle of the two powers for mastery in the Balkans. The understanding existing between them threatened to vanish; the peril of an Austro-Russian war loomed larger. Taking these circumstances into consideration,

[86] Notes regarding conversations with Bismarck in Varzin, August 12-16, 1885; signed in Kálnoky's own handwriting.

[87] Crispi states (*Memoirs*, ii, p. 160) that on October 24, 1885, Bismarck made overtures to Launay regarding the renewal of the treaty, and declared his readiness to give it "more practical and cordial" form. But when Launay remarked "that provisionally the aim was only to smooth the way for improving the working of the existing alliance," Bismarck had no objection to make. The latter expression is perhaps more characteristic than the former of Bismarck's attitude at the time. According to Chiala (*La triplice e la duplice alleanza*, 2d ed., p. 466), Robilant, when asked by Launay whether he intended to suggest an exchange of ideas with regard to the question of renewing the treaty, replied: "che ciò spettava al principe, non a noi."

[88] According to Chiala, p. 467, Robilant replied about the middle of March, 1886, to a second inquiry from Launay as to the desirability of taking the first steps toward the renewal of an improved alliance: "che non giudicava il momento acconcio per intavolare negoziati per il rinnovamento del trattato, il quale, in tutti i casi, non poteva essere rinnovato tel quel."

the value to Austria-Hungary of an alliance with Italy, stronger as she now was financially and in military resources, had decidedly increased — all the more so because it must have been realized in Vienna that Bismarck was by no means inclined to support Austria-Hungary's Balkan policy through thick and thin. On the contrary, it was known that he intended to demand considerable sacrifices of his ally for the purpose of blocking the union of the French military party, at that time making great headway under Boulanger's leadership, with that of Russia.

In view of the possibility of a war on two fronts, even to Prince Bismarck Italy's adherence to the Triple Alliance seemed far more desirable than before. With the growth of this peril in the second half of 1886, Bismarck became increasingly disposed to give a hearing to the proposals brought forward by the Italian government. As late as July, 1886, he had declined Launay's request that Germany take the initiative in renewing the Triple Alliance, on the ground that such a step might be regarded in Vienna as pressure, and that "Germany was only secondarily interested in the prolongation of the treaty." The Italians were referred to their Austro-Hungarian allies, who in the meanwhile had been cautioned to observe the greatest wariness, since Italy was also negotiating with France and would sell herself as an ally as dearly as possible. At the same time Bismarck had expressed doubts as to the advisability of meeting the wishes of Italy, who was already demanding the renewal of the Triple Alliance on the basis of the status quo in the Mediterranean and in the Adriatic, especially as "in view of Italy's well known aspirations towards Albania," no faith can be placed "in the sincerity of the promises she has given regarding the maintenance of the status quo in the Adriatic." [89] In the conversations which took place in July, 1886, at Kissingen, and a month later at Gastein, between Bismarck and Kálnoky, the two statesmen likewise agreed that the existing relation should be allowed to continue unchanged, since an extension of the pre-

[89] Telegram from Széchényi to Kálnoky, July 27, 1886. Among other things, Launay mentioned in a conversation that 'the Italian frontier in Friuli was entirely open; but this question would be exclusively the subject of an *entente à l'amical.*' With regard to the differences between Robilant's and Launay's conceptions, cf. Chiala, *La triplice e la duplice alleanza* (2d ed.), pp. 469 ff.

vious obligations through the assumption of a guaranty of the status quo in the Mediterranean could not be accepted.[90]

The substance of this was made known to Robilant,[91] who was greatly offended by Bismarck's unfavorable attitude. "Italy," he wrote at the time to Launay, "is tired of this unprofitable alliance, and I feel no desire to facilitate its renewal; for I am convinced that it will always remain unprofitable for us. It is possible, however, that Herr von Bismarck is deceived with regard to me, and has imagined, in his ignorance, that I will feel constrained to follow him at all times and under all circumstances. If he believes this, he is grievously mistaken. It is more than probable that I shall not renew the alliance. I shall wait, however, for the proper moment to come before committing myself. I therefore desire that you, for your part, should avoid any exchange of opinions in the matter of the renewal of the alliance. If the Imperial Chancellor wishes to set on foot negotiations to this end, he must take the initiative and let us know his ideas." [92] These were haughty words, written in a moment of excitement — a blazing protest against Bismarck's condescending treatment of Italy.

This mood, however, did not last long. The scanty inclination shown by Salisbury to champion with energy Italian interests in the Orient, together with the fear of France's projects in the Mediterranean, sharpened the desire of the Italians for closer relations with the Central Powers. In the middle of September von Rosty, the Austrian chargé d'affaires in Rome, was able to notify his government that Robilant was ready to negotiate with Vienna and Berlin; he needed only to find a method of procedure "which would protect him against the charge of imperfectly safeguarding Italy's dignity on the part of his countrymen, whose amour propre was very great." The German government met this wish in an

[90] Conversation between Kálnoky and Reuss, September 24, 1886.

[91] Cf. also Chiala, p. 474.

[92] Cf. Chiala, p. 471. In this connection von Rosty reported from Rome on August 14 that Robilant had communicated to the ambassadors in Vienna and Berlin his conception of the conditions under which he believed it desirable to renew the Triple Alliance. He instructed them, however, "not to raise discussions of the matter on their own initiative, but merely to express themselves in accordance with their instructions in case the ministers of foreign affairs should bring up the subject."

accommodating spirit, and began to work in Rome for the renewal of the alliance, thereby letting it be understood that if Robilant were to make fresh overtures he need no longer fear a brusquely unfavorable answer.[93] In fact, Bismarck now showed a much greater inclination to meet the wishes of the Italians. When, toward the end of September, 1886, Launay again made mention in Berlin of the Mediterranean question in connection with the renewal of the Triple Alliance,[94] Bismarck, it is true, referred him once more to Vienna, "where the key between Germany and Italy is to be found," and left it to the Austro-Hungarian government to consider how far it might seem expedient for them "to encourage Italy's loyalty to the treaty, which is not altogether above suspicion, by holding out hopes of territorial acquisitions in the Mediterranean." This time, however, he did not fail to point out the significance of her possible defection.[95] The eagerness shown by Keudell, the German ambassador in Rome, and the numerous conferences between him and Robilant, likewise indicated that the German government, realizing the ever-increasing peril of a Franco-German war, desired a speedy agreement with Italy.

Towards the middle of October the results of German mediation in Rome were imparted to Vienna. Robilant had declined a mere renewal of the treaty of 1882, and had characterized as indispensable a discussion of the Mediterranean questions — especially as regarded the maintenance of the status quo in Tripoli. An alliance with the Central Powers — so Robilant declared — would be of no value to Italy if it gave her no assurance that the allies would not permit an occupation of Tripoli by France. If this were not done, public opinion in Italy would rather favor

[93] Despatch from Rosty, September 16, 1886. In the conversations between the German representative, Count Arco, and Robilant, the question of Francis Joseph's return visit to Rome was broached by the latter. Bismarck thereupon caused inquiries to be made by Reuss, in Vienna, as to the attitude taken there in the matter. Kálnoky replied that a journey to Rome by the emperor would be impossible; he would gladly pay his return visit to King Humbert at any other place, but it was unlikely that this would be agreed to in Italy. Interview with Prince Reuss, September 17, 1886.

[94] Tavera to Kálnoky, September 28, 1886. Telegram.

[95] Ritter von Tavera to Kálnoky, October 1, 1886. Original. Cf. Chiala, pp. 474 ff.

reaching an agreement with France regarding the mastery of the Mediterranean.

One more wish had also been expressed by Robilant. Italy, said he, could not stand by as a disinterested spectator in case Turkey's possessions should be divided up by Russia and Austria; nor could she "allow herself to be taken by surprise by an ally." She must be given an opportunity, by timely notification, to assert her interests in that region.[96] As we have seen, the Italian statesmen knew how to make use of a favorable situation to their own ends. They now expressed in unmistakable terms their wishes for an extension of their sphere of influence on the North African coast of the Mediterranean and in the Balkans. Bismarck, in transmitting the proposals of the Italian cabinet to Vienna, at first refused to commit himself in regard to these claims. Now that the initial step had been taken by the Italians, he said, he would leave it to the Austrian government to get in touch with Robilant either through the intermediary of the German government or by the direct agency of the Italian ambassador in Vienna, Count Nigra; he declared at the same time, however, that any agreement reached by Austria would be assented to in advance by the German government.[97]

This shifting of the decision to Kálnoky's shoulders increased the Austro-Hungarian statesman's responsibility for the results of his action and compelled him to bear constantly in mind the desires of the German Imperial Chancellor, with which he was well acquainted. On principle, Kálnoky would have preferred to decline both the Italian demands. The assumption by Austria-Hungary of an obligation to back Italy's schemes in the Mediterranean, and the direct interference of Italy in the Balkan conflicts, were equally distasteful to him. In the course of his first conversation with Reuss regarding the Italian demands, he re-

[96] Report made by the German Ambassador on October 19, 1886, concerning Keudell's conversation with Robilant on October 5, 1886. The Austrian government had already been informed of the contents of these German-Italian negotiations through telegrams from its representative at the court of Berlin, Ritter von Tavera, on October 9, 12, and 16, 1886.

[97] Telegram from Tavera to Kálnoky, October 16, 1886, and instruction to Reuss, an excerpt from which was handed to Kálnoky on October 19, 1886.

ferred to the fact that he and Bismarck had agreed at Kissingen to assume no guaranty for the maintenance of the status quo in the Mediterranean.[98] He added immediately, however, that in view of the existing situation, he did not propose to offend Robilant by an abrupt rejection of his wishes. He therefore said that he was ready to propose to Robilant the acceptance of the existing treaty as the basis for its prolongation, giving him at the same time an assurance that the Austrian government would "consider such other wishes as the Italians might express, and interpret them in a spirit of accommodation." Kálnoky, referring to Robilant's demands, went on to say: "If the guaranty of Tripoli asked for by Count Robilant means only an assurance that we will pledge Italy our moral and diplomatic support in case of an attack by France on Tripoli — or if he will be satisfied with such an assurance — then, so far as we are concerned, we will raise no objections, for we have no reasons for grudging Italy the possession of Tripoli. If, however, Count Robilant demands that our support in such an event should go as far as active intervention against France — in other words, that we should become involved in a war on sea or on land on account of Tripoli — we must refuse such a guaranty with the utmost decision; and so, I venture to say, must Germany." [99]

With regard to Robilant's proposals concerning the Balkans, Kálnoky suggested an answer to the effect that 'in accordance with our interpretation of the spirit of the existing alliance, it would not have been permissible to reach such an important understanding without the knowledge of our ally, Italy. In such an event — which, moreover, is out of harmony with the entire tendency of our policies — Germany and Austria-Hungary would not fail to inform the Italian government in ample time.' Kálnoky added that he saw no objection to promising Robilant that, in the highly improbable event of such an agreement, the Italian cabinet would be duly acquainted with it. He also suggested an exchange of opinions with Bismarck regarding the possible coöperation of Italy against Russia. "During the negotiations pre-

[98] Cf. pp. 47 f.
[99] Kálnoky's notes on his conversation with Reuss, October 23, 1886.

ceding the conclusion of the present treaty," he said, "a certain inclination in that direction on the part of the Italians was to be observed. The matter, however, was not taken up either by us or by the Germans — partly because we did not consider it necessary to draw Italy into the affairs of the Orient, partly because we doubted whether Italy, occupied as she was by the more immediate French peril, would be in a position to make any important military contribution in the East. Now, however, that Italy has in view an Oriental policy with regard to France, I think it is worth our while to give further consideration to a possible Italian coöperation against Russia." [100]

The cautiousness, the reserve shown in Kálnoky's utterances concerning the Italian demands, aroused Bismarck's displeasure, for he believed Italy's aid was indispensable to the great structure of the alliance built up by him against a double attack by the united military forces of France and Russia. He therefore decided to exert strong pressure on the Austro-Hungarian government in favor of Italy. For this purpose he made use of an effective expedient, employed by him many times before, and brought his aged ruler into the foreground. "Emperor William," he wrote to Vienna, "finds that it would be inexpedient for Germany to remain neutral in the event of a war between France and Italy, no matter what its cause might be. The origin of such a war would, in fact, be of no consequence,[101] for Germany could not permit Italy to be annihilated or reduced to a state of dependence by France." In Vienna also, he went on to say, it should be considered how easily Italy, if she were bound by no treaty, could align herself with Russia in the event of an Austro-Russian war. Bismarck, for his part, laid most stress on the danger of Italy's defection to the camp of the French. "If Italy," he said, "repulsed by the Allies, were to offer herself to France for the price of Tripoli, France would close with her." Bismarck also expressed his con-

[100] Kálnoky's notes on his conversation with Reuss, October 23, 1886.
[101] On October 26 Prince Reuss and Kálnoky had a second conversation; Reuss, acting under Bismarck's instructions, emphasized the point that Germany would have no objection to guaranteeing the status quo in Tripoli, and said that Bismarck would like to know Kálnoky's views in the matter. The latter answered evasively. Notes regarding Kálnoky's conversation with Reuss, October 26, 1886.

viction that Italy would accept less than she was now asking of Germany and Austria-Hungary. He believed himself justified in assuming that she would be satisfied with a promise on the part of the Central Powers to help her in case she "should be attacked by France in her European possessions after protesting against a possible, though very improbable French advance in Tripoli." In the Balkan question also he felt that Italy's assent could be counted on, provided "assurance against surprises were given her" in that region.[102]

The exhortations and counsels directed by Prince Bismarck towards Vienna were not without effect. Kálnoky realized how urgently he needed Germany's help to maintain Austria-Hungary's position in the Balkans, and Bismarck's utterances had given him reason to doubt whether he could count unreservedly on German support in the event of a passage at arms with Russia. In the same speech in which he indicated the limits of his concessions to Russian demands in the Balkans by the words, "We all wish peace, but certainly not peace at any price," he hinted at the differences existing between him and Bismarck with regard to the Balkan question. "It is self-evident," he declared, "that in the case of two great powers of such magnitude, stretching as they do from the Baltic to the Adriatic, and from the North Sea to the lower Danube, each one possesses special interests lying wholly outside the sphere of interests of the other, the protection of which is not included among the obligations of the other."

Kálnoky therefore decided to accommodate the Italians as far as possible, without altogether abandoning the stand he had taken on principle, and informed Berlin that the cabinet of Vienna "had no objections to the pledges, as worded by Bismarck." At the same time, however, he expressed the fear that the demands of the Italians would not be within the bounds of moderation. For this reason he felt it his duty to state with emphasis that Austria-Hungary would have nothing to do with any project that might curtail her freedom of action in the Orient, or "give Italy the right to exert particular influence in any territorial question whatever."

---

[102] Excerpt from the instructions from the German Foreign Office to Reuss; handed to Kálnoky on October 30.

The question of the Adriatic, he said, "is bound to emerge at some time from the hiding place in which it has been lurking of late." [103]

Shortly after this, Robilant took another step which showed that Kálnoky's misgivings had not been without foundation. Toward the end of November, 1886, he submitted to the German government, through Launay, the draft of a supplementary treaty, urgently recommending its acceptance and attempting to establish and justify its substance in great detail. In doing this, he proceeded on the assumption that the treaty of 1882 had not fulfilled Italy's rightful expectations. At the time of its signature the three allies had expressly promised mutual support "within the limits of their own interests" in matters not directly implying the *casus foederis*. Italy, however, was convinced that, so far as her just claims on Tripoli and Morocco were concerned, the provisions of the treaty had been dead letters. Robilant also pointed out that the Italy of 1887 was not the same as the Italy of 1882; with her new financial and military strength she could offer her allies more, and could ask more from them. It was possible for her to enter into relations with France which, if not exactly renewing the old ties of friendship, would serve to preclude any danger of an attack from that quarter. "And as far as our neighbor to the east, Austria-Hungary, is concerned, it must be admitted that public opinion, after accustoming itself to the radical difference in the relations between the two countries before and after the peace treaty of October 3, 1866, is generally agreed that an Austro-Italian conflict growing out of Irredentist agitation appears almost out of the question." The instinct of self-preservation, however, compelled Italy to insist on the safeguarding of her position in the Mediterranean against further aggressions, in places where these were still possible. The proposed obligations to be assumed by the Central Powers would therefore only "restore in favor of Italy the rightful relation of the reciprocal advantages." Acting on these suppositions, and supported by the conviction that a stronger Italian position in the Mediterranean would avert the danger "which might arise from the extension of the sovereignty

[103] Kálnoky to Reuss, November 3, 1886. Copy.

and the influence in the Mediterranean of that nation which one day might be our common enemy," Robilant proposed that the alliance of 1882 should be perfected by the addition of a supplementary treaty, the substance of which he outlined as follows:

The first article would confirm the original treaty and establish the prolongation of its validity for five more years, counting from the day of exchange of ratifications.[104]

The second article was to bring up the discussions of the question of the Orient. Robilant assumed that all three powers must regard it as their purpose to maintain the status quo in that region. This joint programme, he declared, had express reference "to the coasts and islands of the Adriatic and Aegean Seas belonging to the Ottoman Empire." To this end the signatory powers were to pledge themselves to use their influence to prevent any territorial change which might occur there to the disadvantage of one of the parties to the treaty; and to impart to one another any information which might serve mutually to throw light on their own 'dispositions' as well as on those of other powers. However, since account had to be taken of the possibility that events might prove stronger than the wishes of the allied powers, and that the maintenance of the status quo in the aforementioned regions might therefore become impossible, Robilant proposed that, in the event that 'another power should attempt to make a move in that direction' (Russia was of course alluded to), Italy and Austria-Hungary should consider a separate action; for "in view of their geographical position and their greater title to intervene, these two states only from among the group of the allies would be called to appear on the battlefield." If such a case should arise, Germany would only assume a moral obligation to favor the operations of the other two allies; the latter would take steps temporarily or permanently to occupy such territories as might be menaced by a third power. Before the beginning of opera

[104] The wording corresponds exactly with that of the first article of the treaty signed on February 20, 1887, by the representatives of all three powers. See Vol. I, p. 105. The observation is added (at that time Robilant was not thinking of special treaties), "Les stipulations du dit traité d'alliance sont en outre, à partir du jour de l'échange des ratifications du présent traité additionnel, complétées par les clauses contenues dans les articles suivants."

tions, however, an understanding would be reached between Austria-Hungary and Italy as to the reciprocal compensation 'by which the legitimate claims of both parties would be equally satisfied.' [105]

Robilant believed that by this provision "the danger of a clash between the two allies will be avoided, each of the two parties will be assigned its proper task, and, finally, the advantages which they expect to gain from the joint undertakings will be regulated with impartiality and mutual good will."

By the terms of the third article, each of the allies was to be allowed a free hand in certain questions of foreign policy. Robilant made it plain to the Austro-Hungarian and German statesmen that he had particularly in mind the Egyptian question and Italy's relations to England, with whose government he had already entered into negotiations regarding the protection of the interests of both countries in the Mediterranean. "This reservation," he said, "is not merely for the sake of additional clearness; it also possesses for us an especial value, in that it averts all danger of a conflict between the obligations we have assumed toward our allies and the especial demands made by our relation with England; and contains, so to speak, a tacit sanction by the two empires of the combinations which a regard for our interests has obliged us to effect with the English government." [106]

[105] In Robilant's draft, Article 2 reads: "Les hautes parties contractantes, n' ayant en vue que le maintien, autant que possible, du status quo territorial en Orient, s'engagent à user de leur influence pour prévenir sur les côtes et îles ottomanes dans l'Adriatique et dans la mer Egée toute modification territoriale qui porterait dommage à l'une ou à l'autre des puissances signataires du présent traité. Elles se communiqueront à cet effet tous les renseignements de nature à les éclairer mutuellement sur leurs propres dispositions, ainsi que sur celles d'autres puissances.

"Toutefois dans le cas où, par suite des événements, le maintien du status quo dans les régions susmentionnées deviendrait impossible, et que, soit en conséquence de l'action d'une puissance tierce, ou outrement, l'Italie ou l'Autriche-Hongrie se verraient dans la nécessité de le modifier par une occupation permanente ou temporaire de leur part, cette occupation n'aura lieu qu'après un accord préalable entre les deux susdites puissances, basé sur le principe d'une compensation réciproque donnant satisfaction aux intérêts et prétentions bien fondés des deux parties."

[106] Article 3 of this draft corresponds completely in substance to Article II of the German-Italian treaty of February 20, 1887. In wording there are only a few minor stylistic changes. Cf. Vol. I, p. 112.

The greatest stress was laid by Robilant on the provisions of Article 4 of his draft, which had reference to Tripoli and Morocco. "One should cherish no illusions," wrote Robilant. "The possibility of a French advance against Tripoli, or against the portion of Morocco bordering on the Mediterranean, is still to be reckoned with, in spite of the frequent assurances of the French ministers, which were repeated only recently." An extension of the French sphere of influence on the North African coast would be regarded by public opinion in Italy as "a wound inflicted on the national integrity. Any government," he went on to say, "would in such a case be forced to oppose with armed force the carrying out of this plan, or at least to restore the disturbed balance in the Mediterranean by means of suitable compensations. We do not ask our allies to give us armed assistance in preventing a French inroad in Tripoli or Morocco; neither do we ask their help in case we seek compensation for French conquests in Morocco by a gain of territory in Tripoli, unopposed by France. What we do ask of them is this. If we should proceed to meet with armed force a French advance against Tripoli, or if, as the result of French action in Morocco, we should prepare an advance on Tripoli in the face of French resistance; or if, in either of these events, a formal declaration of war should be followed by an outbreak of hostilities between us and France, either in Tripoli or in a part of the French possessions in Europe, then, and only then — after we had taken the initiative in armed action against France — should we consider ourselves empowered by Article 4 to invoke the aid of both our allies and enjoy all the consequences of the *casus foederis.*" [107]

Robilant knew that this demand would meet with opposition from the allies — especially from Austria-Hungary; he knew that the latter would flatly refuse to enter, for the sake of satisfying

[107] With the exception of two places, Article 4 of this draft corresponds word for word with Article III of the German-Italian treaty of February 20, 1887. Cf. Vol. I, p. 112. The variants are as follows: In the draft — which presupposed a treaty binding on all three parties — it is stipulated that the potential war shall be carried on "à la charge du groupe allié"; in the definitive treaty between Germany and Italy, "à la charge commune des deux alliés." In the draft, Italian action "sur la Tripolitaine" is specified; in the definitive treaty, "sur lesdits territoires nord-africains."

Italian ambition, into a war not directly provoked by France. Launay was therefore instructed to emphasize most strongly in Berlin that no mere territorial questions in Morocco or Tripoli were at stake, but the very existence and destiny of the kingdom of Italy. "In view of this, our allies will not deem our demands superfluous." [108]

After mature consideration, the Italian statesmen had first submitted their draft in Berlin and besought Bismarck to use his good offices with the government of Vienna. They knew that on the Spree they might count upon a more accommodating spirit than on the Danube. Bismarck, as a matter of fact, was prepared to make extensive concessions to the Italians. At this moment, with the danger of a war with France continually increasing, he placed far greater value on the aid of Italy, with her new acquisition of military strength, than in 1882, when the Triple Alliance came into being; he was therefore anxious to conciliate the only ally on whom he could count in the event of a French attack — for Austria-Hungary was not pledged to participate in a Franco-German conflict. Moreover, by supporting Italy's interests in the Mediterranean, Bismarck hoped to strengthen the ties that were to bind England to the powers of the Triple Alliance — England, who, at Italy's request (and with Bismarck's hearty approval), was about to assume obligations which, in the event of a Franco Italian war, might easily draw her into the conflict as an adver sary of France.[109]

If the maintenance of an alliance with Italy was to the advan tage of Germany's special interests in case war should break out between herself and France, Austria-Hungary, in Bismarck's opinion, would have even more to gain from such an alliance in case an Austro-Russian conflict were to become inevitable. We know that Bismarck had done everything in his power to bring about a

[108] Instruction from Robilant to Launay, Rome, November 23, 1886, and copy of the Italian treaty draft; the former communicated on December 7, 1886, the latter on December 5. Cf. also Robilant's speech in the Chamber on November 28, as given by Chiala, p. 477.

[109] The negotiations leading, on February 12, 1887, to the Anglo-Italian agreement, which was subscribed to, on March 24, 1887, by Austria-Hungary, will be dealt with in detail in subsequent portions of this work.

peaceable settlement of the serious differences which had arisen between the courts of Vienna and St. Petersburg. He had kept it no secret that if hostilities were to break out, the Austrian government could only count on Germany's help if Russia were the aggressor. He had most emphatically advised Vienna against a break with Russia over Bulgaria, or even over Constantinople; he had advocated taking steps toward lasting friendly relations with the conservative and autocratic government of the Tsar, and had recommended, as a means to this end, the delimitation of separate spheres of influence in the Balkans for the two great powers. However, he had to reckon with the possibility that his efforts would prove fruitless; that Russia's sovereign, swept along by the powerful current of the nationalist movement, would invade Austria in order to put an end to her influence in the Balkans. Firmly resolved that, in such an event, Germany should fulfil her obligations as an ally to the uttermost, he felt it his duty to impress on the statesmen at Vienna that Italy, if repulsed, would be driven into an alliance with France and Russia which would be most dangerous to Germany and to Austria-Hungary.

In order to avoid this, he insistently urged Kálnoky to meet Robilant's wishes as far and as quickly as possible. Kálnoky, however, showed no inclination to follow his advice. He acknowledged the weight of Bismarck's arguments, and declared his readiness to consider Italy's just wishes; but in his conversations with Reuss he emphasized the fact that Italy was asking for more than Austria-Hungary, consistently with her own interests, could concede. Participation by the Dual Monarchy in a Franco-Italian war brought on without direct provocation by France would be too heavy a burden for Austria-Hungary to assume in favor of exclusively Italian interests. In the Balkans, he went on to say, Italy was attempting to gain a footing of equality which had so far not been conceded her by Austria-Hungary, whose freedom of action in those regions would be curtailed thereby; and in return for all this Italy offered no compensating counter-service.[110] Kálnoky refused to accept a treaty which made so unfair a division of obligations and privileges in Italy's favor. He requested time for

[110] Notes regarding a conversation with Reuss, December 8, 1886.

reflection, and insisted on the adoption of provisions which would extend Italy's obligations.

⌐ Kálnoky's attitude was the cause of great disappointment in Berlin. The difficulties with France were growing more serious week by week, and with them increased the danger of a Russo-German conflict. It was imperative to make sure of the Italians — above all, to prevent their fighting at the side of Russia and France as Germany's enemies. In order to bring Kálnoky around, Bismarck informed the Austro-Hungarian representative in Berlin that, in case the renewal of the Triple Alliance should prove impossible, Germany would contract a separate alliance with Italy.[111] The warnings from Berlin had their effect in Vienna; Kálnoky could not deny their weight. In his opinion, the blocking of Russian aggressions in the Balkans was, and would continue to be, the chief purpose of Austro-Hungarian foreign policy, to further which he was ready, as a last resort, to employ armed force. Kálnoky well knew how much depended on Italy's attitude in such an event. Her union with Russia might be fraught with momentous consequences for Austria-Hungary. Even unbenevolent neutrality on the part of Italy would mean the neutralizing of considerable portions of the fighting force of the Dual Monarchy, and would disadvantageously influence the course of an Austro-Russian war. For these reasons Kálnoky had no idea of allowing the ties with Rome to be broken. He slowly gave in, abandoning the stand he had made on principle against the Italian demands, and limiting himself to proposing alterations in Robilant's draft,[112] which were calculated to safeguard Austro-Hungarian interests.

To this end he demanded that the efforts of the allies to maintain the territorial status quo of the coasts and islands in the Adriatic and the Aegean seas belonging to the Ottoman Empire, as emphasized in Article 2 of the draft, should be extended to

[111] Telegram from Tavera to Kálnoky, December 13, 1886. Regarding the differences existing between Bismarck and Kálnoky with reference to the Bulgarian question, cf. Heinrich Friedjung, "Graf Kálnoky," *Biographisches Jahrbuch*, iii, pp. 362 ff. (reprinted in *Historische Aufsätze*, 1919, pp. 327 ff.).

[112] Count Robilant's treaty draft; communicated through Reuss, December 5, 1886; with the changes suggested by Austria-Hungary, December 19, 1886.

include the entire Balkan peninsula, since Austriá-Hungary's interests were particularly concerned in the interior of the peninsula.[113] Moreover, as it did not seem desirable to him "to witness the establishment of the principle of compensations, which is distasteful to us" — he doubtless feared that Italy would extend her aspirations to Austrian territory, particularly the southern Tyrol — he demanded the omission of the passage in the Italian draft relating to this.[114] Finally, he insisted that Italy should bind herself to furnish active assistance, not merely to observe a benevolent neutrality, in case Austria-Hungary should be attacked by Russia.[115] In justifying this demand to the German government, Kálnoky stated that a declaration of such a nature would serve to guarantee the material support of Austria-Hungary by Italy,

[113] He eliminated from Robilant's draft the words "sur les côtes et îles ottomanes dans l'Adriatique et dans la mer Egée," and added in a subsequent place (cf. Vol. I, p. 108) the words "des Balkans ou des côtes," etc. which took account of Austro-Hungarian interests. In the negotiations which took place between Italy and Austria-Hungary after the outbreak of the World War, the interpretation of the words "dans les régions des Balcans" played a decisive rôle. Italy, invoking the terms of Article VII of the treaty of the Triple Alliance, put forward claims for territorial compensation in the event of the occupation of Serbian territory by Austria-Hungary. The government of Vienna replied with the declaration that the wording of Article VII, as well as the origins of this article, made it plain that its provisions applied solely to the occupation of Turkish territory, and that no account had been taken here of non-Turkish territory in the Balkan peninsula. However, in order to strengthen Italy in her then neutral attitude, whch was still regarded in Berlin and Vienna as benevolent, Berchtold issued a statement in Rome on August 23, 1914, after lengthy negotiations carried on simultaneously with the German government, to the effect that the Italian interpretation of the words "dans les régions des Balcans" was accepted "without reservation" by Germany and Austria-Hungary, not only for the present crisis, but as long as the treaty remained in force. (Cf. *Diplomatische Aktenstücke betreffend die Beziehungen Österreich-Ungarns zu Italien in der Zeit vom 20. Juli 1914 bis 23. Mai 1915*, p. 44.) No discussion of the question as to the correct interpretation of the phrase "dans les régions des Balcans" will be attempted here; it is certain, however, that the wording adopted was unfortunate.

[114] In Robilant's draft this passage ran as follows: "The 'accord préalable' between the two powers shall be based 'sur le principe d'une compensation réciproque donnant satisfaction aux intérêts et prétentions bien fondées des deux parties.'" For the definitive wording, cf. Vol. I, p. 108.

[115] Kálnoky gave to this article the following wording: "Si à la suite de pareils événements et sans provocation de la part de l'Autriche-Hongrie une guerre s'éclatait entre cette dernière et la Russie, l'Italie s'engage à faire cause commune avec son allié et à prendre part à la guerre."

whose reliability was greater under the leadership of Robilant, "but still not altogether above suspicion." This assistance, in the event of an invasion "by an army considerably superior in numbers to our own, would result in a most desirable reënforcement of our fighting strength, especially as the German army would probably be needed in the West to deal with France." The degree of seriousness with which Kálnoky made these proposals is indicated by the concluding words of his statement: "I must particularly emphasize the fact that I should not be able to obtain the assent of the ultimate authorities to the supplementary treaty, if, in return for the extensive concessions made by us to Italy, the latter should pledge herself only to a benevolent neutrality without any material counter-service. I could not assume the responsibility of committing Austria-Hungary to possible great sacrifices of blood and treasure in behalf of Italy, if Italy for her part does not consent to make similar sacrifices for us." [116]

[116] Kálnoky to Széchényi, December 20, 1886. In a second letter to Széchényi on the same date (copy) Kálnoky reiterates his views of Robilant's draft and justifies his observations. With regard to his demand for the active participation of Italy in an Austro-Russian war, Kálnoky writes: "For our part, it is no more than a justifiable demand if we claim the right to count on Italy's material aid with the same degree of definiteness as we are pledged to intervene with blood and treasure in Italy's behalf, in questions entirely foreign to our own interests. Since Count Robilant, in the documents which he has submitted to us, dwells again and again on the possibility of active participation in a war against Russia, and since he takes only Austria-Hungary and Italy into consideration in dealing with the questions of the Orient, he gives us a chance to frame our demands in such a way as to make a direct mention of Germany unnecessary." Here also Kálnoky emphasizes the fact that he could not possibly conclude the treaty without a counter-obligation on the part of Italy. He then continues: "I am well aware what great importance is placed by the German cabinet on the conclusion of the treaty; this, in view of France's doubtful attitude, is entirely comprehensible. For us, however, whose frontiers do not march with those of France, and who have no conflict of interests with her, these matters are only of secondary importance, and then only in consideration of our friendly relations with Germany. We are ready to show towards Germany the most unreservedly accommodating spirit; but, just as Italy has conspicuously safeguarded her own interests and advantages in the treaty draft, so it is our duty as well to have an eye to Austria-Hungary's lawful interests." In making his demands, Kálnoky was able to refer to a passage from a private letter from Robilant to Launay which was imparted to him by Reuss, reading as follows: "State plainly that we are a nation to be relied on, and that, unlike the Spaniards, we do not wish to have some one else pull our chestnuts

Kálnoky's hopes of finding approval of his plans in Berlin were not fulfilled. Bismarck wished at all costs to avoid irritating Russia, and was exerting his whole influence to prevent her from joining forces with a France eager for revenge. For this reason he had been insistently urging on Vienna the idea of separate spheres of influence in the Balkans for Russia and Austria-Hungary. In Kálnoky's proposal to include the Balkans in the regions whose territorial status quo was to be guaranteed by the allies, Bismarck now saw a move against his plans.[117] Moreover, Kálnoky's desire to make sure of Italy's active aid in the event of Russian aggression was equally distasteful to him. If this scheme should go through, it might be feared that Austria-Hungary, relying on her own strength and that of her allies — for she had made sure of support from Serbia and Rumania through the treaties of 1881 and 1883 — would provoke a war with Russia in which Germany as well as Italy would be bound to participate If the chances of renewing the Triple Alliance were to be shattered by this demand of Kálnoky, the danger loomed up that Italy would unite with Russia and France and commence the conflict with the Central

out of the fire. Within eighteen or twenty days after the mobilization we shall have 150,000 men on the northwestern frontier for an offensive defensive against France. 200,000 men — that is, six army corps, four divisions of cavalry, and one division of Alpine troops — would at the same time be ready either to cross the Alps to the Rhine, as reënforcements for the Germans, or to march against the Russians through Austria." Kálnoky said that he would be satisfied with two or three army corps of auxiliary troops, but that he must be able to count on these with certainty.

[117] In a long conversation between Széchényi and Count Berchem, who was privy to the negotiations and had been instructed by Herbert Bismarck to receive Kálnoky's communications, Berchem declared "that he really did not understand why the insertion of the words 'des Balcans' before the words 'ou des côtes ou îles ottomanes de l'Adriatique ou de la mer Egée' had been insisted on. This, he thought, would mean renouncing our freedom of action as respects Italy, in case we wished to make a move in the Balkans either independently or with other combinations: for instance, if we should happen to have in view a joint occupation of Macedonia with Russia. I remarked to him that he was considering very remote and hypothetical combinations, whereas we felt obliged to consider the immediate situation, making sure, in return for the obligations assumed by us, of a definite counter-obligation in the event of our sphere of interests being threatened — and this, after all, lies rather in the interior of the Balkan peninsula — or in the event of our being attacked for the purpose of forcing us out of the Balkans." Széchényi to Kálnoky, December 25, 1886.

Powers at their side.[118] These considerations probably determined
the German government to proceed swiftly with the negotiations
with Rome.[119] Toward the beginning of 1887 Robilant sent to
Berlin his reply to Kálnoky's proposals. He declared that they
were unacceptable. What Kálnoky suggested, he declared, were
not merely amendments, but, so far as Austro-Italian relations
were concerned, "radical alterations of the principles of the existing treaty."

"According to the treaty of 1882," he wrote, "we are now at
liberty to take such a position towards possible Austro-Hungarian
moves in the Balkans as will best correspond with our interests.
Should war between Russia and Austria-Hungary arise from the
latter's advances in the Balkans, Austria-Hungary can only ask
us to observe a benevolent neutrality. Were we to accept the Austrian counter-proposal, however, we should be playing an entirely
different rôle; we should, in a certain sense, be assuming a joint
responsibility for everything that Austria did, or planned to do,
in the Balkans; we should be pledged to participate in a war which
does not seem altogether improbable — a war involving difficulties and sacrifices which are not to be calculated. One should in-
dulge in no illusions: we should be assuming one of those historic
responsibilities which not only stamp their impress upon the work
of a minister, but at times are also a determining factor in the life
of a nation for generations to come." [120] Under the circumstances,
continued Robilant, he would prefer to adhere to his own project.
This would preserve the defensive character of the alliance, afford
Italy a guarantee of the maintenance of the balance of power in
the Mediterranean, and, by way of compensation, assure Italy's

[118] Széchényi to Kálnoky. Telegram of January 4 and despatch of January 5,
1887.

[119] On December 31, 1886, Bruck had already informed Kálnoky that Robilant
was annoyed at the way negotiations were being delayed by Bismarck, who 'formerly had always hurried matters along, and could hardly wait for the moment to
arrive for concluding the treaty.' This was not Launay's opinion. According to
Chiala, p. 477, Launay wrote at the same time to Robilant, "Je persiste à croire que
nous parviendrons à une entente, car le Prince de Bismarck et le Comte Herbert
sont bien disposés à notre endroit."

[120] Robilant to Launay, January 1, 1887. Copy communicated to Kálnoky by
Herbert Bismarck.

help to Germany in case she were attacked by France, or to Austria-Hungary in the event of a Russo-Turkish or Franco-Russian alliance. If Kálnoky nevertheless insisted on alterations, they must be so worded as to preserve the balance between the obligations and counter-obligations assumed by the allies. Following out these statements, Robilant proposed the alternative either of accepting Article 2 of the supplementary treaty as worded by him — that is, without entering into particulars regarding an Austro-Russian war, but retaining the final clause objected to by Kálnoky, governing the indemnifications of each party in the event of an occupation of Balkan territory by Italy or Austria-Hungary; [121] or of accepting Kálnoky's project providing for Italian participation in an Austro-Russian war. In this latter event Robilant demanded not only the retention of the above-mentioned compensation clause, but also the addition of another clause to the following effect: "Austria-Hungary and Italy reserve the right to conclude, at a suitable time before the beginning of hostilities, a special agreement intended to regulate, on the basis of just indemnification, the territorial changes (*combinaisons*) which might possibly take place as the result of a joint war." [122]

The German government held that Robilant's new proposals were justified. Herbert Bismarck, who had previously notified Széchényi orally of the substance of Robilant's note, said that in view of the fact that Italy "would have to stake blood and treasure" if Austria-Hungary and Russia were to go to war, her demands for a corresponding compensation were not unreasonable. It also seemed to him "very prudent and proper" that a definite agreement in this matter should be reached in advance. "If this were not done, there would always be the danger that the two allies might disagree at the end of a victorious campaign and come to blows with one another. As a result of this, the advantages would go to the adversary whom they had just conquered."

[121] Cf. p. 56, note 105.
[122] "L'Autriche-Hongrie et l'Italie se réservent de stipuler, au moment opportun, avant l'entrée en campagne, un accord spécial [originally 'ultérieur'; this was replaced at Robilant's request by 'spécial'] destiné à régler sur la base d'une compensation équitable les combinaisons territoriales qui pourraient éventuellement résulter de la guerre entreprise en commun."

These observations, made by Herbert Bismarck in his own name, as Secretary of State, were followed by the statement that the Imperial Chancellor, to his great regret, was unable to assent to the insertion of the words "des Balcans," which Kálnoky had suggested and so warmly sponsored. "That would plainly be alluding to Bulgaria," said Herbert Bismarck, "and Bulgaria is regarded by us as belonging within the Russian sphere of influence. Our assent to a provision aimed against that sphere is rendered all the more impossible by the fact that we would thus be coming into conflict with our secret agreement with Russia, which is still in force."

Széchényi replied that the words "des Balcans" had no special application whatever to Bulgaria, but covered the Balkan states in general, "since our interests," as he put it, "centre in the interior of the Balkan peninsula, not in its islands and coasts." This did not impress Herbert Bismarck, who said that it made very little difference; "Bulgaria in any case was included in that region." [123] Shortly after, he sent to Vienna a copy of Robilant's instruction to Launay, together with the new Italian draft for the treaty, and at the same time communicated through Reuss "that we (Germany) find both of Robilant's proposals acceptable, and that we should be pleased if Count Kálnoky could accept the Italian point of view within the limits defined by them." "We hope," he continued, "that he will find it to his own good interests to send us an answer which will satisfy Rome and make it possible to proceed towards a conclusion of the treaty."

The attitude of the German government evoked Kálnoky's deepest displeasure. He felt that Bismarck was not giving sufficient consideration to Austria-Hungary's special interests; that he was over-emphasizing the danger of a war with France, and that he was observing too considerate an attitude towards Russia. A speech, delivered by Bismarck in the German Reichstag on January 11, 1887, strengthened his conviction. "The whole problem of the Orient," the Imperial Chancellor had declared, "involves no question of war for us. We shall allow no one to put a leading-rope about our necks and embroil us in difficulties with Rus-

sia." [124] This was a direct threat against Austria-Hungary. In uttering it, Bismarck doubtless had no idea of forsaking his ally in case she were attacked by Russia; but he plainly let it be known just how far he was willing to follow her lead. His speech was at the same time a warning that Italy might be driven into the enemy's camp, an admonition not to refuse Robilant's new demands.

He failed, however, of his purpose. Kálnoky stated in his reply that "Prince Bismarck's declarations in his recent speech in the German Parliament, in which he proclaims to the world at large that Germany has no interests in the Orient, and that it is a matter of indifference to him who holds sway in Bulgaria or in Constantinople, has had no inconsiderable weight" in determining the attitude of the cabinet of Vienna.[125] On January 16 the decisive conference with Reuss took place.[126] Kálnoky spoke in a heated, vehement tone; his utterances sounded like an ultimatum to the German government. He declined to give any consideration whatever to Robilant's new demands. But this was not all. He also withdrew the concessions formerly offered by him, and announced that he now had in view merely the renewal of the treaty of 1882, without any alterations.

"The more evident it becomes to friend and foe," he said to Prince Reuss, "that Austria-Hungary will have to defend single-handed her lawful interests on her southeastern frontiers, the more our enemies are heartened, and our friends discouraged by this fact, the greater care we must take to assume no obligations which would involve us in complications outside our own sphere of interests. At a moment when our people are speculating, with pardonable solicitude, as to the perils which may beset the monarchy to the southeast, and as to the sufficiency of our forces to withstand the various hostile elements which threaten us in that quarter, it would be indeed a heavy responsibility unnecessarily to assume obligations which might draw us into a conflict with France over incidents in the far west, or in Tripoli or Morocco,

[124] Horst Kohl, *Die politischen Reden des Fürsten Bismarck*, xii, p. 183.
[125] Private letter from Kálnoky to Széchényi, January 20, 1887.
[126] Copy of a private letter to Reuss, Vienna, January 17, 1887.

where we have no interests whatever, and bind us 'de porter se-cóurs et assistance avec toutes nos forces' for the purpose of protecting Italy and her shores against French attacks by land and on sea." [127]

Austria-Hungary, he went on to say, needed all her strength now, and for the immediate future, in the south and southeast; she therefore could not live up to such a promise without doing violence to her own interests. It was best to state this fact frankly. Italy, moreover, was showing no serious intention of supporting Austria-Hungary against Russia. "There may also be some doubt as to her ability to do so," Kálnoky pursued, "if the danger of war with France becomes more imminent. We are therefore of the opinion that it would be as fitting for Italy to drop the demands she has made on us exceeding those stipulated in the first treaty as for us to renounce the counter-claim of military assistance from Italy, which we have demanded for our part. We also believe that the vague Italian claims for compensation, on which such stress is laid, could only serve to bring about differences and dissensions when it comes to practical settlements." Clear-cut understandings, he said, alone could avail. This was particularly true of the provisions relating to the Balkan peninsula. Kálnoky expressed the fear that in case Austria-Hungary were to limit her freedom of action in the Orient in favor of Italy, she might be drawn into conflict with the obligations she had assumed towards Russia. Now, too, he recognized the validity of the objection brought by Herbert Bismarck, in connection with the imminent renewal of the League of the Three Emperors, against the insertion of the words "des Balcans" in Article II of the supplementary treaty. "As regards this question," declared Kálnoky, "it would be advisable, in our opinion, to limit ourselves to the originally proposed promises that Italy shall be notified in due season, and with due regard to her interests, of any changes in the status quo in the Orient, which we wish to maintain, and that above all she shall be safeguarded against surprises." At the same time, he had no wish to disturb the existing friendly relationship with Italy, which he con-

[127] Report of Prince Reuss, January 17, 1887. At the request of Prince Reuss, Kálnoky had read this report before it was sent to Berlin.

sidered from the standpoint of peace and of the monarchical interests, and appreciated at its full value. He persisted, however, in believing that the alliance of 1882 fulfilled these purposes, and urged that "a way be found at the proper moment for securing a more extensive reciprocal support" through "another interpretation" of Article IV of the treaty.[128]

Kálnoky knew that in making these declarations he retracted that to which he had already given his assent; but he felt that the interests of his sovereign and his country obliged him to risk the displeasure of his allies and the dangers to the monarchy which might result from a sudden change in Italian policy.[129] The consternation of the German statesmen was, in fact, very great. Reuss expressed his amazement and alarm at Kálnoky's utterances not only to Kálnoky himself but to Emperor Francis Joseph, with whom he requested an audience on the same day. "I have spoken to His Majesty regarding this matter," he wrote to Kálnoky on the evening of January 16, "and said to him what I said to you — that I am extremely surprised and alarmed by your communication, and that I foresee the painful impression which will be caused in Berlin by this statement, for which they could not possibly be prepared." At the same time he asked Kálnoky "whether there can be no more discussion of Tripoli, not even in the noncommittal sense of Prince Bismarck's proposal, which you will surely recall, and which you expressly accepted first on November 3, and again later, in conversation with Monts." [130]

Kálnoky, however, stood firm. On January 17 Reuss sent the very unsatisfactory results of his negotiations to Berlin, where, as he had predicted, a most painful impression was caused. A deluge of reproaches was poured on the head of the Austrian am-

[128] Report of Prince Reuss, January 17, 1887.

[129] Kálnoky to Széchényi, January 20, 1887; to Bruck, January 22, 1887. Kálnoky did not then believe that, in case the treaty of the Triple Alliance were not renewed, Italy would attack Austria-Hungary from the rear in the event of an Austro-Russian war. "We consider that we are protected for the present against a rear attack from Italy," he wrote Széchényi, "by the fact that Germany and Italy have common interests in regard to France, and will therefore maintain their alliance in any event."

[130] Reuss to Kálnoky, January 16, 1887.

bassador, Count Széchényi. Herr von Holstein, who was even then an influential figure in the Foreign Office, expressed his concern over this "not easily comprehensible decision" of Count Kálnoky. What would become of Austria-Hungary, he asked, if she failed to come to a peaceful settlement with Russia, and at the same time cast off her Italian ally? Bismarck — so Holstein declared — had given Vienna the well-meant advice either to reach a friendly understanding with Russia regarding the spheres of interest of the two powers in the Balkans, or else to attack Russia in alliance with other nations. There seemed to be no other practical alternative. "If Germany is attacked by France at the same time that Austria-Hungary is attacked by Russia, she can guarantee her ally none too strong a support. Austria, however, is too weak to overcome her powerful adversary single-handed. Why, therefore, this holding aloof from Italy?" To Széchényi's objection that no reliance could be placed on the Italians, Holstein replied that this distrust was not unjustified, but that it was a question, not of a permanent alliance, but of acquiring a "paid corps of auxiliaries, like the mercenaries of the Middle Ages." In order to dispel Kálnoky's fears that Italy might demand indemnification in the Tyrol as the price for participation in an Austro-Russian war, Holstein declared, after a consultation with Launay, that Italy had no such idea. He held it to be self-evident that compensations could be exacted only "in the districts which had caused the war." "As far as these are concerned," added Holstein, "it might be impossible in any event to prevent Italy from establishing herself in Albania." [131]

Count Herbert Bismarck, recently appointed Secretary of State in the Foreign Office, also expressed himself to the same effect. He informed Vienna through Reuss that it was useless to think that Italy would be willing to renew the Triple Alliance of 1882 as it stood, and reminded Kálnoky of the declaration to this effect made by Robilant in September, 1886. At the same time he exerted every effort to dispel the fears of the Austro-Hungarian minister, assuring him, as Holstein had previously done, that Italy had no idea of territorial acquisitions in southern Tyrol, and that

[131] Széchényi to Kálnoky, January 21, 1887. Copy.

neither she nor the German government counted on Austro-Hungarian 'action' in the West in the event that Germany should become involved in war with France.[132] All these efforts were fruitless. Kálnoky's attitude remained unchanged and the deadlock in the negotiations continued. Italy would not renew the old treaty without the proposed alterations; Austria-Hungary would not accede to Italy's wishes, particularly to those which might draw her into a conflict with France. There appeared to be no way out of the dilemma.

Finally, however, the desire of the three powers to renew the Triple Alliance, the value of which was fully appreciated by the various signatories, reached fulfilment in spite of all difficulties. On January 27, 1887, Bismarck instructed Reuss to inform the Austrian government that Count Robilant was ready to abandon his original scheme, according to which the supplementary treaty was to be signed by all three powers, its various articles binding the signatories in equal degree, as in the case of the Triple Alliance of 1882. Instead of this, the treaty of 1882 was to be renewed as it stood, and at the same time two supplementary agreements, one with Germany and one with Austria-Hungary, would be concluded. From the latter the provisions objected to by Kálnoky, in so far as they related to Tripoli and Morocco, would be omitted; Austria-Hungary would thus incur obligations toward Italy only in the matter of her Balkan policy. As regards this point, Robilant adhered to the alternative proposed by him toward the beginning of the year. This, as we know, provided for the indemnification of Italy in the event of a temporary or permanent occupation of Balkan territory by Austria-Hungary; moreover, if Austria-Hungary wished Italy to participate on her side in an Austro-Russian war, the question of the compensation to be received by Italy in return for her services was to be settled before her entrance into the field.[133] Prince Bismarck, in imparting these new proposals of Robilant to the cabinet of Vienna, also let it be known that the Italian Minister of Foreign Affairs

[132] Copy of a letter from Herbert Bismarck to Reuss, January 24, 1887, and Széchényi's despatch to Kálnoky, January 26, 1887.
[133] Cf. p. 65.

had definitely resolved that, in case Kálnoky should not accept the Italian proposals, he would conclude a dual alliance with Germany, "who had raised no objections to his first scheme." [134]

The decisive moment had arrived for Kálnoky. Should he accept Robilant's proposals, or decline them? He knew that Bismarck was backing Robilant. He could assume that the Imperial Chancellor had taken a prominent part in drawing up the new project of compromise — that it was due to him that Austria-Hungary was no longer called upon to pledge herself to intervene in behalf of Italian interests in North Africa, or to send her soldiers against France for the sake of Tripoli or Morocco. In his conversations with German and Italian statesmen, Kálnoky had always stressed the fact that he was unable to advise his sovereign to sign the treaty principally because Austro-Hungarian troops might thus be engaged in the West at a moment when they were needed in the East to defend the vital interests of the monarchy. With this obstacle removed, should he now, in the face of the ever-increasing danger of a bloody conflict with Russia, deeply offend one ally and drive the other into the enemy's camp? To be sure, there still remained the demands which Italy wished to exact from Austria-Hungary in the event of territorial changes in the Balkans, and in return for the participation by Italian troops in an

[134] Excerpt from Prince Bismarck's despatch to Reuss, January 27, 1887. In connection with the point of controversy raised by the new project, I give herewith the passages in Bismarck's despatch relating to this matter: "According to the notes which I was able to take, the instruction read to me by Count Launay ran as follows: 'Pour déférer à l'opinion du prince et pour épuiser tous les moyens propres à maintenir l'Autriche-Hongrie dans le groupe allié, je puis me décider à admettre pour ce que regarde cette puissance le simple renouvellement du traité de 1882 avec un engagement séparé concernant sa politique en Orient, mais ceci sous la condition que l'arrangement séparé entre l'Autriche et l'Italie *comprenne toute la teneur de l'article 2 tel qu'il figure dans le projet que par mon télégramme du 1 janvier je déclarais, en suite de la première réponse de Vienne, être prêt à adopter en lieu et place de mon projet originaire.* L'alinéa I de l'article 2 est purement platonique et ne reproduit qu'une déclaration que tous les cabinets ne cessent d'échanger entre eux; s'il était établi à lui seul et formait tout le texte de l'arrangement séparé, il serait sans valeur et laisserait la porte toute grande ouverte à toute sorte d'éventualités le jour où le maintien du status quo ne serait plus possible d'après le jugement de l'Autriche. Il faut donc compléter l'alinéa premier par l'alinéa deuxième, qui seul nous prémunit contre toute surprise, et qui assure aux mouvements des deux puissances en Orient la base d'une entente préalable.'"

Austro-Russian war. We know how Kálnoky shrank from limiting his freedom of action in his Balkan policy, and how well he realized the dangers which, sooner or later, would beset his country were Italy to extend her sphere of interests to the Balkans or seize territory on the farther shore of the Adriatic. After mature reflection, however, he decided that a bird in the hand was, after all, worth two in the bush.

"In view of developments in the East while the negotiations were in progress," he wrote to Széchényi, "it would have been impossible for us to assume obligations which might have drawn us into war with France. This would have run counter to our interests, without being of any real profit to Italy. Now that this insurmountable difficulty has been removed by the elimination of Articles III and IV, we can overlook many other objections, and accept the last draft submitted to us by Prince Bismarck without change. We also agree to the proposed manner of renewing the old treaty." [135] He went on to say that he must express only two wishes, on the observance of which Emperor Francis Joseph laid especial emphasis. These related to the proposed indemnification of the Italians. Kálnoky insisted categorically on the acceptance of a clause stating "that Austria-Hungary regards her continued occupation of Bosnia and Herzegovina, which will end as a matter of course in a permanent annexation by Austria-Hungary, as included in the existing status quo; and that neither this occupation, which has already lasted for years, nor the consummation of the annexation, would empower Italy to put forward claims for compensations." [136] In addition to this, he demanded a clear declaration that under no circumstances should the Trentino be included in the territorial compensations which might be accorded Italy in return for assisting Austria-Hungary in a war against Russia.[137]

[135] Kálnoky to Széchényi, February 2, 1887. Private letter (summary and copy).

[136] Draft of the Austro-Italian treaty after the last modifications had been made, January 30, 1887. The decisive words are as follows: "basé sur le principe d'une compensation réciproque pour tout avantage territorial ou autre que chacune d'elles obtiendrait en sus du status quo actuel."

[137] Kálnoky to Széchényi, February 2, 1887. The passage contemplating the participation by Italy in an Austro-Russian war, and the compensations to be guar-

Kálnoky's accommodating attitude caused the greatest rejoicing in Berlin. Herbert Bismarck declared that he did not doubt for a moment that both of Kálnoky's justifiable demands would be accepted by the Italians, and requested that plenipotentiaries be immediately sent for the signing of the treaty, which, he hoped, would take place on February 12.[138] At the last moment, however, a new difficulty presented itself. The Italian government, moved doubtless by the bad news from Massowah, declared that it had never intended to give Austria-Hungary Italy's active support in an Austro-Russian war, unless Austria-Hungary assumed a like obligation in the event of hostilities between Italy and France over Tripoli and Morocco.[139] At the same time Launay presented a new version of the Austro-Italian treaty, in which no mention was made of Italian participation in an Austro-Russian war, or, correspondingly, of Italy's compensations.[140] It was to no pur-

anteed to Italy in return, read as follows in the treaty draft of January 30, 1887: "Si à la suite de pareils événements et sans provocation de la part de l'Autriche-Hongrie une guerre éclatait entre cette dernière et la Russie, l'Italie s'engage à faire cause commune avec son allié et à prendre part à la guerre. L'Autriche-Hongrie et l'Italie se réservent de stipuler au moment opportun, avant l'entrée en campagne, un accord special destiné à régler, sur la base d'une compensation equitable, les combinaisons territoriales qui pourraient éventuellement résulter de la guerre entreprise en commun." This passage was later eliminated at Italy's instigation. See p. 77.

[138] Széchényi to Kálnoky, February 4, 1887.

[139] Robilant to Launay, telegram, February 5, 1887 (copy). "J'ai encore relu mon télégramme du 25 janvier, et je ne réussis vraiment pas à m'expliquer de quelle façon le malentendu que V. E. me signale a pu se former. J'avais eu soin en effet de dire très-nettement dans ce télégramme ·que l'arrangement séparé entre nous et l'Autriche-Hongrie ne devait reproduire que le premier et le deuxième alinéa de l'article deux. Si en parlant du deuxième alinéa, je me suis référé à mon télégramme du 1 janvier, c'est parce que je tenais à ce que cet alinéa fût conçu d'après le texte cité dans ce télégramme, c'est-à-dire contenant la mention explicite des Balcans, et non d'après le texte de mon projet originaire, où cette mention n'existe pas. Si, au contraire, j'avais eu l'idée de faire également figurer dans l'arrangement séparé italo-autrichien le *casus foederis* envers la Russie, je l'aurais évidemment annoncé, tandis que rien dans mon télégramme du 25 janvier laisse supposer une pareille intention." Kálnoky's interpretation is shown by his private letter to Széchényi (February 2, 1887), in which he says: "Moreover, Article II applies to Germany only as far as the close of Paragraph 2, while the whole remaining portion of Article II. according to Count Robilant's final version, would remain binding with regard to Austria-Hungary." He transmitted at the same time a copy of a draft "as it stands after the last negotiations." Cf. note 137, *supra*.

[140] This wording corresponds verbatim to that of the final treaty. Cf. Vol. I,

pose that Herbert Bismarck referred to the original text of Robilant's declaration, and pointed out that Italy had made the promises which she was now disavowing. Launay only replied that the wording had not been fortunate; that a part of the blame was his, since he had failed to make Robilant's comments sufficiently clear.[141] Even Prince Bismarck's efforts to bring Robilant around were fruitless. The latter's reply was so brusquely unfavorable that all hope was abandoned in Berlin of coming to terms with the Italians.

Bismarck therefore found it necessary to bring fresh pressure to bear on the Austrian government. He pointed out the danger that Italy — her hopes blighted by the recent defeat at Dogali, her pride wounded, unable to stand alone, and repulsed by the Central Powers — might fling herself into the arms of France and Russia. The menacing spectre of a coalition of France, Russia and Italy, directed against the Central Powers, rose once more before Bismarck's eyes and spurred him on to make every attempt to avert the peril. On February 10 he counselled Vienna with the greatest urgency to accept the draft as it stood. He declared that the main object — namely, the safeguarding of Austria-Hungary against an attack from the south while she was waging war on Russia — had been attained through Italy's promise of benevolent neutrality; the substance of the supplementary treaty was non-committal. Even the pledge of reciprocal compensations was dependent on an agreement which had previously to be reached at a suitable time, and which Austria-Hungary could always prevent whenever she wished.[142] Soon after this Holstein expressed himself to the same effect to Széchényi. He referred angrily to the "*pourboire* paragraphs," but emphasized the necessity of yielding.

p. 108. In the draft, however, there are lacking the words inserted into the final treaty after "compensation réciproque" and before "et donnant," etc., at Kálnoky's request. Cf. p. 73. These words read as follows: "pour tout avantage territorial ou autre que chacune d'elles obtiendrait en sus du statu quo actuel."

[141] Széchényi to Kálnoky, February 6 and 9, 1887. In the letter of February 6, Széchényi states that the conversation between Herbert Bismarck and Launay had been very stormy. It had ended with Bismarck's remark: "je dois vous prévenir que votre gouvernement désobligerait fortement mon père en faisant échouer cette affaire au moment où il devait la croire parfaitement réglée."

[142] Excerpt from a note to Reuss; communicated February 10, 1887.

Széchényi replied that he was not at the moment in a position to do so; he wrote, however, to his friend Kálnoky that there were certain cases — and this certainly seemed to be one of them — when benevolent neutrality was worth as much as a whole army. "It is annoying," he added, "but nevertheless true, that the Italians, who gain a province after every defeat, are now to be enabled to gather in booty without having fired a shot. And in the last analysis they will not even observe the neutrality which they have promised. That is the sort of thing one must expect from a country where the mob wields the sceptre." [143] A few days later Kálnoky was informed by Reuss that the two conditions stipulated by him at the beginning of February had been accepted by Italy.[144]

On February 18, Bismarck, as though wishing to help his Austrian colleague to bear the heavy burden of responsibility, informed Kálnoky that he had thoroughly examined the new treaty draft, and felt that he was able to recommend with the greatest conviction that it be accepted unchanged. He pointed out that the wishes of Emperor Francis Joseph and Kálnoky had been respected in the new version. "A wording fully satisfying all parties and eventualities in the case of so complicated an agreement would be hard to find," he said. "For this reason we have from the first abstained from suggesting alterations, although we should have been glad to give a different reading to many passages in our own separate agreement. This wish must be sacrificed to the great purpose which we wish to attain through the renewal and extension of the treaty of the Triple Alliance." [145] The pressure exerted by these representations, and still more the realization that, under the existing circumstances, Italy's benevolent neutrality implied no mean advantages for the Dual Monarchy in view of the ever-increasing peril of an Austro-Russian war, caused Kálnoky to abandon his opposition. He therefore let drop the

[143] Széchényi to Kálnoky, February 12, 1887.

[144] Extract from a private letter from Herbert Bismarck to Reuss, which was communicated to Kálnoky on February 17, 1887.

[145] Extract from Prince Bismarck's letter to Reuss. Communicated on February 18, 1887.

provision relating to the conditions under which Italy should participate in an Austro-Russian war,[146] and instructed Count Széchényi to sign the treaties.[147] This was done at three o'clock in the afternoon of February 20 in Prince Bismarck's conservatory.[148] It was decided to inform the public — which had already profited by certain indiscreet communications of the Italian press [149] — that the Triple Alliance had been renewed. Its substance, as previously, was to be kept secret.

There were, in all, four documents which were signed that day in Berlin. First, an additional treaty, subscribed to by the representatives of all three states. This contained only the confirmation of the Triple Alliance of May 20, 1882, and the establishment of the duration of the new treaty until May 30, 1892.[150] Second, a separate treaty between Austria-Hungary and Italy, containing four articles, the first of which — the only one of real importance — governed the conduct of both powers in questions relating to' the Near East. By means of a wording which took into account the wishes of both governments, this article primarily expressed the desire for the maintenance of the territorial status quo in the Orient as long as possible. It pledged them to use their influence to avert any territorial changes in these regions which might take place to the disadvantage of either party. Furthermore, they promised to impart to one another all information of a nature to

[146] The wording of this passage is given on p. 74. The necessity of taking precautions lest Italy claim compensations in the Tyrol for her participation in an Austro-Russian war — an eventuality already foreseen by Kálnoky — was thus clearly eliminated.

[147] In his communication to Bruck of February 15, 1887, Kálnoky gave detailed report in this matter. Among other things, he wrote: "At the last moment Count Robilant, using the more or less valid pretext of a misunderstanding, has again interpreted away and revoked the promise which had already been made to us of military assistance from Italy in the event of an emergency. I shall offer no opinion as to whether this decision was influenced by the bad news from Massowah (1), and I have avoided being drawn into a discussion of the matter. It has not been difficult to forego these possible auxiliary troops, on the practical value and timely despatch of which I never placed great reliance, and to let drop the provision relating to them."

[148] Széchényi to Kálnoky, February 23, 1887.

[149] Baron Bruck to Kálnoky, February 26, 1887.

[150] Compare the text, Vol. I, pp. 104 ff. May 30 was selected at Italy's request, because the ratifications had been exchanged on May 30, 1882.

throw light on the measures [151] taken by themselves as well as by other powers. "However," the text continues, "if, in the course of events, the maintenance of the status quo in the regions of the Balkans [152] or of the Ottoman coasts and islands in the Adriatic and in the Aegean Sea should become impossible, and if, whether in consequence of the action of a third power or otherwise, Austria-Hungary or Italy should find themselves under the necessity of modifying it by a temporary or permanent occupation on their part, this occupation shall take place only after a previous agreement between the two powers aforesaid, based upon the principle of a reciprocal compensation for every advantage, territorial or other, which each of them might obtain beyond the present status quo,[153] and giving satisfaction to the interests and well founded claims of the two parties." [154]

It is beyond doubt that the acceptance of this article implied a great victory for Italy. She had attained one of her chief aims; recognition by Austria as a power with equal rights in the Balkans. From now on she could be sure of not being overlooked in the event of a division of Turkish territory in that region. Her hopes of an extension of Italian territory on the farther shore of the Adriatic now had a real foundation, which was doubly precious at a moment when her far-reaching colonial plans in Africa had proved impracticable. All this had been attained by Italy without pledging herself to participate in an Austro-Russian war — not even if her ally should be attacked by Russia, for in such a case Italy was bound to observe only a benevolent neutrality. She could take part in the conflict, however, if she saw fit to do so, and exact payment with new concessions.

The provisions of the separate treaty concluded on the same day between Germany and Italy were no less favorable to the

[151] The word *dispositions* is here perhaps equivalent rather to " Massnahmen " than to "Absichten," which represents it in the official German translation. On this point see Fraknói's observations, *op. cit.*, p. 43.

[152] The words "des Balcans" were inserted at Austria-Hungary's request. Cf. p. 61, note 113.

[153] The words "en sus du status quo actuel" were inserted at Kálnoky's instance. Cf. p. 73.

[154] Cf. the text, Vol. I, p. 109.

latter power. This treaty included seven articles. The first, corresponding to the first article of the Austro-Italian treaty, contained the promise of both Powers to maintain the status quo in the Orient; however, the reciprocal pledge given by Germany and Italy to exert all their influence towards averting territorial changes was expressly limited to the Turkish coasts and islands in the Adriatic and Aegean seas. This eliminated the provisions contained in the Austro-Italian treaty regarding the circumstances under which a temporary or permanent occupation of Balkan territory by one or the other power might take place.[155] The second article expressly stipulated that the joint measures contemplated in Article I had no relation to the Egyptian question. Both powers reserved for themselves a freedom of decision as regards Egypt, in so far as this did not run counter to the principles laid down by the alliance of 1882 and the present treaty.

The most notable concessions agreed to by Bismarck in order to keep Italy in the alliance formed the substance of Articles III and IV of this treaty. They dealt with the possibility of a war between France and Italy, and laid upon the German government considerably more extensive obligations than those established by the treaty of 1882. At that time Germany had promised only to come to Italy's assistance in case she should be the victim of an unprovoked attack by France. Now she assumed the further obligation to assist Italy actively, under certain conditions, if she were to undertake an offensive war against France. "Should France" — so reads Article III of the German-Italian treaty — "extend her occupation or her protectorate or her sovereignty, under any form whatsoever, in the North African territories, whether of the vilayet of Tripoli or of the Moroccan empire, and, as a result thereof, should Italy, in order to safeguard her position in the Mediterranean, feel that she must herself undertake action in the said North African territories, or even have recourse to extreme measures in French territory in Europe, the state of war which would thereby ensue between Italy and France would constitute ipso facto, on the demand of Italy and at the common charge of the two allies, the *casus foederis* with all the effects fore-

[155] Cf. the text, Vol. I, pp. 110 ff.

seen by Articles II and V of the treaty of May 20, 1882, as if such an eventuality were expressly contemplated therein." [156] In order that no exaggerated estimate be formed of the sacrifices which Bismarck made to the Italians through this compromise, it is well to remember that, at the time when he caused the treaty to be signed, he already knew that England had simultaneously assumed the obligation to protect Italian interests in North Africa.[157]

Article IV of the German-Italian treaty was particularly profitable to Italy. It read as follows: "If the fortunes of any war undertaken in common against France should lead Italy to seek for territorial guaranties with respect to France for the security of the frontiers of the kingdom and of her maritime position, as well as with a view to the stability of peace, Germany will present no obstacle thereto; and, if need be, and in a measure compatible with circumstances, will apply herself to facilitating the means of attaining such a purpose." [158] What Bismarck meant by these "guaranties" and for what reasons he was ready to fulfil Italy's wishes in this respect, may be learned from the observations he let fall to Crown Prince Rudolph shortly after the conclusion of this treaty. It was necessary, he said, "to mollify Italy as far as possible and bind her to the Central Powers by means of gifts, such as could be made in the shape of Nice, Corsica, Albania, and territories on the North African coast." [159]

The fourth document, which was signed the same day by the representatives of all three powers, was intended [160] to express the

[156] See Vol. I, p. 113. No information is to be found in the Vienna State Archives regarding the negotiations which led to the conclusion of the German-Italian separate agreement.

[157] Cf. Vol. I, pp. 94 ff.

[158] Cf. Vol. I, p. 113. The Austrian government first learned of the contents of this article when a copy of the German-Italian separate agreement was given it upon the conclusion of the treaty. In the drafts in Kálnoky's possession there is no mention of such a promise on the part of Germany. It would appear that the negotiations relating thereto were not entered into until the last weeks before the conclusion of the treaty, when the idea of a single treaty, binding on all parties, was dropped.

[159] Crown Prince Rudolph's report of his conversation with Prince Bismarck, March 17, 1887.

[160] Cf. Vol. I, p. 115. As Széchényi informed Kálnoky on February 20, Holstein had told him, by instruction from Bismarck, that Robilant had proposed this. Bis-

idea that the joint additional treaty as well as the two separate treaties formed one great whole, and were designed to serve in common the same purpose, the preservation of peace.[161]

marck had not been favorably impressed by this eleventh-hour request, "in which he saw only a wholly superfluous formality, another instance of a distressing desire for endless new projects; but in consideration of the fact that 'pock-marked men are twice as sensitive as others,' and that the paper contains nothing that is not obvious and simple, he had not refused his assent." Széchényi telegraphed to Kálnoky and immediately received authorization to sign.

[161] Julius Hansen, in his book *Ambassade à Paris du Baron de Mohrenheim* (*1884–1898*), page 91, says: " In addition to the official treaty of the Triple Alliance, to which Crispi caused the military protocols to be added, oral agreements also existed between King Humbert and Emperor William, according to which these two monarchs gave their word of honor to remain true to the alliance, and to exert pressure on their ministers in order to forestall any possibility of its rupture. These confidential agreements were communicated to Emperor Francis Joseph, who also subscribed to them. This understanding, reached in 1889, was recorded by means of autograph letters which the three sovereigns exchanged with one another. This is the truth of the matter." It is doubtful, however, whether this was "the truth of the matter." No protocols governing military conventions were added to the treaty of 1887. No such military convention yet existed. Negotiations to this end came to nothing. Not until January, 1888, was a convention of this nature concluded between Germany and Italy. Austria-Hungary participated in it only in so far as the passage of Italian troops to the western frontier for the support of Germany was concerned (cf. p. 86, note 173). The "autograph letters" of the sovereigns were not to be found in the Vienna State Archives. Their existence is also argued against by the fact that Francis Joseph, according to Hansen's assertion (p. 92), is said to have demanded "that the general nature of the alliance, as it is characterized in the diplomatic treaties, should be expressed in plain, intelligible terms. It should be made unmistakably clear that the treaty has a purely defensive purpose, establishing the *casus foederis* only in the event that one of the three allied powers should be attacked; and that the *casus foederis* is not to be established if one of the allies should deem it opportune to enter into action at its own peril." The purely defensive nature of the Triple Alliance is so clearly defined in the treaty itself that no especial emphasis of this fact by Francis Joseph was called for.

CHAPTER III

THE THIRD TREATY OF THE TRIPLE ALLIANCE
MAY 6, 1891

THE renewal of the Triple Alliance in February, 1887, was accomplished only after prolonged negotiations, and was dearly paid for by the Central Powers; while the mutual distrust between Italy and Austria-Hungary remained undispelled.[162] In fact, the points of friction had multiplied through Italy's freshly acquired right to a decisive voice in the Balkan questions. At first, however, the beneficent results of the new and more effective coöperation of the three powers were evident. The Triple Alliance became a bulwark against French projects of revenge as well as against Russia's efforts to extend her sphere of influence in the Balkans, both of which perils assumed more threatening proportions during 1887, and, toward the end of that year and the beginning of 1888, brought Europe to the verge of war. The structure erected by Bismarck's masterly skill for the safeguarding of peace had as its core the alliance between Germany, Austria-Hungary, and Italy, around which numerous other powers were grouped as more or less stalwart buttresses.

Two agreements, concluded with the assistance of Germany in February and March and in December, 1887, between England, Austria-Hungary, and Italy [163] assured to the last two powers —

[162] As an evidence of the lack of confidence in the straightforwardness of the Italian policy felt by the statesmen of the Central Powers accredited to the Italian court, the fact may be cited that on February 26, 1887 — the ratifications of the treaty of the Triple Alliance of February 20 had not then been exchanged, and a change of ministry was imminent — Bruck wrote the following words to Kálnoky: "In the case of a war between France and Germany, the Italians will probably wait to see how the first battles turn out; only then will they decide whether to participate actively or to assume a passive attitude. There will probably be much noise and little action."

[163] Cf. the texts of these two agreements, Vol. I, pp. 94–103, 124–133. In a subsequent portion of this work the negotiations preceding their conclusion will be treated in detail. Some light is thrown on this matter by the literary legacy of Crispi,

and thus indirectly to the Triple Alliance — the coöperation of the British fleet against French advances in the western Mediterranean and also against the Russian menace of Constantinople and the Dardanelles. The more intimate association of England with the Central Powers, a "moral extension of the Triple Alliance across the English Channel," [164] was thus obtained. In May, 1887, the coöperation of Spain was secured in the event of joint action in the Mediterranean.[165] As the result of this step — prompted also by Germany — Spain might be made use of against France, just as Rumania,[166] allied to the Central Powers since 1883, might be employed against Russia.

The assistance of Milan of Serbia, whose personal dependence on Austria-Hungary — to whom he owed the maintenance of his throne — was continually increasing, could be definitely counted upon in the event of a conflict with Russia. These taken together, were powerful forces, which might well deter any adversary from beginning hostilities. We know, however, that Bismarck's measures for the protection of Germany went still further. On June 18, 1887, before the expiration of the agreement signed in 1881 and renewed in 1884 between the three empires, he concluded a treaty of reinsurance with Russia, without the knowledge of the Austrian government, which pledged Russia to neutrality in case Germany should be attacked by France, and laid upon Germany a similar obligation in case Austria-Hungary should advance against Russia.[167] This security on all sides and against every eventuality enabled Prince Bismarck to pursue toward allies and

especially *Questioni internazionali*, pp. 179 ff. Bismarck's letter to Salisbury of November 22, 1887, is of the greatest interest. Its text will be found in J. V. Fuller's *Bismarck's Diplomacy at its Zenith* (Cambridge, 1921); and (translated into German) in Hammann, *op. cit.*, pp. 154 ff.

[164] H. Oncken, *Das alte und das neue Mitteleuropa*, p. 47.

[165] The agreement between Spain and Italy was concluded on May 4, 1887. Austria-Hungary and Germany also subscribed to it. See Vol. I, pp. 116–123.

[166] The treaty between Austria-Hungary and Rumania was concluded at Vienna on October 30, 1883. Germany subscribed to it on the same day, and Italy on May 15, 1888. See Vol. I, pp. 78–89. In a subsequent portion of this work this treaty and its repeated renewals will be dealt with.

[167] Cf. Otto Hammann, *Zur Vorgeschichte des Weltkrieges*, pp. 33 ff., and the literature cited there. Further details regarding the treaty of reinsurance will be given in the comments on the Austro-Russian treaties. Cf. the text, Vol. I, pp. 274–281.

opponents alike those tactics of threats and promises, admoni-
tions and pleadings, pacifications and elucidations, by means of
which he attained the goal he held unswervingly before him, the
maintenance of the peace of Europe. It was a dangerous game
that he was playing. Only a master like himself could hope to
bring the ship of state through all the rocks and shoals into safe
harbor. As Emperor William I once said, he was like a rider who
juggled on horseback with five balls, never letting fall one.[168]
There were moments when he himself was frightened at what he
had done — when he feared that the irreconcilable differences between the Balkan policies of Russia and Austria-Hungary would
burst the Dual and Triple Alliances asunder.

Outwardly, however, Bismarck gave no signs of these misgivings. Even in the days when his differences with the cabinet of
Vienna had reached an alarming acuteness, he had unremittingly
praised the Dual Alliance, as well as the Triple Alliance, as the
strongest safeguard of peace. "Italy and Germany are living in
peace with Austria-Hungary," he declared in February, 1888,
"and they have the aim in common with Austria-Hungary to
ward off the perils which threaten them in common." In these
efforts he was strongly supported by Francesco Crispi, who had
been guiding the policy of Italy since July, 1887. Crispi was a
faithful partisan of the Triple Alliance, whose earnest desire
it was not only to strengthen the ties of friendship with Germany,[169] but also to eliminate the ceaselessly arising difficulties
which blocked the way to a better relationship between Italy and
Austria-Hungary. To this end he entered into negotiations with
Kálnoky in August, 1888,[170] broke up the Irredentist societies for
Trieste and Trent in the following year,[171] and induced King

---

[168] Hermann Hofmann, *Fürst Bismarck, 1890–1898*, iii, p. 183.

[169] With regard to Crispi's negotiations with Bismarck, cf. Crispi, *Memoirs*, ii,
pp. 207–240.

[170] This did not prevent Crispi from reverting to the old custom and complaining
once more about the bad treatment which his countrymen were alleged to be receiving in Austria. To Herbert Bismarck, who appeared in Rome with Emperor William
II in the fall of 1888, he spoke of the necessity of safeguarding the Italian frontiers
against Austria. Cf. Crispi, *Memoirs*, ii, p. 348.

[171] As regards Crispi's attitude, cf. Palamenghi-Crispi, *Questioni internazionali*, p.
106.

Humbert to affirm in Berlin his faithful adherence to the Triple Alliance. This attitude did not go unrewarded. Bismarck gave his most outspoken support to the Italian government when France, angered by Crispi's friendliness toward the Central Powers, began a vigorous tariff war against Italy and caused her weaker adversary serious losses. At the same time Bismarck negotiated with England for the purpose of securing for his ally the coöperation of the British fleet in the event of a French attack on the Italian coast. At Crispi's request, the cabinet of Vienna also used its influence at London in behalf of Italy. Crispi's efforts to secure Austria-Hungary's assent to a military convention on land and at sea fell flat,[172] however, although the German government, which had concluded an agreement with Italy in the beginning of 1888 providing for reciprocal military support on land,[173] vigor-

[172] As early as March, 1889, Crispi had brought forward a proposal for a naval convention, which, however, was refused by Kálnoky. (Bruck to Kálnoky, March 12, 1889; Kálnoky to Bruck, March 19, 1889.) Kálnoky took the stand that in discussing the eventuality of coöperation between the fleets, wholly different political questions and wholly different acts would necessarily be contemplated. Events in the eastern basin of the Mediterranean would have a much more profound and direct significance for Austria-Hungary than those which might take place off the western coasts of the Mediterranean. This difference between the scenes of action, as well as between the interests in question, would offer an almost insuperable obstacle to any attempt to realize in concrete form the idea of coöperation between the two fleets. "Our fleet is excellent," he said, "but in size it is not to be compared with those of the Great Powers. I can therefore only repeat that the basic requisite of a prudent Italian foreign policy is to make sure of England's protection. Until this is done, I consider Italy incapable of action, since fear for the safety of her coasts would paralyze the country and its people, and would prove stronger than the most energetic premier."

[173] The text of this German-Italian agreement is not available. Austria-Hungary was involved in it to the extent that she incurred obligations for the transportation and sustenance of Italian troops that were to fight in the West with Germany against France. The basis for Austria-Hungary's coöperation was established in a memorandum signed on January 28, 1888, by Baron Karl von Steininger, the Austro-Hungarian military attaché in Berlin, Count Alfred Schlieffen, the German representative, and Count Victor Emmanuel Dabormida and Cavalier M. Albertone, the representatives of Italy. This memorandum bears the title: "Mémoire indiquant les vues échangées à Berlin entre les délégués militaires des trois puissances centrales pendant le mois de janvier 1888." The introductory words read: "Dans le cas où la guerre viendrait à éclater entre les trois puissances centrales d'une part et la France et la Russie de l'autre, tandis que la plus grande partie des forces italiennes attaquerait la France sur la frontière des Alpes, le reste se joindrait aux forces le l'Alle-

ously supported Crispi's demands in Vienna. It was due to Kálnoky's wish not to offend Crispi that he did not brusquely decline
his proposals; he remarked instead to Count Nigra, who had pre-

magne, destinées à opérer au delà du Rhin dans le but de concourir avec elles aux
opérations actives qui seraient dirigés contre la France sur ce théâtre de guerre."
It provided for the transportation of six army corps and three cavalry divisions,
grouped in one or two armies, the commanders of which were to receive their military orders from the commander of the German army. Since the union of these
troops with the Germans was to take place "à travers le territoire" of Austria-Hungary, that state put three transport routes at their disposition: (1) Cormons-
Vienna-Wels-Passau; (2) Pontafel-St.Michael-Selzthal-Salzburg; and (3) Ala-
Innsbruck-Arlberg-Bregenz or Innsbruck-Kufstein. Further provisions dealt with
the number of trains, the beginning of the transportation, etc. The more detailed
provisions were to be incorporated in a separate agreement between Austria-Hungary and Italy. As a matter of fact, an agreement of this nature — "Conventions in
the event of the transportation of troops of the royal Italian army through the imperial and royal Austro-Hungarian territory, concluded on the basis of the memorandum drawn up in Berlin in January, 1888, by the military plenipotentiaries of the
three allied great powers" — was signed toward the beginning of February by Emil
Ritter von Guttenberg, and Giovanni Goiran.
Political significance lay in the fact that Austria-Hungary insisted on the inclusion, at the end of the memorandum drawn up in Berlin, of the reservation: "The
Austro-Hungarian government reserves the right to remain neutral and not to permit the transportation of troops in question to take place, in case the war should be
confined to Germany and Italy on one side, and France on the other." Count Launay,
the Italian ambassador in Berlin, objected to this clause. At his request Széchényi
telegraphed to Kálnoky (January 22, 1888) that Launay urgently requested the addition of the following supplement to Austria-Hungary's reservation: "Il est entendu
que par cette réserve l'Autriche-Hongrie n'entend déroger en rien aux accords stipulés
en 1882 et renouvelés en 1887." Kálnoky replied (telegram to Széchényi, January
23, 1888) that Launay was to be assured that memorandum was a wholly "informal" document, which in no case could encroach upon treaty provisions; Kálnoky
moreover had no objection to the adoption of the following supplement: "Il est entendu que par cette réserve l'Autriche-Hongrie n'entend déroger en rien à ses engagements avec l'Italie." This was the wording given to the supplement in the
memorandum of January 28, 1888.
In the period between October, 1887, and April, 1888, deliberations also took
place concerning the coöperation of Italian with Austro-Hungarian troops; this,
however, finally came to nothing. The idea had originated with Crispi, and Kálnoky supported the project. In a letter to Baron Bruck dated December 28, 1887,
Kálnoky refers to this: "At the time of the treaty negotiations with Count Robilant,
the latter proposed to us a military coöperation with the Italian army. An article in
the treaty to this end was at first contemplated; later, however, when we limited the
scope of the treaty obligations, this was dropped again." Kálnoky went on to emphasize the great advantage accruing to the monarchy from support by Italian
troops. The only question was whether Italy was reliable and how much she would

sented them and pointed to the example set by Germany, that although Germany and Italy might have to defend their frontiers against a common adversary, this was not the case with Austria-Hungary and Italy. He stated with perfect frankness that there was as little reason for hoping that Austria-Hungary, if threatened by war with Russia, would send strong contingents of troops to a Franco-Italian war as that Italy would help Austria-Hungary against Russia if she were obliged to defend herself by land and on sea against the French.[174] However, since he had promised further consideration of the matter in case concrete propositions were made by Italy, Count Nigra transmitted to him at the beginning of August, 1889, the draft of a military convention between Austria-Hungary and Italy.[175] Even now Kálnoky did not

demand. "I have no reason," wrote Kálnoky, "to cast doubt on Italy's trustworthiness as an ally, but I also have no proof that she would remain unreservedly faithful under all circumstances. If Italian troops were to fight side by side with those of the Dual Monarchy, and in this manner their interests were to be bound all the more closely to the common cause, this would furnish us with one more substantial guaranty, and thus a lasting feeling of friendship might arise between the two neighboring states through this brotherhood of arms; while, on the other hand, it would be a matter of concern if the Italian army were to stand intact and eager for war at a moment when our troops and reserves might be well nigh exhausted by a hard conflict." All this made it advisable to make sure of Italy's coöperation. He pointed out, however, that there were many reasons for caution; "Modesty and unselfishness," he wrote, "are qualities with which Italy cannot be reproached. For this reason we must make up our minds that the price which Italy will ask for her aid may give rise to many disagreeable arguments — even to the possible breaking off of the negotiations." Kálnoky therefore felt at the time that he could only recommend general discussion. In February, after the conclusion of the military conference in Berlin, he went further. Bruck was commanded (instruction of February 4, 1888) to get information regarding the number of troops that Italy could spare — Kálnoky had in mind two army corps, which might be employed against Russia — and the price she intended to ask for her assistance. The negotiations came to nothing, however, since the danger of war with Russia no longer appeared so threatening. Hansen's remarks (*op. cit.*, pp. 94 ff.) regarding the conclusion of military agreements are therefore incorrect.

[174] Report by Kálnoky of a conversation with Count Nigra, Vienna, July 28, 1889.

[175] Count Nigra to Kálnoky, Vienna, August 7, 1889 (original). The enclosure reads: Convention maritime:

    1ère hypothèse: Déterminer une action concertée de l'Italie et de l'Autriche-Hongrie dans la Méditerranée.

    2ème hypothèse: L'Autriche-Hongrie se limiterait à assurer les eaux de l'Adriatique

decline to enter into further negotiations, though he was firmly resolved not to agree to Crispi's projects; he wished to keep matters dragging on until the Italian's excessive apprehension should be dissipated.

The relations of the allies were thus steadily improving toward the end of the eighties. Differences kept recurring, indeed, between Italy and Austria-Hungary, but they were superficially less evident, or were smoothed over by Bismarck's mediatory activities whenever they threatened to become critical. It is therefore intelligible that the dismissal of the Imperial Chancellor in March, 1890, should have caused misgivings to arise in Rome and Vienna lest the Triple Alliance come to grief through the loss of one of its creators. The events of the next few months, however, proved that any fears of this nature were groundless. General Caprivi, Bismarck's successor, immediately professed himself a loyal supporter of the policy of the Triple Alliance, and Kálnoky and Crispi gave assurances to the same effect.[176] Kálnoky's speech in the Austro-Hungarian Delegations, the address made by Crispi to the representatives of the Dual Monarchy and of Germany in Rome, as well as the declarations of William II and Francis Joseph I to Launay, were all of the same tenor; they emphasized the significance and the value of the Triple Alliance, and expressed the determination to sustain it.[177] But in all these utterances nothing

contre l'ennemi pour le cas où les forces navales italiennes seraient engagées en totalité dans la Méditerranée.

Convention militaire:

1ère hypothèse: Déterminer le rôle des deux armées dans le cas où la guerre serait limitée, au moins pour quelque temps, à l'Italie.

2ème hypothèse: Déterminer le rôle des forces alliées pour le cas où la guerre éclaterait en même temps en Orient et en Occident.

Further negotiations concerning the naval convention took place in the following years, particularly 1891. (Acts in State Archives.) They finally led, on December 5, 1900, to the conclusion of a convention according to which certain zones of operation were designated for the fleets of Austria-Hungary and of Italy. Only within these zones were they to advance against the enemy. This convention was replaced by another (June 23, 1913), providing for joint action in case of war: printed in Vol. I, pp. 282–305.

[176] Documents in the State Archives. Cf. Palamenghi-Crispi, *Questioni internazionali*, pp. 3 ff.

[177] The strained relations between Italy and Austria-Hungary in the summer of 1890, resulting from the Slavophile policy of Count Taaffe, were only ephemeral. At

was said about a prolongation of the treaty, which was to expire on May 30, 1892.

According to Crispi, the matter was mentioned for the first time on the occasion of his meeting with Caprivi at Milan, in November, 1890. England's approach to the Triple Alliance, brought about by the treaty of July 1, 1890, between England and Germany, unquestionably made it easier for Crispi to bring up the idea of its renewal. After his return to Rome he gave the Austro-Hungarian ambassador, Baron Bruck, a detailed account of his conversations with the Imperial Chancellor, dwelling on the fact that he had emphasized at Milan Italy's deep interest in the prolongation of the Triple Alliance. "No Italian statesman," he had said to Caprivi, "could think or feel otherwise; every one of us will strive to stand by the Triple Alliance, and, as a logical conclusion, to plan for the renewal of the existing treaties. France has reverted to her old policy and is ceaselessly working to undermine the monarchical form of government and the monarchical spirit, especially among her Latin neighbors. Thus is the revolution striving to spread out and strike its first roots in Spain,[178] Portugal, and Italy, in the hope that it can transfer its activities in like manner to the Germanic and Slavic peoples. Here in Italy this subversive effort has of late grown stronger every year; leaving other political considerations out of the question, it has in itself become sufficiently serious to impress on the Italian statesmen the ever increasing necessity of maintaining the most intimate relations of alliance with the Central Powers, and of seeking in this

that time, it is true, Crispi expressed the doubt whether the exasperation of public opinion in Italy by Count Taaffe's attitude would permit of the renewal of the Triple Alliance in 1892; at the same time, however, he declared that such a renewal was to Italy's interests: "Italy," he wrote to Nigra, "must be sure of her frontiers. Since unfortunately she can no longer count on the friendship of France, she must cling to Austria-Hungary at any price, in order to prevent her from concluding an alliance with France and the Pope which would bring with it incalculable consequences. Austria-Hungary, moreover, forms a barricade protecting Italy against dangerous foes [i. e., the Slavs]."

[178] At that time Crispi suggested the support of the monarchical principle in Spain and Portugal. Cf. *Questioni internazionali*, p. 9. During the course of the next few months the powers of the Triple Alliance entered into negotiations at Madrid regarding the matter. Documents in the State Archives.

a guaranty of the royal house of Italy, which alone can keep the nation great and united."

Crispi also informed Caprivi that for this reason he was anxious to renew the existing treaties before the time of their expiration — all the more so because certain "little additions or little alterations would seem to be desirable." The discussion of these, he said, might be begun at once. As one of these "little alterations" he proposed the consolidation of the three treaties concluded in 1887 into one. "By so doing," said Crispi to Bruck, "we should attain greater security and a more uniform coöperation; the territories of the various parties would be better safeguarded against any attack, and, above all, conditions of greater intimacy would be brought about. These Italy needs — but they would likewise be in harmony with Austria-Hungary's interests.[179]   The more uniform are the agreements," added Crispi, "the better it will be; for not only will every misunderstanding be thus automatically eliminated, but each one of the three states would be following the same lines of policy. This is not exactly the case at present; little difficulties keep arising which, at critical moments, might assume great proportions." Crispi believed that General von Caprivi had fully appreciated these observations of his, and had appeared to be favorably disposed toward them.

The next step was to get Kálnoky's assent.[180]   The Austro-Hungarian statesman knew immediately what Crispi sought to obtain by his proposals. Germany was to assume obligations for the whole nexus of Near Eastern questions; Austria-Hungary for the Italian sphere of interests in North Africa. It seemed improbable to him that Caprivi had not seen through the Italian plans, or had lightly given them his approval.[181]   According to the first information sent to Kálnoky by Caprivi regarding his conversations with Crispi, these questions had not even been mentioned in Milan.[182]   When Kálnoky again inquired how matters stood, Ca-

[179] Bruck to Kálnoky, November 18, 1890.

[180] Ibid.

[181] Kálnoky to Széchényi, November 27, 1890. Summary and copy for Emperor Francis Joseph, with the Emperor's marginal note: "Very good and clear."

[182] Széchényi to Kálnoky, November 19, 1890 (original). In Crispi's Diary (Palamenghi-Crispi, pp. 8 foll.) the text is in harmony with Crispi's statement to

privi declared most explicitly that "Crispi has not uttered a syllable regarding the renewal of the existing treaty of Alliance before its expiration." [183] The discussion, he said, had been limited to German-Italian relations.[184] In regard to these Crispi had doubtless spoken of changes desired by him, but had made no definite. demands. 'Not the remotest allusion had been made by him' to the treaty between Austria-Hungary and Italy, or 'to the question of giving this treaty a wording identical with that existing between Italy and Germany.' From further remarks of the Imperial Chancellor, however, Széchényi became convinced that although Caprivi had no idea of expecting the Austrian government to follow Germany's lead and assume extensive obligations in North Africa in behalf of Italian interests, he would nevertheless be displeased if Kálnoky should take exception on principle to Crispi's desire to combine the three treaties in one.[185]

Bruck: "Ricordai che il 30 maggio 1892 cioè da qui a 18 mese scade il trattato di alleanza delle tre monarchie. Soggiunsi . . . Necessario rivedere . . . se vi ha altro da aggiungere." The suspension-points are inserted by Palamenghi, who doubtless left out certain passages for reasons of secrecy.

[183] Caprivi went on to say: "The latter (the German-Italian treaty) was discussed only so far as Signor Crispi expressed the wish to have it renewed in due season. Herr von Caprivi thereupon hastened to express a similar wish on the part of the German government; he was much pleased, however, that the Italian premier had made no mention of expediting the renewal. He (Caprivi) had feared this and was prepared to reply with a decisive 'No.' He felt really relieved that he was not obliged to do so."

[184] Crispi asserted after his fall in July, 1891, that he had also spoken with Caprivi about the necessity of securing for Italy an "adjustment of frontiers," which would also have been attainable if the matter had been properly approached: "Chiedere per compenso almeno una modificazione delle frontiere; l'avremmo potuto ottenere sapendo agire, à Vienna se l'aspettavano e Berlino avrebbe pesato sopra Vienna." Cf. Fraknói, p. 50, text and note. The latter assertion is certainly incorrect. It is doubtful, however, whether Crispi really discussed this question seriously with Caprivi. In the face of Caprivi's communications to Széchényi, this can hardly be believed.

[185] Széchényi to Kálnoky, November 30, 1890 (original). The reading is as follows: "Crispi has evidently believed that he can most safely approach us with his projects if he does so indirectly, by invoking a community of ideas with the German Imperial Chancellor. In so doing his over-fertile imagination has again led him too far. He appears, moreover, to have made his calculations without taking account of Caprivi's love of the truth and his accurate memory." Bruck, however, declared (Bruck to Kálnoky, December 16, 1890): "I believe that Crispi was really sincere in this matter, and was attempting no trickery. . . . Crispi still believes that the Ger-

Kálnoky's need of learning the views of his German colleague grew all the greater when Count Nigra shortly after read him a letter in which Crispi "sets forth — in great detail, it is true, but with no real definiteness whatever — his ideas and wishes, the approval of which by Germany he believes he has already obtained in Milan." [186]   In replying to Nigra, Kálnoky pointed out how hard it would be for Italy to assume new obligations. He acknowledged the necessity for the Triple Alliance and the desirability of renewing it; he said, however, that if Crispi designated the considerable differences existing between the Austro-Italian and the German-Italian separate treaties of 1887 as "little variations," and believed that he could easily eliminate them, he need only make the attempt. He would soon realize — as Robilant had realized in 1887 — that the "differences in the geographical situations and the direct political interests of each one of the three powers must also entail real differences in their respective claims and obligations." These could hardly be smoothed out so easily and unceremoniously. "Or is Italy in a position," asked Kálnoky, "to give us such assistance against Russia as Germany has promised us, in return for further obligations which we might assume in the West or in the Mediterranean?" So far, he pursued, Italy has promised in the treaty to observe only benevolent neutrality in an Austro-Russian war, and Crispi must be aware that if a great European conflagration were to break out his country would be obliged to send her whole army westward. "Even Germany has always refused up to the present to meddle in questions of the Orient and the Balkans; yet she would be forced to do so if the article in the Austro-Italian treaty relating to these matters were equally binding on all parties. Austria-Hungary, for her part, has neither reasons nor interests which would lead her to fly to arms for Tripoli or Morocco." Kálnoky drew from these premises the conclusion that the existing treaties between the Central Powers and Italy rested "on an entirely just basis," and that in them the capacity of each party found the fullest possible expression. He

man Imperial Chancellor has given full approval to his proposals, possibly going on the assumption that silence gives consent."

[186] Cf. the letter from Crispi to Nigra, December 4, 1890, in Palamenghi-Crispi, *Questioni internazionali*, pp. 12 f.

could not see what purpose would be served by making changes. "That which is good is not made better by disturbing it unnecessarily."

In spite of all this, however, Kálnoky respected Caprivi's wish and did not decline to enter into further negotiations with Crispi; he asked instead for "precise, practicable proposals." At the same time, referring to the demands made by Crispi at Milan for a commercial policy which would end in a tariff league of the three powers,[187] he declared that Austria-Hungary, as well as Germany, was interested in reaching an understanding with Italy in commercial and economic fields, but that the conclusion of the pending negotiations between the Austro-Hungarian and German delegates must take precedence over any other agreement of a commercial nature, and that neither Austria-Hungary nor Germany would enter into any commercial treaty directed against France.[188]

[187] In his above mentioned letter to Nigra of December 4 (cf. *Questioni internazionali*, p. 12), Crispi gives information regarding this point. As Bruck reported in his second note of November 18, 1890, Crispi had made the proposal to Count Caprivi to combat the French 'blockade system' by similar steps "which would paralyze this measure, for otherwise the commercial and industrial interests of these states will be hard hit." Crispi had also emphasized the political side, "since a common interest in commercial and industrial questions would bind the respective countries closer together." He had pointed to the fact that "the first steps toward an understanding" between Berlin and Vienna "had already been taken," and expressed the wish that Italy should not be excluded. Caprivi had expressed his readiness to enter into negotiations with Italy also after the conclusion of the German-Austrian negotiations. (Széchényi to Kálnoky, November 19, 1890.) Crispi states for his part (Palamenghi-Crispi, *Questioni internazionali*, pp. 10 and 12 f.) that he had proposed to Caprivi that France's threat to apply the autonomous tariff should be answered by a counter-threat. A customs union (*lega doganale*) of the powers of the Triple Alliance could not easily be managed, but a system of preferential tariffs was feasible. There were also political reasons for Caprivi's promise to give this matter consideration. He believed that customs quarrels between the allies might decrease the popularity of the alliance in all three countries, but that a new commercial treaty would heighten it. Cf. Otto Hammann, *Der neue Kurs*, p. 18; H. Oncken, *Das alte und das neue Mitteleuropa*, pp. 62 f.

[188] Kálnoky to Bruck, December 13, 1890. Draft. Cf. *Questioni internazionali*, p. 14. No discussion of questions of commercial policy will be attempted here. It goes without saying that these were of significance as regards the attitude of the various governments in matters of foreign policy. At the time that Kálnoky expressed himself in the manner stated above, negotiations were being opened in Vienna which led on December 6, 1891, to the conclusion of the German-Austrian commercial treaty. Cf. *Die Handelspolitik des Deutschen Reichs vom Frankfurter Frieden bis zur Gegenwart* (Berlin, 1899), pp. 155 ff.

Kálnoky informed the Foreign Office at Berlin of his conversations with Nigra,[189] stating at the same time that he had no objection to an anticipatory renewal of the Triple Alliance, in case this could be accomplished without changes. In Berlin, however, there appeared to be little inclination to take immediate steps in this direction. Caprivi said that he had no idea of tying his hands thirteen months before the expiration of the treaty. He also pointed out that the separate treaty between Germany and Italy was far more complicated than that between Austria-Hungary and Italy. "In the course of the summer of 1889," he said, "Crispi alarmed us more than once over Tripoli; and it is by no means impossible that before the treaty in question expires we may witness the development of events which will result in such a disturbance of affairs in Africa that it may eventually be to our own interest to cause changes to be made in our treaty relations."[190] The results of this opposition of the German government to a hasty settlement with Italy immediately became manifest. The negotiations began to drag, and the whole month of January, 1891, went by without another step having been taken.

At this time there occurred an event which caused a change in the policy of the cabinet of Berlin. Crispi, the faithful supporter of the Triple Alliance in Italy, fell a victim to the miscarriage of his colonial policy, and Marquis Rudini, whose Francophile tendencies were as well known in Berlin as in Vienna, took his place. On assuming office, indeed, he declared that there would be no change of foreign policy[191]; but his actions in the first few weeks showed that a change had already taken place. Italy's relations with France became noticeably better; the influence of the French ambassador in Rome increased. Vienna and Berlin were notified from well informed sources that negotiations were under way between Paris and Rome which were intended to conciliate the two governments and break up the Triple Alliance. In April, 1891, Baron Bruck, the Austro-Hungarian ambassador in Rome, learned from trustworthy informants that a representative of the Roth-

---

[189] Kálnoky to Széchényi, December 30, 1890.
[190] Széchényi to Kálnoky, January 3, 1891. Original.
[191] Rudini to Kálnoky, February 11, 1891. Original. Cf. Chiala, pp. 532 ff.

schilds had held out great promises of a financial nature in case Italy were to remain neutral in a Franco-German war, or "observe a 'hands-off' policy in the event of the reconquest of Alsace and Lorraine." [192] These disquieting tidings were in contradiction to the official declarations of Rudini, who repeatedly gave assurances of his loyalty to the Triple Alliance; but Kálnoky and Caprivi both lacked faith in the trustworthiness of his protestations. The latter particularly considered it most important under the circumstances to bind the unreliable ally to the Central Powers by still another tie.

This desire grew month by month more urgent. Reports from Paris and St. Petersburg showed that the alliance with Russia which had long been desired and asked for by the French statesmen was on the verge of consummation. The Tsar, offended by Germany's failure to renew the 'reinsurance treaty' concluded for three years in 1887, worried by reports of far-reaching agreements between the British and German governments, and enraged by William II's friendly policy toward the Poles, overcame his distaste for the republican form of government in the West and joined the increasingly powerful party which for a long time had favored alliance with France and which saw Russia's salvation in a war with Germany.[193] The German government, realizing the danger which threatened it, bent all its efforts toward the immediate renewal of the Triple Alliance, for which it was now ready to pay with sacrifices. Continuous pressure was straightway brought upon the cabinet of Vienna, which, regarding the situation with more composure, had so far refused to consider the assumption of

[192] Bruck to Kálnoky, telegram of April 27, 1891, and despatch of May 5. Illuminating observations in this matter are to be found in a despatch of Count Hoyos, the Austro-Hungarian ambassador in Paris, dated May 21, 1891. Count Hoyos stated that it could not be determined whether Rothschild was acting in agreement with the French government, or whether he merely wished to know, before starting financial negotiations in Italy, if he could do so without violating any "patriotic duty." Eckardt, however, states in the volume *Berlin, Wien, Rom*, published anonymously by him (pp. 130 f.), that the French government replied to Italy's attempt to contract a loan in Paris by the statement that it would be time enough to think of money matters when the political situation had been settled — i. e., when Italy had either renounced the Triple Alliance or revealed its contents in Paris.

[193] Cf. André Tardieu, *La France et ses alliances*, 3d ed., pp. 12 ff.

fresh obligations. When, toward the end of March, Rudini proposed the resumption of negotiations,[194] Kálnoky instructed Bruck to let the Italians know that since a more extensive support of their Mediterranean policy could only be expected of Austria-Hungary in return for corresponding obligations which Italy would not be willing to assume, he would recommend the renewal of the treaty of 1887 without any alterations. His arguments, which he also brought forward in numerous interviews with Count Nigra, appeared to make some impression upon Rudini.

Toward the beginning of April the Italian minister announced his readiness to proceed with the renewal of the existing treaties as quickly as possible,[195] and stated at the same time that he realized "that no change in the present relations [with Austria-Hungary] seems possible, since Italy is not in a position to offer a counter-service in return for any possible service which might be done for her." [196] He hoped, indeed, that Austria-Hungary would make common cause with Italy in Mediterranean questions; but he understood that these could not be precisely defined. As a compensation, so to speak, for the abandonment of this demand, Rudini requested the good offices of the Austrian government in London for the purpose of prompting England, who had pledged herself to Italy only as regards the eastern basin of the Mediterranean, to assume similar obligations for the western portion of this sea as well. This desire was intelligible, since all the Italian coasts were exposed to attack in the event of a war with France.[197] A short while later Count Nigra repeated this request, which was the more favorably received in Vienna and Berlin because England's rapprochement with the Triple Alliance was held by Kálnoky and Caprivi to be desirable from their own point of view.[198]

[194] Bruck to Kálnoky, March 25, 1891. Original.

[195] Telegram from Bruck to Kálnoky, April 5, 1891.

[196] Bruck to Kálnoky, April 7, 1891. Original.   [197] Ibid.

[198] Kálnoky to Bruck, April 13, 1891 (copy). Detailed information will be given in subsequent portions of this work concerning the negotiations carried on to this end with England. Cf. Eckardt, op. cit., p. 131, who states that the British premier had made the assurance of English protection of the Italian coasts, as requested of him, dependent on the previous renewal of the Triple Alliance. After receiving this information Rudini exclaimed, "Now the renewal of the treaty for the sake of England has become inevitable!" Cf. H. Oncken, op. cit., p. 60.

At the same time negotiations between Nigra and Kálnoky for the renewal of the Triple Alliance were set on foot once more. The questions of the unification of the treaties of 1887 and of possible changes in substance were discussed in detail. Kálnoky had hopes of a satisfactory outcome. On April 9, he wrote his friend Szé-chényi that Nigra appeared to have convinced the Italian premier that "the existing stipulations would have to be accepted as a basis, and very likely also as the probable final result — at least so far as the treaty with Austria-Hungary was concerned." Kálnoky hoped that his advice would be taken and that "with the exception of a few details," a simple prolongation would be found sufficient.[199] This was also the prevailing view in Berlin at that moment. Caprivi answered Rudini's request for a rapid conclusion of the negotiations by saying that he was ready immediately to renew the treaty of alliance with Italy, "but only as a prolongation of the existing treaty, without the alteration of a single word."[200] He remarked to the Austro-Hungarian ambassador at the time that even so Germany's obligations, as defined by the treaty, were so much greater than Italy's counter-obligations that for military reasons alone he would not renew the treaty; general political considerations, however, had determined him to take the step. He also expressed the hope that his proposals would prevail in Rome.[201]

Scarcely a week later the alliance of France with Russia caused a complete reversal of his opinions. He was now inclined to take into consideration not only Rudini's wish for the formal unification of the treaties of 1887, but also the extensive demands of the Italian government as to matters of substance. We have but scanty information regarding the negotiations carried on from this point to the conclusion of the new treaty on May 6, 1891. They took place, with Kálnoky's approval, at Berlin.[202] Since Austria-Hungary had but little real concern in them, the German government was no longer under the necessity of keeping Kálnoky

[199] Kálnoky to Széchényi, April 9, 1891. Draft.
[200] Telegram from Széchényi to Kálnoky, April 11, 1891.
[201] Széchényi to Kálnoky, April 12, 1891. Original.
[202] Kálnoky to Széchényi, April 9, 1891. Draft.

informed as to the progress of affairs. On April 20, Nigra presented at Vienna a copy of the treaty draft, over which his colleague at Berlin had to negotiate with the chief German statesmen. Kálnoky soon convinced himself that it entailed no new obligations for Austria-Hungary.

The project of the Italian government provided for the union of the three treaties of 1887 in one.[203] Kálnoky and Caprivi, who had at first refused to sanction this change of form, now raised no objection. Kálnoky immediately gave his approval; and the German Foreign Office, in marked contrast to its earlier attitude, declared that it was the more ready to give its assent "because the unity and connection of the various existing treaties has already been recognized in the final protocol of the treaty of 1887." [204]

Rudini's draft provided for fourteen articles and one protocol. Articles I to V corresponded verbatim to the first five articles of the treaty of 1882. Article VI, regarding the question of the Orient, was of the same tenor as paragraph 1 of the first article of the Austro-Italian separate treaty of 1887.[205] For Germany, who, through the elimination of Article I of the German-Italian separate treaty of 1887, figured as a cosignatory to the abovementioned Article VI, this meant an increased burden; for she was now pledged to exert her influence for the maintenance of the status quo throughout the entire Turkish Orient, whereas her previous obligations were limited to the "côtes et îles ottomanes de la mer Adriatique et dans la mer Egée." [206] Article VII (ex-

[203] First draft of Marquis di Rudini. Kálnoky made the following notation on this: "Received from the Italian ambassador as preliminary communication; conditional upon the formal communication from Berlin, where the negotiations are taking place." April 20, 1891.

[204] Marschall to Reuss, April 25, 1891. Communicated by Reuss to Kálnoky, April 27, 1891. Copy. Cf. the text of the final protocol, Vol. I, p. 114.

[205] See Vol. I, p. 109.

[206] In the treaties of 1887 the stipulations regarding the Orient were not identical for Austria-Hungary and for Germany. The obligations assumed by the latter to prevent a territorial change which might be harmful to the two signatory powers was limited "sur les côtes et îles ottomanes dans la mer Adriatique et dans la mer Egée." As this limitation was no longer to the liking of the Italians, Rudini united the Austro-Hungarian and German declarations, which were now worded alike, in Article VI. Article VII related to Egypt; Article VIII contained the second part of Article II of the separate treaty of 1887 between Italy and Austria-Hungary. Since

clusion of the Egyptian question, and liberty of action in regard thereto) contained an unimportant innovation providing for Austria-Hungary's accession to the provisions contained in Article II of the German-Italian separate treaty of 1887. Article VIII, governing the attitude of Austria-Hungary and Italy in the event of a change in the Balkan situation, corresponded verbatim to the second paragraph of Article I of the Austro-Italian separate treaty of 1887,[207] and was still limited to these two powers.

Article IX and portions of Article X, on the other hand, were, wholly new. They had no bearing on Austria-Hungary, but they entailed for Germany a considerable extension of those obligations in North Africa which she had pledged to Italy through the, separate treaty of 1887. Not only was Tunis coupled with Tripolitania and Morocco as the North African territories whose status quo Germany must maintain, but mention was also made in Rudini's draft of the "status quo de fait et de droit" instead of the "status quo territorial." In case of need, Germany was also bound to support Italy in any action which she might feel called upon to undertake, in the event of a disturbance of the status quo in North Africa, for the purpose of restoring the balance and obtaining just compensations.[208] Article XI, which referred to a

Germany, however, succeeded in bringing about the reinstatement of the clause "sur les côtes . . . mer Egée," it became necessary to abandon the joint article regarding these questions of the Orient. Article VI now contained the provisions regarding the Orient, in so far as they concerned Germany; the opening words "Les hautes parties contractantes" had therefore to be changed to "L'Allemagne et l'Italie"; Article VII contained the provisions referring to Austria-Hungary, and Article VIII, those referring to Egypt.

[207] Vol. I, p. 109.

[208] In Rudini's draft Article IX is worded as follows: "L'Italie et l'Allemagne s'engagent à s'employer pour le maintien du status quo de fait et de droit ¹ dans les régions nord-africaines sur la Méditerranée, à savoir la Cyrenaïque, la Tripolitaine, la Tunisie, et le Maroc.² Les représentants des deux puissances dans ces régions auront pour instruction de se tenir dans la plus étroite intimité de communications et d'assistance mutuelles. Si malheureusement ³ le maintien du status quo devenait impossible, l'Allemagne s'engage ⁴ à appuyer l'Italie en toute action sous la forme d'occupation ou autre prise de garantie, que cette dernière devrait entreprendre ⁵ en vue d'un intérêt d'équilibre et de légitime compensation.⁶" After further negotiations the following changes in this draft were accepted in compliance with German demands. ¹ "territorial" instead of "de fait et de droit." ² "et le Maroc" was eliminated. ³ "en suite d'un mûr examen de la situation l'Allemagne et l'Italie re-

possible acquisition of territory by Italy at the cost of France, corresponded literally to Article IV of the German-Italian separate treaty of 1887, and did not involve Austria-Hungary. The remaining articles contained stipulations regarding the secrecy, the duration, and the ratification of the treaty. The duration was fixed by Rudini at six years.

The draft of a protocol, the incorporation of which in the new treaty was insisted on by Rudini, came as a real innovation. The first paragraph of this protocol dealt with the commercial relations of the three powers. Its contents, the result of lengthy negotiations on the part of the Italian government with representatives of the Central Powers, were, as Marschall, then German Secretary of State, justly remarked, "rather of a decorative nature, considering the restrictions with which it began and ended." [209] Above and beyond the treatment accorded to the most favored nation, the three powers — under reserve of the consent of the respective parliaments — promised one another every facility and every special advantage in economic matters (finances, customs, railroads) which would be compatible with their own interests.[210] Of greater value to Italy was the second paragraph of the protocol, which had to do with England's assistance in the North African territories bordering on the Central and Western Mediterranean. This had already been promised, in principle at least, for the territory of the Turkish Empire in the Orient. The three powers, in accordance with the promises received by Italy from the governments of Berlin and Vienna during the negotiations, also pledged themselves to attempt, at a suitable moment and so far as cir-

connaissaient l'une et l'autre que" was inserted after "malheureusement." 4 "après un accord formal et préalable" was inserted after "s'engage." 5 "dans ces mémes régions" was inserted after "entreprendre." 6 At the conclusion, "Il est entendu que pour pareille éventualité les deux puissances chercheraient à se mettre également d'accord avec l'Angleterre" was added.

[209] Marschall to Reuss, April 25, 1891; communicated by Reuss to Kálnoky, April 27. Copy.

[210] At the time when the treaty of the Triple Alliance was renewed, the negotiations regarding the commercial treaties between Germany and Austria-Hungary had come to a favorable conclusion. The negotiations between the Central Powers and Italy were then begun in the course of the summer of 1891. On December 6 the commercial treaties between Germany and Austria-Hungary were signed, together with the treaties between these two states and Italy.

cumstances permitted, to induce England to subscribe to the provisions of Articles IX and X of the new treaty.[211]

Count Kálnoky had little fault to find either with the substance of the protocol or with the whole draft of the treaty. He had Reuss make the proposal in Berlin that in case the treaty were not denounced one year before the date of expiration, it was to be considered as renewed for another term of years.[212] The decision of all other questions he left to the German government, for on it alone would fall the burden of the concessions exacted by Rudini. It is not within the province of this work to describe the negotiations carried on between Germany and Italy until the end of April; the documents at our disposal would not be adequate for this.[213] A comparison of Rudini's draft with the definitive text of the treaty, however, shows that the German statesmen succeeded in securing substantial alterations, which considerably limited the scope of the obligations assumed by Germany. These changes, which were effected in the important Articles VI and IX of the Italian draft, provided in the former for the reinstatement of the text of the treaty of 1887,[214] and in the latter for the insertion of several clauses.[215]

[211] The wording of the draft is identical with that of the final treaty. See Vol. I, pp. 160–163. Details will be given in subsequent parts of this work concerning the negotiations carried on to this end with England. Cf. the chapter "La triplice alleanza e l'Inghilterra" in Palamenghi-Crispi, *Questioni internazionali*, pp. 256 ff. The rapprochement between England and the powers of the Triple Alliance was very disquieting to their opponents. Barthélemy-Saint-Hilaire wrote at that time "The Triple Alliance tomorrow will be the Quadruple Alliance. England, the only nation with which we could possibly form an alliance without demeaning ourselves, goes where her interests lead her — that is, to a union with the three powers which are determined to block Russia's desires for world conquest." Cf. Singer, *op. cit.*, p. 103.

[212] Marschall to Reuss, April 25, 1891. Communicated by Reuss to Kálnoky, April 27, 1891. Copy.

[213] Marschall's often mentioned letter of April 25, 1891, contains information regarding the attitude of the German government toward Rudini's draft. We have a private letter from Prince Reuss to Kálnoky (May 3) in which he suggests certain stylistic alterations in the two drafts communicated the day before; likewise a draft of Kálnoky's answer of May 4, in which he assents to Prince Reuss's proposals and expresses similar wishes on his own part.

[214] Cf. p. 98, note 206.

[215] Cf. p. 99, note 208.

In accordance with Kálnoky's suggestion,[216] it was also provided that the treaty, the duration of which was fixed at six years, should be prolonged for another term of six years in case it were not denounced one year before the date of expiration. By the end of April the treaty text had been drawn up in Berlin; on May 2 Prince Reuss delivered the new draft in Vienna.[217] Kálnoky accepted the unimportant alterations suggested by Reuss,[218] and recommended that the treaty be signed as soon as possible. He was pleased with the result which had been attained.[219] "As far as the form is concerned," he wrote Széchényi, "respect has been paid to the wishes of the Italians that the stipulations of the earlier separate treaties should be gathered together in one instrument, thus giving a more pregnant expression to the character of the Triple Alliance.   As for the actual substance, it corresponds throughout, so far as Austria-Hungary is concerned, to the treaty of 1887. From the German standpoint as well, no important changes, such as the Italians had in view, have been made. The protocol annexed to the treaty is an innovation introduced at Italy's suggestion; it contains, however, merely declarations which are partly matters of course, partly of a theoretical nature." On May 6 the signing of the treaty took place at Berlin,[220] and on the 17th of the same month the ratifications were exchanged.[221] At Italy's wish, and by consent of the Central Powers, it was decided to follow the procedure of 1887 and inform the public that the Triple Alliance had been renewed. The contents of the treaty were to be kept secret, as previously.[222]

[216] Marschall to Reuss, April 25, 1891; imparted to Kálnoky by Reuss on April 27. Copy.

[217] Reuss to Kálnoky, May 3, 1891. Original.

[218] Kálnoky to Reuss, May 4, 1891. Draft.

[219] Kálnoky to Széchényi, May 4, 1891. Draft.

[220] Széchényi to Kálnoky, May 7, 1891. Original.

[221] Cf. Vol. I, p. 159, note. In the document of ratification of the Italian treaty, Kálnoky also intended to include the protocol, but refrained from doing so at the request of the German government, which declared that protocols had not been included in the earlier documents of ratification, and that it was best "to abide by the old procedure in all matters concerning which new agreements had not been reached." Reuss to Kálnoky, May 13, 1891. Kálnoky to Széchényi, May 13, 1891.

[222] Kálnoky to Bruck, June 22, 1891.

CHAPTER IV

THE TACIT RENEWAL OF THE THIRD TREATY OF THE TRIPLE ALLIANCE

THE treaty of the Triple Alliance of 1891 was concluded for a period of six years; it expired in May, 1897; but, according to the stipulations of Article XIV, the duration of the treaty was to be prolonged for another six years in case no one of the allied governments made use of its right of denunciation one year before the date of expiration. In 1895 the question of the renewal was first mentioned — by Italy. Crispi was then Premier, and Blanc Minister of Foreign Affairs; the former had been the most ardent promoter of the Triple Alliance, the latter an untiring defender of the idea of a union with the Central Powers in the years 1880 to 1882.[223] No doubt could be entertained as to the genuineness of their intentions to maintain Italy's relations with Germany and Austria-Hungary as defined by the treaty. In 1892, indeed, Crispi had bitterly reproached Rudini for not having taken precautions at the time of the conclusion of the new treaty of the Triple Alliance which would have prevented Italy from getting the worst of it in the commercial treaties [224] concluded later with the Central Powers, toward the end of 1891. He also complained that Italy had been the chief sufferer under the Triple Alliance.[225] At that time, however, he was the leader of the Opposition. As head of the

[223] The Italian Ministers of Foreign Affairs, during the years 1891–93, had been profuse in assurances that they would stay faithful to the Triple Alliance. On the accession to office of Brin (May, 1892) he sent the following message to Vienna: "After exhaustive examination of the secret agreements between the friendly powers, Minister Brin takes this occasion to give us the assurance that these treaties and the political course determined by them will find in him as true and sincere an executor as in his predecessor, whose attitude in this matter he is definitely determined to follow." Kálnoky to Bruck, May 23, 1892.

[224] The commercial treaties between Italy and the Central Powers were signed on December 6, 1891. Cf. the text of the Austro-Italian treaty in the *Reichsgesetzblatt* of 1892, part vi, no. 17, pp. 111 ff.; also found in Ludwig Bittner's *Chronologisches Verzeichnis der österreichischen Staatsverträge*, iii, p. 433, no. 4686.

[225] Cf. *Questioni internazionali*, p. 97; Singer, p. 108.

Italian ministry after 1893, he professed to be a friend of the Central Powers, though his friendship was somewhat more tempered than during his earlier period of office. Through Blanc he sharply repelled the charges brought by the Radicals, who blamed the Triple Alliance for the decay of trade relations between Italy and France,[226] and expressed the conviction in his speeches in the Chamber, as well as in his conferences with the chief statesmen of the allies, that Italy's interests would best be served by unswerving adherence to the Triple Alliance.

This realization did not prevent Crispi from making frequent reference to the sacrifices exacted from Italy by this fidelity. Toward the beginning of 1895, Crispi, as well as Blanc, declared that France had for years let it be openly known that Italy could have Abyssinia, Tripoli, and Heaven knows what else, if only she would desert the Triple Alliance. Considerations of honor had prevented Italy from listening to a word of this; and yet now (Crispi went on to say) she was being attacked in Abyssinia, and was forced to stand by, powerless, and watch France proceeding brazenly and unhindered toward her chief goal, the establishment of a North African state. Blanc went so far as to forecast the overthrow of the Italian monarchy, the victory of the Radical and Republican parties, and, consequently, the dissolution of the Triple Alliance,[227] in case the Central Powers did not support Italy's plans for the extension of her domain in the Mediterranean countries. These utterances explain the fact that as soon as the renewal of the treaty was mentioned, the Italian statesmen attempted to obtain the binding assent of Germany and Austria-Hungary to Italy's acquisition of Tripoli. The Central Powers, however, firmly declined this request, refusing also to take up the question of the prolongation of the alliance.[228] As a result, no further negotiations were entered into during 1895.

[226] Singer, p. 113.   [227] Bruck to Kálnoky, February 16 and 19, 1895.
[228] Kálnoky to Szögyény, March 23, 1895. Telegram. Count Lanza, in Berlin, was informed by Marschall to the same effect. As the latter told Szögyény, the Italian was given to understand "that Baron Blanc's tendency to construe the Triple Alliance as a sort of 'association for profit', which was bound to pledge to one of the parties the unrestricted aid of the others for such acquisitions as it pleased, is absolutely rejected here." Szögyény to Kálnoky, March 30, 1895.

A good opportunity for the initiation of negotiations first presented itself toward the beginning of the year 1896. This was the time when the tension between England and Germany had become so great that the outbreak of open hostilities appeared possible. Italy, supported by England, was then fighting in Abyssinia; but after her first few initial successes she realized that her hopes were illusory. In December, 1895, the vanguard of the Italian army suffered a severe defeat; and the future might have worse in store. Then came reports of German 'courtesies' proffered to the Russian court, of efforts toward a rapprochement on the part of the cabinets of Vienna and St. Petersburg which could only serve to show the passive attitude observed by the Austro-Hungarian government toward the Russian menace of Constantinople. All this caused fear in Italy lest the old League of the Three Emperors should come to life once more and Italy should find herself isolated. It was even believed that an agreement might be reached between Austria-Hungary and Russia for the partition of the Balkans, and anxious thought was given to the contingency that Italy might come away empty-handed .from the division of the spoils. Prompt action was requisite to avert such a possibility.

For this purpose, Italy intended to renew the Triple Alliance, but, at the same time, to pledge the Central Powers more deeply than before to her interests. Count Nigra, most experienced of Italian diplomats, was called to Rome at the beginning of January, 1896, to give his advice. Nigra, who knew the aims of the courts of Vienna and Berlin, took pains to dispel the misgivings of the Italian ministers; apparently with success, as far as Crispi was concerned, for the latter declared his readiness to renew the Triple Alliance as it stood. Demands were made in other important circles, however, that Austria-Hungary should assume the same obligations with regard to the western basin of the Mediterranean as those binding Germany in the same region. Germany was also to take the same pledges for the eastern basin of the Mediterranean which Austria-Hungary had already assumed. Nigra advised against this, characterizing these wishes as unattainable; he well knew the strong disinclination of the Central Powers to accede to

such demands. For the purpose of calming the excited state of mind of the leading Italian statesmen, however, he recommended the German and Austro-Hungarian representatives in Rome to observe a certain spirit of accommodation, and advised them, when the treaty was renewed, to give a more precise wording to the already existing obligation of the allies "to proceed to an agreement concerning pending questions of a general political nature before a single power adopts an attitude towards them, or seizes the initiative." [229]

Baron Pasetti, the Austro-Hungarian ambassador in Rome, with whom Count Nigra repeatedly discussed the matter, gave his heartiest assent to the idea. For the sake of satisfying Italy's ambition, which had received a terrible blow through the defeats in Abyssinia, he recommended that she should not be robbed of the hope of finding in Tripoli a substitute for East Africa. "I have already had to listen to the Italians lamenting in every key that they have been the 'victims' of the Triple Alliance," wrote Pasetti, "and this conviction is not to be eradicated by any amount of argument — particularly because Italy has been treated so roughly by France since she joined the Triple Alliance. The prospect of gaining Tripoli and of securing at least the moral and diplomatic support of her allies to this end would once more make Italy a willing member of the alliance, and even if no help is to be expected of her in the moment of need, it is nevertheless to our interest to keep her among us. Desire to have a part in every thing; eagerness for new conquests, for a great success; fear of an unexpected *coup* which might procure this success for some one else and not for them — all these beset the Italian statesmen. Every confidential conversation comes back to this theme, even if the subject of discussion is the agreement with England." [230]

Pasetti had appraised the situation correctly. In February, 1896, Crispi wrote to the Italian ambassador in Berlin: "A treaty

[229] Despatch from Pasetti, January 25, 1896.

[230] Ibid. On February 8, 1896, Pasetti wrote to Goluchowski that the German ambassador, Bülow, "had never seen such satisfaction in the countenance of Nigra, who as a rule stays in Rome only against his will, and then only for a short time. His whole manner showed his pride in a well administered lesson on European politics."

of alliance, even if concluded only for the purpose of averting war, loses a great part of its value if it is not calculated to safeguard the interests of the allies in times of peace. . . . The Italian people has not yet lost its illusions regarding the alliance with Germany, but if matters go on in this manner, who can make sure that it will not have lost them even by tomorrow? In case circumstances should compel the Italian government to fulfil obligations laid upon it by an alliance with Germany which had become unpopular, it would remain faithful to its international duties; but it would be in a delicate position towards its people and its allies." [231]

Both in Vienna and in Berlin, the attitude was again unfavorable; but Crispi and Blanc, influenced by the difficult situation in which Italy found herself as the result of further disasters in Abyssinia, urged no further action for the time being. Shortly after this Crispi fell and Rudini took his place. This meant an aggravation of the situation, for Rudini, who had long advocated a closer connection with France, immediately declared that he would hold to the Triple Alliance, but not to the aggressive attitude adopted by Crispi toward France. He would make efforts, he said, to establish better relations with that neighboring state, which, in economic and financial matters, had the power to do Italy so much good and so much harm; Italy could be on as good terms with France as Germany or Austria-Hungary, without doing violence to the "defensive nature" of the Triple Alliance.[232] A short while later he summoned Count Nigra to Rome for further consultations. Nigra once more succeeded in influencing the premier favorably to the Triple Alliance. Rudini now declared his readiness for a tacit renewal of the existing treaty, but he expressed at the same time a desire that the protocol annexed to the first treaty of the Triple Alliance of 1882, in which it was expressly specified that the alliance was not directed against England, should be embodied in the new treaty. This protocol had not been included in the treaties of 1887 and 1891, since Austria-Hungary and Italy had concluded the "accord à trois" with England in 1887,[233] and

[231] Fráknoi, pp. 54 f.
[232] Pasetti to Goluchowski, March 16, 1896.
[233] The agreement of December, 1887, is referred to. See Vol. I, pp. 124–133.

the treaty of 1891 had expressly left room for the union of England with the powers of the Triple Alliance. Rudini based his request on the fact that the efforts to secure England's assent to a renewal of the "accord à trois" had come to nothing, and that, in view of the present tenseness of her relations with Germany, her accession to the Triple Alliance was not to be thought of. He therefore felt it desirable to fall back on this protocol, since Italy, in the event of an alliance of France with England, could not undertake to wage war on these two powers.[234] In spite of all Pasetti's efforts to wean him from the idea, Rudini transmitted notes verbales containing this project to Berlin and Vienna.[235]

In Berlin his proposal was brusquely rejected. In an instruction given on March 31, 1896, to Bernhard von Bülow, the German ambassador in Rome, and transmitted to Count Agenor Goluchowski, who had been guiding the foreign affairs of Austria-Hungary since May, 1895, the German government declared that the protocol had been added in 1882 at the express wish of Mancini, who feared that Article III of the treaty of May 20, 1882, might possibly be regarded as "operative against England as well"; that Count Kálnoky, whose views were approved by Prince Bismarck, had long stood out against any such declaration, for he feared indiscretions on the part of the English which would have caused the world to believe that the treaty of the Triple Alliance was directed particularly against France and would have aggravated the relations of the allies with that Power; but that Kálnoky had finally yielded to the insistence of the Italians, and Bismarck had followed his lead. In the archives, however, there existed a declaration made by Prince Bismarck on May 22, 1882, to the effect that German diplomacy had had no part in the draw-

[234] Pasetti to Goluchowski, March 27, 1896. Telegram and despatch of the same date.

[235] Note verbale from Italy, March, 1896. It reads as follows: "Dans l'éventualité de la prorogation tacite du traité d'alliance, conclu le 6 mai entre l'Italie, l'Allemagne, et l'Autriche-Hongrie, le gouvernement royal d'Italie croît devoir rappeler aux deux H.P.C. qu'il reste entendu que les déclarations ministerielles échangées en mai 1882 concernant l'Angleterre, dont copie est ci-jointe, demeurent en vigueur pour la même durée du traité susmentionné. Le gouvernement du roi attacherait du prix à recevoir du gouvernement I. et R. une assurance analogue."

ing up of the documents relating to the treaty with Italy. At that time — 1882 —(the instruction continued) it would not have been out of the question for England to take action with other powers, such as France or Russia, against one of the states of the Triple Alliance; now, however, and for some time to come, an Anglo-Russian or an Anglo-French joint action lay beyond the bounds of possibility.

"Since a duel between Germany and England — which, for reasons of common sense, we consider to be as remote as an Anglo-French combination — would, according to Article III, establish no *casus foederis*, the Italian supplementary proposal has no occasion; it satisfies no existing need. If we were to make concessions to the Italian cabinet which are unquestionably superfluous, we should at least have to be convinced that these superfluous demands did not have an aspect objectionable to us. The exact opposite is true, however. Three great political divisions exist today in Europe: the Triple Alliance, the Franco-Russian group, and England. The defensive nature of the Triple Alliance caused it to take into consideration such aggression as might occur under certain prescribed circumstances rather than the individual aggressors. It is this general character of its provisions which gives the Triple Alliance its objective quality. A power which feels it has been offended or thwarted by the Triple Alliance admits at the same time that its aggressive projects have been frustrated by it. The Triple Alliance assumes an entirely different character, however, if a provision be added to the effect that England can under no circumstances be the object of the *casus foederis*. From that time onward the Triple Alliance, from the point of view of its signatories, would be directed against the Franco-Russian group alone, and the tension foreseen in 1882 by Count Kálnoky and Prince Bismarck as the result of the supplementary provision determining our relations with France, would now also extend to the relations of the Triple Alliance — and especially of Germany — with Russia. We have very recently shown that whenever a legitimate Italian interest is involved we take no heed of any possible displeasure which might be caused in St. Petersburg or in Paris by our support of Italy. We are determined, however, not to do un-

necessary violence to our relations with Russia if no Italian interest is at stake. Apart from the fact that the wording of Article III excludes any possibility of calling on Italy for help in the event of war between Germany and England, the agreements of May 6, 1891, give Italy still further guaranties in this direction; mention may be made of Article VIII, whereby Italy is granted full liberty as regards the Egyptian question, and the protocol, which expressly gives her permission to seek a rapprochement with England." [236]

The German ambassador in Rome expressed the views of his government with the greatest vigor. At first, to all appearances, he was successful. Rudini declared that he was willing to forego his demand; [237] but shortly after — on April 27 — he sent to Vienna and Berlin the draft of a note which he proposed formally to submit in the event that the Central Powers gave their assent. This note stated that in case England and France were to join forces with hostile intent against one of Italy's allies, Italy would not regard the *casus foederis* as established, since in view of her geographical position and the inadequacy of her fighting forces, she would be in no position simultaneously to take the field against both of these adversaries. [238] The Italian government emphasized

---

[236] Instruction of the German government to Bülow, March 31, 1896. Copy transmitted to Goluchowski. On April 1 Szögyény telegraphed from Berlin that Secretary of State Marschall had begged Lanza not to ask for this superfluous "ministerial declaration." Marschall had said to him "that the German government would in any case have to refuse the supplementary declaration in question, since it was entirely unnecessary as far as Italy's attitude toward England was concerned, and might give occasion for indiscretions on the part of Italy which, for no purpose whatever, might cause the relations of the powers of .the Triple Alliance with Russia and with France to suffer."

[237] Szögyény to Goluchowski, April 4, 1896 (telegram). As Goluchowski telegraphed on April 5 to Szögyény, he had taken no action when Nigra handed him the same note. He was delighted, he said, to hear that Italy had abandoned her demand. "A formal renewal of the declaration of 1882," he said, "would have seemed objectionable to me at the present moment; it is an open question, however, whether it is not really continuing in force — whether, in other words, it was not also tacitly prolonged simultaneously with the main treaty, of which it is a constituent part." This opinion was not shared by Marschall. Szögyény to Kálnoky, April 12, 1896.

[238] Szögyény reported on April 12 that, according to communications made by Bülow to the German government, Rudini and the minister of foreign affairs, the Duke of Sermoneta, had declared, on the occasion of their renunciation of the re-

the fact in Berlin that it expected no answer from Germany — that it would be satisfied with an official acknowledgment of its communication on the part of the German government.[239] This declaration left no room for doubt in Berlin that, in the event of France and England becoming the adversaries of Germany, Italy wished to be relieved of the obligations which, according to the treaty, she would be obliged to assume if Germany were involved in war on two fronts. The German government, however, declared that it was wholly unable to regard the Italian note "as a correct interpretation of the text of the Triple Alliance and of the declarations made to the German plenipotentiaries," and that it was not in a position to accept this note without protest. If the Italian view were correct, the alliance would evidently be aimed against Russia, and its inherently defensive character — directed as it was against possible attacks rather than against individual adversaries — would thus be lost.[240] The rejection of the Italian

newal of the declaration of 1882, that "they would frankly admit that, on account of her geographical situation, and especially of her extended coast line on the Mediterranean, Italy could not undertake to enter into war simultaneously with these two adversaries, with their formidable maritime strength. However, since such an eventuality appears most improbable, the Italian government is glad to conform with the wishes of the German cabinet and to withdraw its proposal regarding the supplementary declaration in question."

[239] Szögyény to Goluchowski, May 23, 1896, and Goluchowski's instruction to Rome of the same date.

[240] The German government transmitted to the cabinet of Vienna the draft of the reply it had determined to make to Count Lanza, the Italian ambassador, in case he should formally state the wishes of his government. It reads as follows: "Projet du réponse 29. April 1896 (copy): Le gouvernement de S. M. l'empereur d'Allemagne donne acte à M^r l'ambassadeur d'Italie d'une communication faite par S. Exc. à la date du 27 de ce mois, et d'où il résulte que le gouvernement italien ne croit pas être en mesure d'agir contre une coalition anglo-française, si cette coalition venait à se réaliser. La réserve que le gouvernement italien vient de formuler aux termes de cette déclaration n'atteint pas les intérêts allemands, puisque ceux-ci se trouveraient le cas échéant sauvegardés par le nouveau groupement des puissances européennes qui serait la conséquence immédiate de la coalition susdite. Le gouvernement allemand ne saurait cependant reconnaître à cette réserve la qualité d'interprétation soit du texte des traités intervenus entre l'Italie, l'Allemagne, et l'Autriche-Hongrie, soit du langage tenu par la diplomatie allemande; car la pointe d'hostilité directe et prédominante contre la Russie qu'une pareille interprétation donnerait à la triple alliance modifierait absolument le caractére essentiellement impersonnel de ce pacte défensif qui vise des aggressions éventuelles plutôt que des adversaires individuels."

request by the German government was sharp, and hardly left room for hope that the cabinet of Vienna would meet it. The attempt, nevertheless, was made, for at the time it was generally supposed in Rome that Austria-Hungary, who had no idea of becoming involved in war with the two great powers of Western Europe, and who then contemplated Russia only as her adversary, would have no objection to such a limitation to Italy's obligations, and might even be inclined to support her wishes in Berlin.

In their first supposition the Italians did not go astray. Count Goluchowski declared that he saw no reason for not tacitly accepting such a note from Italy, "since, in fine, it was only an act of loyalty for the Italian cabinet to state frankly that Italy would be in no position to appear as the adversary of France and England, if these two powers were to join forces against the Triple Alliance." However, when he had learned from conversations with Count Eulenburg, the German ambassador in Vienna, and from the despatches of the Austro-Hungarian ambassador in Berlin, Szögyény, that the German government had taken a firm stand against any such concession, he likewise declined to consider the Italian demands.[241] Under these circumstances Rudini's only course was to refrain from submitting his note.

In the meanwhile, however, May, 1896, the term stipulated in the treaty, had gone by without use having been made by Italy of her right of denunciation. The treaty of the Triple Alliance of 1891 was therefore tacitly prolonged for another term of six years. Rudini's displeasure at the rejection of his proposals by the German government, and his wish to give expression to Italy's friendly feelings toward England, continued nevertheless to exist. In a speech delivered on July 1, 1896, before the Italian Chamber, he asserted that it was both necessary and profitable for Italy to adhere to the Triple Alliance, which efficaciously safeguarded her chief interests; he added, however, "that friendship with England formed the indispensable complement to the Triple Alliance. In the interests of Italy and her allies, the Italian government intended to improve the agreements of the Triple Alliance; the pos-

[241] Goluchowski to Pasetti, May 23, 1896.

sibility of such an improvement had been expressly stipulated in the treaty itself " [242] Rudini's utterance caused strong disapproval in Berlin. Through its official organ, the government declared that there must have been some mistake; nothing was known in Berlin of any intention to alter the recently prolonged treaty.[243] Rudini, seeing that he must retreat, let it be made known that he had only intended to suggest the possibility of improving the Triple Alliance in case an opportunity to do so should be recognized.[244] To the Austro-Hungarian ambassador, he said that he had been reproached by the Opposition for having twice let slip an opportunity for improving the treaty stipulations, and had thus allowed himself to be led into a theoretical assertion of the perfectibility of this, as of every other, treaty. At the same time he most emphatically denied having entertained any idea of a change at that particular moment.[245]

[242] Cf. Schultess, *Geschichtskalender*, 1896, p. 241.
[243] Szögyény to Goluchowski, July 2, 1896. Cf. Singer, p. 121.
[244] Ibid.
[245] Telegram from Pasetti from Rome, July 4, 1896. Shortly after a great sensation was caused by a newspaper article by Crispi — who was a member of the Opposition — in which he declared that Rudini had concluded the new treaty of the Triple Alliance for a long period and brought about a guaranty of Italy's possessions. Crispi's article also occasioned negotiations between the powers of the Triple Alliance. Documents in the State Archives.

CHAPTER V

THE FOURTH TREATY OF THE TRIPLE ALLIANCE
JUNE 28, 1902

THE tacit renewal of the Triple Alliance in May, 1896, had wrought no change in Italy's relations with her allies. The statesmen continued to dwell on the community of their interests; sovereigns and ministers, at the occasion of their meetings and in their speeches, extolled the Triple Alliance as a gage of peace and vowed fidelity to it. Many variations of expression were given to the thought first shaped by Prince Bismarck: "We keep coming together again, because we can't get along without one another. An alliance of such powers as the Triple Alliance can always say of itself, *Nemo me impune lacessit*, and will always be in a position to defend itself." [246] This recognition of the value of the Triple Alliance to the general as well as the particular interests of each of its members was felt especially by the Italian statesmen, who knew that for the present they would be unable to attain their ambitious ends without the support of the Central Powers. For this reason even those among them, who in their hearts longed most desperately for a dissolution of this *mariage de convenance*, clung fast to the Triple Alliance, and did everything in their power either to smooth over the ever-arising difficulties with Austria-Hungary which threatened to disrupt the alliance, or, if this were not possible, at least to hit upon some modus vivendi.

This was especially true as regards the Balkan problem. In Italy there was no hope — perhaps even no desire — for a permanent solution of this question, so vital to both powers; but it was thought best to put off the conflict until there was some hope of terminating it successfully. For this reason Rudini and Visconti-Venosta agreed with Goluchowski at Monza (November, 1897) to advocate in future the maintenance of the status quo in the Balkans, and, if this should prove impracticable, to work

[246] Singer, p. 115.

for the autonomous development of the Balkan states.[247] The Albanian question was now becoming more and more an object of interest to public opinion in Italy, and occupying an increasingly important place in the thoughts and feelings of the nation; the contest for 'the other shore' of the Adriatic was more and more insistently urged by the representatives of all classes, and the leading statesmen of Austria-Hungary and Italy were constrained to renew and strengthen the oral agreements of Monza, with special regard to Albania, through an exchange of notes which took place in December, 1900, and in February, 1901.[248]

Other negotiations between Austria-Hungary and Italy were going on simultaneously with these: negotiations touching the interests of all three allied powers, and dealing primarily with the military preparations desirable in view of a possible conflict. A naval convention, concluded at Berlin, on December 5, 1900, provided for the coöperation of the naval forces of the allies in case they should become involved in war with France and Russia.[249] Notwithstanding this, the efforts of governmental circles in Italy to maintain correct relations with the Central Powers met with opposition from a great part of the Italian nation, and fresh recruits were continually joining that body of statesmen who advocated a closer understanding with France.[250] The governments of Vienna and Berlin learned from the despatches of their ambassadors in Rome how cleverly this attitude was being fostered, openly and secretly, by the French representatives, particularly Camille Barrére, French ambassador to Italy from 1897, and how their influence was increasing.

The Cretan affair, in 1897, in which Italy ranged herself with the adversaries of her allies, had already shown that Italy was

[247] Notes by Goluchowski concerning his negotiations with Rudini and Visconti-Venosta at Monza, November, 1897.

[248] In the introduction to the treaties between Austria-Hungary and Italy a detailed discussion will be given of these notes of December 20, 1900, and February 9, 1901, respectively. See Vol. I, pp. 196–201, for the texts.

[249] Naval agreement of December 5, 1900; not to be found in the State Archives. Cf. p. 88, note 175.

[250] The despatches of the Belgian government recently published by the German government (*Zur europäischen Politik 1897–1914*, i, pp. 41 f., 90 ff., 102 ff., etc.) contain, among other things, some interesting information on this matter.

going her own way.[251] In November, 1898, Italy concluded a commercial treaty with France, thus ending a tariff and financial war which had lasted more than a decade, with results most disastrous to her trade and finances. In the spring of 1899, France and England had given assurances regarding Tripoli which disclaimed in favor of Italy any interests on their part. Both these developments paved the way to a more friendly understanding between France and Italy.[252] In 1900 these two powers reached an agreement regarding their spheres of interest in the Sudan; in 1901 the assurances given two years previously by the Western Powers with regard to Tripolitania were renewed and extended. All this increased Italy's coyness in her negotiations with the Central Powers, as was shown during the discussions held between the allied governments, beginning with the fall of 1900, regarding the renewal and alteration of the existing commercial treaties. The demands of the Italians, especially as concerned the continuance of the favorable tariff on wines,[253] were so energetically supported by the Italian press that Count Nigra was compelled to remind his countrymen of the great dependence of Italy on the Triple Alliance. This attitude of the more prudent elements, however, could not stem the increasingly powerful current of anti-Austrian feeling. Then, too, when Victor Emmanuel III mounted the throne at the end of July, 1900, after the assassination of King Humbert, who had cherished ties of intimate friendship with the German rulers, Frederick III and William II, he showed a certain coolness toward his allies. In March, 1901, Zanardelli, Italian Premier since the beginning of 1901, and an ancient foe of Austria-Hungary, expressed his strong sympathies for France, and declared

---

[251] Cf. Albert Billot, *La France et l'Italie* (1905), ii, p. 395.

[252] See Appendix C.

[253] The provisions regarding the wine tariff, which are to be found in the commercial treaty of 1891, are given in the *Reichsgesetzblatt, l. c.*, p. 205, Nr. 2, Tarif A, and p. 215, Nr. 77, Tarif B. The latter reads as follows: "If, while the treaty is in force, a tariff of 5 francs 77 centimes or less should be fixed for the import of wines into Italy, this tariff shall also be applied to all wines coming from Austria-Hungary; Austria-Hungary pledges herself, in this case, to give to Italian wines *ipso facto* the special favors specified in N. 5 III. . . . The tariff shall in this case be 3 florins 20 kreuzer per hundred kilogrammes, and shall be applied to all wines imported by cask into Austria-Hungary by land or by sea."

significantly that in future Italy would assume obligations only after mature reflection. The ministry, he said, would have to occupy itself with commercial as well as political treaties. The former expired before the latter; and Italy's foreign policy would be guided by the outcome of the negotiations regarding commercial matters.[254]

In June, 1901, strong attacks were made in the Italian Chamber against Austria-Hungary, particularly against her advance in Albania. Some clamored for the dissolution of the Triple Alliance; others insisted that its prolongation should be made conditional on the conclusion of a special agreement regarding Albania and Tripoli.[255] Prinetti, Minister of Foreign Affairs, rejected these demands, on the ground that 'the Triple Alliance had given a firm foundation to Italian policy, and had effectually served to maintain the peace of Europe.' It was the same Prinetti, however, who, toward the end of the year, answered Guicciardini's interpellation [256] as to the relations between Italy and France by declaring that 'the negotiations with the French government had resulted in a complete unanimity of views on both sides regarding their spheres of interest.' [257] These utterances of so prominent a statesman, and the echo aroused by them in France, caused a disagreeable sensation in Vienna and Berlin, and gave rise to exhaustive discussions of the Triple Alliance between the two cabinets.

The Under Secretary of State of the German Foreign Office, von Mühlberg, pointed out at this time that the negotiations between Paris and Rome with regard to the question of Tripoli were not "affairs of yesterday." There could be no objection in Berlin to good Franco-Italian relations; but it was extraordinary "what remarkably favorable soil was found on the banks of the Tiber by the liberalistic French solicitations, which had been growing more numerous of late." Italy's greed for territory, he declared, was the cause of this. Her efforts for expansion could only find sup-

---

[254] Cf. Singer, p. 136.   [255] Cf. Singer, pp. 137 f.

[256] Francesco Guicciardini was considered a special authority on the Albanian question, regarding which he had published important studies. Cf. Chlumecky, pp. 83 f., and others.

[257] Cf. Singer, p. 138.

port in a rapprochement with France; and in this fact lay peril for the Triple Alliance and for the peace of Europe. When the Triple Alliance was prolonged, therefore, "not an iota" should be changed.[258] The misgivings of the German government were shared in Vienna; they grew greater when in 1902 Barrére, the French ambassador in Rome, spoke of the Franco-Italian agreement regarding interests in the Mediterranean as perfect,[259] while Delcassé offered the Italians other people's territory on the Adriatic for the purpose of diverting them from the Mediterranean.[260]

But the statesmen of Germany and Austria-Hungary gave no outward evidence of their apprehension. On January 8, 1902, Bülow delivered a speech in the Reichstag in which he answered reports of the dissolution of the Triple Alliance with the following

[258] Szögyény to Goluchowski, December 22, 1901. At the same time Pasetti reported from Rome (December 24, 1901) that he had heard from well informed sources that France's efforts were directed toward "getting Italy to renew the Triple Alliance, with the added stipulation that the *casus foederis* should not be established if France were to attack the German Empire single-handed. Italy would then be pledged to furnish military aid only if Germany were attacked by both Russia and France." The Belgian minister in Berlin reported shortly after (March 20, 1902) to Brussels: "chacun sait que l'ambassadeur de France à Rome a fait tous ses efforts pour empêcher le renouvellement de la Triple Alliance ou au moins pour y faire introduire des modifications qui lui auraient ôté toute valeur pratique." *Zur europäischen Politik 1897 bis 1914*, Unveröffentlichte Dokumente, i, p. 103.

[259] Pasetti to Goluchowski, January 14, 1902. Cf. also Singer, p. 139.

[260] Cf. Chlumecky, *Österreich-Ungarn und Italien*, p. 23. Prinetti, with whom Pasetti discussed both these utterances, declared that he felt it worth while to repeat his former assertion, that Italy's alliance with Austria-Hungary and the German Empire, the commercial treaties with these States, and the friendly relations with France formed a whole, a political system, which must be maintained. This, he said, was also the view of Premier Zanardelli and the king. He said that he was ready to enter into negotiations that very day regarding the matter. The Triple Alliance (he continued) had no offensive aim; he had therefore been able to promise France that Italy would assume no obligations which might militate against the safety or the peace of the French. He had given France no written pledge, only an oral one. No guaranty for the observance of this had been demanded save that the stipulations of the future treaty of alliance should be imparted by him. There was, indeed, one way of pacifying France: the publication of the treaty. Prinetti declared that Nigra favored this, and that he himself was not opposed to it; but that he realized the difficulties which lay in the way of publication. The understandings regarding Tripoli and the Balkan peninsula, in particular, were not of a nature to be made public. Pasetti to Goluchowski, January 14, 1902.

assurance: "The Triple Alliance is still enjoying the best of health, and I believe and hope that its case is similar to that of persons incorrectly reported dead, who now live all the longer for it." He then emphasized the fact that the Triple Alliance did not prevent the establishment of good relations between its members and other powers. The excitement over the Franco-Italian agreements was unjustified, since these agreements were not directed against the Triple Alliance. "In a happy marriage the husband must not become mad with jealousy if his wife dances an innocent single turn with another man. The main point is that she should not run away from him; and she will not run away from him if she is happiest with him." [261] The desire to maintain the Triple Alliance, Bülow concluded, not because it was an absolute necessity, but because it was "an exceedingly serviceable bond of union between states, which by virtue of their geographical position and their historical traditions should by rights be good neighbors," had determined the line of action followed by the German government in the pending negotiations regarding the renewal of the alliance.

In order to meet the difficulties which might be expected to arise from the prospective territorial and economic demands of the Italians, the German cabinet announced that a renewal of the Triple Alliance was unnecessary, since, if no notice was given to the contrary, it would always be automatically prolonged for another period of six years. Appeal was made to a declaration to this effect, which Germany had made on May 7, 1899, on the occasion of the renewal of the treaty with Rumania, and in which, in default of denunciation, the automatic prolongation of the treaty every three years was expressly stated.[262] This interpretation, however, was received with no enthusiasm either in Rome or in Vienna. It was pointed out by the Italians that no such provision existed in the treaty of the Triple Alliance, and the responsible statesmen of Austria-Hungary lost no time in recognizing the

[261] Cf. Singer, p. 141.
[262] Cf. Vol. I, p. 177. According to Szögyény's report of December 18, 1901, it was the German ambassador in Constantinople, Marschall von Bieberstein, who expressed this view on the occasion of his visit to Berlin. Szögyény and Lanza did not agree with him.

justice of the Italian demand for a formal renewal.[263] As a matter of fact, the negotiations were begun at once. They soon showed that Germany's misgivings had not been groundless. Prinetti, the Italian minister of foreign affairs, declared that his assent to the renewal of the treaty must depend on a satisfactory solution of the pending commercial questions. The retention of the wine-tariff clause in the Austro-Italian commercial treaty, as demanded by Italy, was the chief bone of contention. Pasetti, the Austro-Hungarian ambassador in Rome, pointed out in vain that it was imprudent "to amalgamate political and economic questions to such an extent as to make the solution of the one dependent on that of the other." In Italy the idea was artificially fostered that found expression in the slogan, "No commercial treaty, no alliance." Prinetti persisted in his demand.

Soon, however, he also presented new requests of a political nature to which conditions in the Balkans had given rise. The insurrection in Macedonia, never really subdued, had broken out once more. The various Christian peoples — Bulgarians, Serbians, Greeks — at variance among themselves, but filled with a common hatred of the Turk, had risen once more against their oppressors, and the bloody contest was dragging on without reaching any decision. Since the Porte was too weak to restore quiet, and the oppressed peoples were too inimical one to another to achieve any permanent results, the Great Powers, at the re-

[263] Goluchowski to Szögyény, January 17, 1902. Pasetti's despatch of January 14, 1902, is accompanied by a "Memorandum regarding the Clauses of Prolongation of the Secret Treaties," drawn up by him. This states, *inter alia*, that "Since no notice was given to the contrary in 1897, the Triple Alliance, according to Article XIV of the treaty, runs from May 6, 1891, to May 17, 1903. If no notice to the contrary should be given in 1903, the treaty, according to the principles laid down in the German note verbale of May 7, 1899, for the interpretation of the treaty clause, is to be regarded as automatically prolonged as a whole. Now the Italian government certainly accepted this interpretation with regard to its accession to the secret treaty between Austria-Hungary and Rumania; but there was no statement by it to the effect that it recognized the application of the German interpretation to the Triple Alliance." Pasetti therefore proposed that this principle of the automatic prolongation of the treaty of the Triple Alliance, in case no notice to the contrary was given before a stipulated time, should be established by a joint protocol, to be signed by the representatives of the three powers. Nothing came of this proposal, however.

quest of both sides, intervened as guarantors of the treaty of Berlin. To Russia and Austria-Hungary, as the two great powers most intimately concerned, fell the leading rôles; and it was this which filled Prinetti with apprehension. He feared that Russia would either intervene in behalf of the liberation of Macedonia, support the Slavic Balkan states in making territorial acquisitions in that region, and gain for herself the hegemony of the Balkans, or else come to an agreement with Austria-Hungary providing for separate spheres of influence in the Balkans for the two rival powers. The situation called for preventive measures. Prinetti informed Vienna that he felt it to be of the greatest importance that the German Empire should be more extensively pledged to the support of the status quo in the Balkan peninsula than she had hitherto been. The situation in that region, he said, gave him great concern — not with regard to Albania, of course, for in that matter Italy and Austria-Hungary could always come to an understanding, since neither power sought for territorial acquisitions there; but 'Macedonia and the future shaping of affairs in that region formed a perplexing problem. If the Slavic element were to get the upper hand in the Balkan peninsula, under the guidance of Russia, or if Russia were to come into possession of Constantinople and the Straits, Italy would be reduced to the level of a second-rate Power in the Mediterranean, helplessly wedged in between France and Russia. England, unfortunately, was not to be counted upon. Although no fixed term had been set to the agreement of 1887, it had lost its value since the conclusion of the Anglo-French understanding of 1899.[264] Would England take action to prevent Constantinople from falling into Russia's hands?'[265]   The Triple Alliance, Prinetti concluded, must therefore arrive at a more definite understanding and counter these Russian plans of conquest.

The German government in answer referred Prinetti to Vienna as the place where discussions concerning Balkan problems must

[264] Allusion is made here to the agreement of March 21, 1899, regarding the partition of Africa. Cf. Friedjung, *Das Zeitalter des Imperialismus*, pp. 220 ff., and the literature mentioned there.

[265] Pasetti to Goluchowski, January 14 and 27, 1902.

take place. Germany would give her approval to any decision of the cabinet of Vienna.[266] Prinetti now became somewhat more explicit. He insisted on the acceptance by Vienna of the provisions in Articles VI and VII of the treaty of 1891, which contemplated the possibility of a Slavic move against Constantinople;[267] for the sake of pleasing France, he also recommended a statement in the preamble of the treaty making it plain that 'Italy had assumed no pledges which might contain a menace to France.'[268] It is plain enough now that Italy wished to strengthen the ties that bound her allies to her interests, while at the same time avoiding any stipulation which might work harm to her friendly relations with her neighbor France, strengthened as they were by recent agreements.[269]

In Berlin, however, no inclination whatever was shown to accede to these far-reaching Italian demands. Some of them were bluntly refused,[270] while the German cabinet sought first of all to secure the adoption of the principle of an automatic renewal of the treaty every three years, unless notice to the contrary were given in due season.[271] Once more this view failed of acceptance. The Italian ministers demanded as before the renewal of the treaty, and insisted that consideration be given to the wishes expressed by them, which they now proceeded clearly to define. All three powers were to pledge themselves, by Article V, to "oppose" any attempt of another great power to change the territorial status quo in the Orient.[272] For Germany, who heretofore had declared only her willingness to see to it that the territorial status

[266] Pasetti to Goluchowski, January 21, and Szögyény to Goluchowski, January 24, 1902. Telegrams.

[267] Pasetti to Goluchowski, January 27, 1902; first despatch.

[268] Prinetti had also approached the Germans with similar demands. Bülow declined them on the ground that in his latest speeches 'he had emphasized the purely defensive character of the alliance in such a decided way that it appeared superfluous to make further special mention of this fact in the text of the treaty.'

[269] Pasetti to Goluchowski, January 27, 1902; second despatch.

[270] Szögyény to Goluchowski, January 29, 1902.

[271] Ibid. Bülow, however, expressed the opinion that the Italians would not assent to this.

[272] "Les trois puissances s'engagent à s'opposer à toute tentative d'une tierce grande puissance de modifier le statu quo territorial en Orient," etc.

quo was maintained "on the Turkish coasts and islands of the Adriatic and Aegean Seas," this would have meant a considerable augmentation of her duties without any counter-service whatsoever on the part of Italy. A similar disproportion characterized the desire of the Italians to give to Article VII of the treaty a wording which would have bound all three allies to support throughout the Balkan states the principle laid down by Austria-Hungary and Italy in 1901 for Albania, providing for the promotion of autonomous development in the event of an inevitable alteration of the status quo in the Balkans. The Italians, moreover, demanded a free hand in Tripoli,[273] and consideration of their wishes in the matter of commercial policy.[274]

Wedel, the German ambassador in Rome, asserted that his government would assume no such guaranty of the status quo in the Orient.[275] Shortly after this Goluchowski also declined the Italian demands, in so far as they implied new burdens for Austria-Hungary. He informed Rome that he did not share Italy's fear of Russian aggression against Constantinople; that nothing of the sort was to be expected now or in the immediate future, for Russia was well occupied with her vast undertakings in Eastern Asia. "Just as it was impossible to foresee, when the Triple Alliance was first concluded, how affairs in the Orient would develop, so we are today confronted with uncertainty in this respect. It can not therefore be regarded as the task of the Triple Alliance to determine in advance the solution of the questions involved in the problem of the Orient. The treaty of the Triple Alliance, con-

[273] This demand for a free hand in Tripoli was due to the fact that Italy, in view of the agreements reached between her and France, felt that she had no more need of a guaranty from the Central Powers 'that France should not possess herself of this region.' As Pasetti informed Goluchowski on January 27, Prinetti had said that 'since France had of her own accord abandoned all designs in this direction, and had pledged herself by specific declarations, the aforesaid guaranty could now lapse — all the more so (Prinetti continued) because he was at that very moment negotiating with the British government for the purpose of obtaining from it declarations similar to those given by France. Lord Currie had voluntarily proposed this to Prinetti, who received the suggestion with pleasure. Thus Italy's interests on the North African coast were adequately protected.'

[274] Pasetti to Goluchowski, January 30, 1902. Telegram.

[275] Ibid. Prinetti remarked in this connection to Pasetti that he thought "that the proposition did not go overfar, as the term 'oppose' did not imply armed force."

cluded for purely defensive purposes, was primarily intended as a mutual safeguard against disturbances of the peace of Europe, to the preservation of which its existence has contributed substantially. The provisions of the treaty provided for the continuance of the concert between the three powers in the event of occurrences rendering impossible the maintenance of the status quo in the Orient, much as they desired its preservation. In case these changes should take place, they pledged themselves to the joint protection of their interests, to the degree in which these should be jeopardized." The treaty as it stood, Goluchowski concluded, took full account of these facts; and as the alterations proposed by Prinetti promised no improvement, it would be better to let them drop, especially as Germany could not agree to them.

Still more energetically did Goluchowski reject Prinetti's demand for a guaranty of the future autonomous development of all the Balkan states — a demand which touched Austro-Hungarian interests in a particularly sensitive spot. He declared that the interchange of ideas which had taken place in 1897 between himself and Visconti-Venosta "was based on the special interests which Austria-Hungary and Italy have to safeguard in the Adriatic, and which might be directly menaced by a shift of the territorial balance of power on the Albanian coast." This basis would no longer exist if all the Balkan States were to be similarly included. "This would lead to discussions for which the necessary premises do not as yet exist, and which may be deferred until called for by the future turn of events." From these reflections he drew the conclusion that it would be to the best interests of all parties concerned to renew the treaty of 1891 as it stood. He declared his willingness, however, to subscribe to a supplementary protocol giving the Italians a free hand in Tripoli — on the express condition that this should give rise to no obligation on the part of Austria-Hungary to participate in a war against France.[276] On the other hand, he flatly declined to retain the wine-tariff clause favoring Italy.

The Austro-Hungarian proposals, like those of Germany, which were fundamentally identical, fell on deaf ears in Rome. Prinetti

[276] Goluchowski to Pasetti, February 6, 1902.

refused to continue the negotiations on this basis,[277] and at the beginning of March he sent to Vienna and Rome his draft of the newly-worded Articles VI and VII of the treaty of the Triple Alliance of 1891.[278] This draft, which was identical with his oral demands of January, 1902,[279] was once more rejected by von Bülow and Goluchowski. Bülow pointed out that the proposed modifications would alter the purely defensive character of the alliance, and that, as a matter of fact, they were unnecessary, since ample guaranties were offered by the existing wording. Agreements of a commercial nature, he declared, lay beyond the province of the Triple Alliance.[280]

Count Goluchowski gave extremely detailed reasons for his opposition to the new Italian proposals. The altered wording of Article VI, he said, "would bind the powers of the Triple Alliance to oppose (de s'opposer) any change of the status quo in the Balkans and in the islands of the neighboring seas which might be to the detriment of the interests of any one of those powers. Such a pledge would also imply that the powers of the Triple Alliance were resolved to use armed force in preventing any change of the status quo which did not please them." Such a decision was quite

[277] Pasetti to Goluchowski, February 12, 1902.
[278] Pasetti to Goluchowski, February 26, 1902. Telegram.
[279] Nigra presented the draft on March 3, 1902. It read as follows: "Article VI. Les hautes parties contractantes, n'ayant en vue que le maintien, autant que possible, du status quo territorial en Orient, conviennent de s'opposer, le cas échéant, à toute tentative de la part d'une tierce grande puissance quelconque de modification territoriale dans les régions des Balcans ou dans les îles des mers adjacentes, et plus spécialement dans celles de ces régions et îles qui sont soumises à la domination ottomane, qui porterait dommage à l'une ou à l'autre des puissances signataires du présent traité." The conclusion of this article runs like that of Article VI of the treaty of 1891. Cf. Vol. I, p. 154. "Art. VII: L'Italie et l'Autriche-Hongrie s'engagent au cas où l'état de choses actuel dans ces régions ne pourrait être conservé et des changements s'imposeraient, à employer leurs efforts afin que les modifications du status quo se réalisent dans le sens de l'autonomie. Les deux puissances s'engagent en outre en général et comme disposition mutuelle de part et d'autre, à rechercher en commun et toutes les fois qu'il y aurait lieu les voies et moyens les plus propres à concilier et à sauvegarder leurs intérêts réciproques. Si par suite des événements l'Italie et l'Autriche-Hongrie se voyaient dans la nécessité " . . . From here on the text corresponds word for word with Article VII of the treaty of 1891. Cf. Vol. I, pp. 154, 156.
[280] Szögyény to Goluchowski, telegrams of March 5 and 8, 1902, and despatch of March 10.

impossible on the part of Germany; and Austria-Hungary, too, could "not look with favor on a wording which perverted the peaceful tendency of the Triple Alliance, and which might be regarded by a power outside the Alliance" (i. e., Russia) "as a menace aimed against herself. The Italian Minister of Foreign Affairs has pointed out in this connection that any action directed against the status quo in the Orient could, in case of necessity, be brought to a stop by a mobilization on our eastern frontiers. We can hardly be expected, however, to expose ourselves to the danger of a war in which we could not count on the help of our allies."

Goluchowski was also unable to assent to Prinetti's request for the inclusion in Article VII of new agreements, such as the exchange of declarations between Austria-Hungary and Italy with regard to Albania. The Triple Alliance, he said, serves primarily to maintain the status quo in the Orient, and states only in the most general terms the points of view which would determine the attitude of the allies in case all their efforts should fail to preserve this status quo from change. Questions of detail could only be dealt with in the future; this, moreover, was a matter to be settled by Austria-Hungary and Italy alone. "It would therefore be premature to come to any conclusions as yet regarding the extent to which the principle of autonomy was to be applied to other portions of Turkey in Europe, besides Albania."[281] Goluchowski's answer plainly indicated that he did not intend to allow any strengthening of Italy's influence in the decision of questions in the Balkans.

The Italians, nevertheless, did not give up. Count Lanza, the Italian ambassador in Berlin, kept urging the acceptance of his government's proposals. As regards the commercial question, he scored a success, if only a limited one. The German government insisted that negotiations for the renewal of the commercial treaty with Italy could only begin when the new customs tariff had been passed by the Reichstag and had acquired legal force, and that for reasons of internal policy it was unable to promise not to denounce the existing commercial treaty before the conclusion of the new one. Germany was ready, however, to make a confidential, but

[281] Goluchowski to Pasetti, March 5, 1902.

binding declaration that she would do everything in her power to prevent the lapse of treaty relations, and that she cherished the greatest hopes of concluding a new commercial treaty based on the new customs tariff, which would be satisfactory to both parties.[282]

Prinetti, seeing that his other proposals, especially those relating to the Balkans, were meeting with stiff opposition in Berlin and Vienna, decided to bow to the inevitable. At the middle of March he announced his readiness to renew the existing treaty as it stood; he demanded, however, that account should be taken of Italy's wishes in regard to Tripoli, as well as the Balkan and commercial questions, through an exchange of notes.[283] He now expressed his wishes in the following form: "The allies of Italy declare their disinterestedness toward any action which she may undertake 'at her own risk and peril' in Tripolitania or in Cyrenaica. As regards the commercial question, the three powers declare their fixed intention to conclude a new commercial treaty, and, until this shall take place, to maintain the validity of the existing treaty. Moreover, Austria-Hungary declares, with regard to the wine clause, that the treatment to be accorded in future to Italian wines imported into Austria-Hungary shall not be more unfavorable than previously."

Pasetti immediately refused this last demand; the others he listened to in silence.[284] There appeared to be no inclination in Berlin or Vienna to accede to these somewhat tempered demands. The negotiations, it is true, were begun, but they led to no result.[284a] New attempts to reach an understanding were then made on the occasion of a conference in Venice between Bülow and Prinetti. This was not altogether fruitless. Prinetti was willing to renounce his proposed alterations in the treaty when Bülow had convinced him of the desirability of being able to point to the fact that no changes had been made in it as far as Russia and England were concerned. Bülow, for his part, cherished the

[282] Szögyény to Goluchowski, March 10, 1902.
[283] Pasetti to Goluchowski, March 20, 1902.
[284] Pasetti to Goluchowski; telegram of March 20, and letter of March 27, 1902.
[284a] Szögyény to Goluchowski, March 24, 1902 (telegram); Goluchowski to Pasetti, March 21, 1902.

amazing belief that he could conciliate Prinetti by holding out the prospect of a written statement of his conviction that neither now nor in the near future would Russia lay hands on Constantinople. This was intended to allay the fears of Victor Emmanuel III. He also promised to embody in a separate declaration an interpretation of Articles IX and X of the treaty of the Triple Alliance which would meet Italy's wishes.

The negotiations regarding questions of commercial policy were more difficult. Prinetti insisted that a lapse of the treaty must be avoided. He proposed that instead of terminating the existing agreements, they should be prolonged until the end of 1905 at the latest, with the provision that in case new commercial treaties were concluded before that date, the existing treaties would be regarded ipso facto as duly terminated. The firmness of Prinetti's conviction that political and economic interests should be put on a footing of equality is shown by the fact that he proposed to Bülow that the Triple Alliance should for the present be renewed for three years only, lest Italy, in the event of a lapse of the commercial treaty, should find herself politically allied for a long term of years to states with which she was economically at variance.[285] No agreement in this matter was reached either at Venice or in the further negotiations which took place in the course of the next few weeks in Vienna, Rome, and Berlin.[286] On the occasion of a visit of Bülow to Vienna, he joined with Goluchowski in urging once more upon Rome the speediest possible renewal of the treaty of the Triple Alliance as it stood, proposing at the same time the elimination of the protocol which, at Italy's request, had been annexed in 1891 to the main treaty. The first part of this protocol, dealing with matters of commercial policy, contained only meaningless assurances; the second part had been rendered superfluous through England's withdrawal from the Mediterranean agreements which she had entered into.[287] However, before the German and Austro-Hungarian ambassadors could make the

---

[285] Pasetti to Goluchowski, March 31, 1902. Telegram.

[286] Goluchowski to Szögyény, April 4, 1902; Szögyény to Goluchowski, April 4 and 5, 1902.

[287] Goluchowski to Szögyény, April 12, 1902.

requisite representations in Rome, Prinetti had instructed Nigra and Lanza to communicate to Vienna and Berlin the proposals which had been formulated by him on the basis of the negotiations in Venice.[288] They were flatly rejected by both governments.[289]

Again it seemed as though no agreement could be hoped for; but once more the recognition by all parties of the necessity of adhering to the Triple Alliance brought the two sides together. Prinetti decided to forego his demands in so far as they related to the Balkans, and limited his wishes to compromises regarding Tripolitania [290] and the commercial treaty; while Bülow declared that he was ready to meet Italy's wishes in these two matters [291] and caused inquiries to be made in Vienna regarding the willingness of the Austrian government to take similar action.[292] At the same time Goluchowski received letters from Pasetti which indicated how bitterly Prinetti had taken his rebuff, and emphasized Victor Emmanuel III's great anxiety not to be left in the lurch by his allies in the matter of Tripoli.[293]

All these influences served to bring about a more kindly disposition on the part of the cabinet of Vienna toward Prinetti's proposals. On April 18, 1902, Goluchowski empowered Pasetti to inform Rome that, although Austria-Hungary's disinterestedness in respect to the affairs in Tripoli was to be assumed from the

[288] Memorandum from Nigra, handed to Goluchowski on April 14, 1902; annex to Goluchowski's instruction to Pasetti of April 15, 1902. Pasetti delivered the official answer to Nigra's memorandum on April 27, 1902. It forms an annex to Pasetti's despatch to Goluchowski, May 6, 1902.

[289] Goluchowski to Pasetti, April 15, 1902; and Szögyény to Goluchowski, April 14, 1902. Telegram.

[290] As Pasetti telegraphed to Goluchowski on April 16, Count Wedel, the German ambassador, had succeeded in persuading Prinetti "that the present wording of Article IX contains in itself the fulfilment of his wishes; but since there is no mention in it of Austria-Hungary, he desires a separate declaration of disinterestedness from us in addition to the treaty."

[291] Szögyény to Goluchowski, April 16, 1902.

[292] Szögyény to Goluchowski, April 16, 1902. As early as the beginning of April, the German government had sought to influence Goluchowski in this direction. Bülow to Goluchowski (undated); transmitted by Reuss about the beginning of April.

[293] Pasetti to Goluchowski, April 16 and 18, 1902.

treaty of the Triple Alliance itself, she was ready to give a written promise to take no steps "which might hinder Italian action in Tripoli or in Cyrenaica in the event that the existing status quo in this region should, as the result of particular circumstances, undergo a change and Italy were to find herself forced to resort to such measures as her own interests might dictate." This declaration, however, would only be given by Pasetti after the formal renewal of the treaty of the Triple Alliance.[294] Goluchowski also met Prinetti's wishes regarding the commercial treaty. Pasetti was instructed to hand Prinetti a confidential unsigned memorandum expressing the firm purpose of Austria-Hungary to do everything in her power to prevent a lapse of the treaty between Austria-Hungary and Italy, "since the lack of an understanding in economic matters was regarded in Vienna as dangerous in the extreme, not only with regard to Austria-Hungary's own interests, but also because of its harmful reaction on the political relations of the two states." [295]

Count Goluchowski's declaration concerning Tripolitania satisfied Prinetti, but not his proposed solution of the commercial question. The Italian minister declared that he shrank from the thought that a customs war might break out a year and a half after the conclusion of a six year term of alliance. Out of consideration for his sovereign, he would not venture to accept such a proposal, which would only strengthen the anti-monarchical movement in Italy. He therefore returned to his original proposal first to establish the duration of the treaty of the Triple Alliance at three years, prolonging it only after the conclusion of the commercial treaty.[296] Both Goluchowski [297] and Bülow firmly declined to consider this,[298] though they stated at the same time that

[294] Goluchowski to Pasetti, April 18, 1902. In substance and, to a certain extent, in form Goluchowski's declarations follow the proposals communicated to him by the German government about the beginning of April.

[295] Ibid.

[296] Pasetti to Goluchowski, April 19 and 22, 1902.

[297] Goluchowski to Szögyény, April 22 and 24, 1902; Goluchowski to Pasetti, April 24, 1902.

[298] Szögyény to Goluchowski, April 23 and 24, 1902; Bülow to Wedel, April 23, 1902.

in view of the approaching parliamentary debates they must insist on the signature of the treaty of the Triple Alliance with the greatest possible expedition. The energetic measures taken by the Central Powers met with success. Lanza and Nigra, who, together with Giolitti, were summoned to Rome, supported the efforts of the German and Austro-Hungarian ambassadors,[299] and, as the result of their combined efforts, Zanardelli's opposition and the objections of the king were finally overcome. In conformity with the agreements concluded toward the end of April with Berlin and Vienna,[300] Prinetti issued on May 3 the written declaration of his willingness to renew the treaty of 1891 without alterations or additions; [301] at the same time, however, he expressed the wish that, in view of the imminent debates in the Italian Chamber, the signature of the treaty should be postponed until July 1, 1902, at the latest, "in order that attacks from the Opposition may be met with the assertion that the renewal of the Triple Alliance has not yet taken place." [302] Both Goluchowski and Bülow announced their willingness to accede to this request.[303] At the wish of the Italian statesman they also renounced their plan of consummating the renewal of

[299] Pasetti to Goluchowski, April 22, 27, and 30, and May 6, 1902.

[300] Goluchowski to Pasetti, April 29, 1902.

[301] Prinetti's declaration, dated May 3, 1902 (original), annexed to Pasetti's despatch of May 6, 1902. It reads as follows: "M^r. l'ambassadeur! Le traité d'alliance du 6 mai 1891 arrivant à l'échéance du 17 mai de l'année prochaine, les trois gouvernements alliés ont entrepris en vue du renouvellement de cet acte un échange d'idées qui a heureusement abouti à un accord complet sur tous les points qui formaient l'objet de leur examen. Je suis donc maintenant en mesure, ayant pris les ordres de S.M., de déclarer à V. Exc., avec priére de vouloir bien en faire part à son gouvernement, que le gouvernement du roi est prêt, pour ce qui le concerne, à renouveler le traité du 6 mai 1891 dans son texte actuel sans aucune modification ni addition. Le gouvernement du roi désire et il propose aux gouvernements alliés que la signature du nouveau traité ait lieu 1.er juillet prochain." As Pasetti informed Goluchowski on May 6, 1902, this agreement was attained only after a long struggle. Lemonon's statement (L'Europe et la politique Britannique, p. 457, note 1), "En 1902, la triple-alliance fut renouvelée, mais dans des conditions sans doute différentes de celles dans lesquelles elle avait été précédemment prorogée," is without foundation.

[302] Pasetti to Goluchowski, May 4, 1902.

[303] Goluchowski to Szögyény, May 4, 1902; Szögyény to Goluchowski, May 5, 1902.

the Triple Alliance by means of a simple protocol,[304] and finally assented to his suggestion that the protocol of 1891, which they had long refused to renew on account of its superfluity, should be added to the new treaty document. Pains were taken in Berlin to point out that this had been done because 'the fact that the treaty had been accepted without alteration was thus all the more clearly emphasized.' [305] For the same reason the cabinet of Berlin had already decided to renounce the idea of an automatic renewal of the alliance on the expiration of the fixed period for giving warning.[306] On June 28 the new treaty was signed in Berlin; [307] on June 30, in conformity with his promise, Pasetti communicated the note which determined Austria-Hungary's attitude in the matter of Tripoli.[308] The exchange of ratifications took place in Berlin on July 8, 1902.[309]

[304] On May 13, Mühlberg, the Under-Secretary of State in the Foreign Office, transmitted to Count Szögyény, by instruction of the Imperial Chancellor, the draft of the protocol by means of which the renewal of the Triple Alliance was to be consummated. It reads as follows: "Protocole. Les soussignés" (here follow the names and titles of the three plenipotentiaries, Bülow, Szögyény, and Lanza) "munis de pleins-pouvoirs qui ont été trouvés en bonne et due forme se sont réunis aujourd'hui à Berlin et sont convenus de ce qui suit: 1°. Le traité d'alliance conclu à Berlin le 6 mai 1891 entre les puissances signataires du présent protocole et ratifié à Berlin le 17 mai de la même année est confirmé de nouveau et continuera à rester en vigueur dans toute son étendue à l'exception de l'article XIV, remplacé par la disposition présente, pour l'espace de six ans à compter de l'échange des ratifications du présent protocole; mais s'il n'avait pas été dénoncé un an à l'avance par l'une ou l'autre des H.P.C., il restera en vigueur pour un autre espace de six ans. 2°. Le présent protocole sera ratifié et les ratifications en seront échangées à Berlin dans un délai de trois semaines ou plus tôt si faire se peut. En foi, etc. Fait à Berlin en triple exemplaire le 1er juillet 1902." The Austro-Hungarian government gave its assent, but the Italians declined this project and demanded a formal treaty. After further negotiations the Central Powers yielded. Szögyény to Goluchowski, June 7, 11, and 14, 1902; Pasetti to Goluchowski, June 5, 1902.

[305] Goluchowski to Szögyény, June 16, 1902, and Szögyény to Goluchowski, June 18, 1902.

[306] Szögyény to Goluchowski, May 14, 1902.

[307] Szögyény to Goluchowski, June 28, 1902. Wedel to Goluchowski, the same date. Wedel particularly emphasized the services rendered by Goluchowski "in preserving unchanged the well tested foundations of our alliance and removing all obstacles which lay in our common path."

[308] Pasetti to Goluchowski, July 1, 1902. Cf. the text, Vol. I, p. 232.

[309] Szögyény to Goluchowski, July 8, 1902. Telegram.

CHAPTER VI

THE TACIT RENEWAL OF THE FOURTH TREATY
OF THE TRIPLE ALLIANCE

THE treaty of 1902, like that of 1891, was concluded for six years, and was likewise to be valid for six years more in case none of the allied powers availed itself of the right to denounce it one year before the date of expiration, or to demand its revision. The period allowed for denunciation was to come to an end on July 8, 1907; and the relations between the allies had in the meanwhile undergone such changes that this date was looked forward to with some apprehension by all the powers concerned. Italy's rapprochement with France had made substantial progress since 1902. A few days after the signing of the fourth treaty of the Triple Alliance, Delcassé had said in the Chamber: "Italy's policy, as the result of her alliances, is aimed neither directly nor indirectly against France. In no event can these alliances constitute a menace to us, either diplomatically or through protocols or military conventions. In no event and in no way can Italy become the tool or the accomplice in an attack on our country." [310]

These utterances were at variance with the provisions of the Triple Alliance. They were not taken very seriously, however, by governmental circles in Vienna and Berlin — not even when Count Monts, the well informed German ambassador in Rome, reported, at the beginning of 1903, that Italy had concluded a far reaching agreement with France which was in direct opposition to the pledges assumed by her toward her allies. [311] The course of events showed that Monts's information had been cor-

---

[310] *Journal officiel*, Chambre des Députés, 1902, p. 2084 (3 juillet).

[311] Count Monts, in an article in the *Neue Freie Presse* of February 23, 1919, stresses the fact that at that time no credence had been given his statements in Berlin. Details concerning the contents of this treaty, concluded between France and Italy in November, 1902, were given in an article in *Le Temps* on December 22, 1918. See Appendix C, below. Cf. also G. von Jagow, *Ursachen und Ausbruch des Weltkrieges* (1919), pp. 41 f., note.

rect. Italy's leaning towards the Western Powers grew more marked from year to year.[312] Especially after the governments of France and England had peacefully settled their differences by the treaty of April 8, 1904, and were bound by a close community of interests,[313] the government leaders of Italy felt that the interests of their country demanded that they should avoid anything which might displease the statesmen in Paris or contain the germs of possible hostilities with France. Until now they had been able to hope that if war broke out between France and Italy, England would join forces with them, or at least observe a benevolent neutrality. In such an event they must now count on England's participation in the war as an ally of France and an adversary of Italy. They realized that it would be impossible to protect their country against the combined fleets of these two states, and feared that the assistance of the Central Powers, guaranteed them by the treaty, would in any case come too late to be of avail in safeguarding their far extended coast line, exposed as it was to enemy attacks. As we know, they had already informed their allies that they could not promise to join them in a war against the two Western Powers.[314]   The more imminent grew the danger of an Anglo-German war, and consequently of a European conflagration, the more irksome the Italian statesmen found their obligations.

In addition to this, public opinion in Italy expressed itself more clearly from year to year against the continuance of friendly relations with Austria-Hungary. The cry for an extension of Italy's sphere of influence on the farther shore of the Adriatic grew continually more insistent after the miscarriage of her colonial plans. As the conviction became firmer that the fulfilment of these aspirations must take place against Austria-Hungary's will, and not

---

[312] In the fall of 1903 Victor Emmanuel referred in Paris to "the happily terminated work of rapprochement" between France and Italy. Cf. H. von Liebig, *Die Politik von Bethmann-Hollwegs* (1919), i, p. 56; K. Helfferich, *Vorgeschichte des Weltkrieges* (1919), i, p. 29.

[313] Cf. Friedjung, *Das Zeitalter des Imperialismus*, i, pp. 407 ff.; E. Lemonon, *L'Europe et la politique britannique* (*1882–1911*), pp. 344 ff.; Debidour, *Histoire diplomatique de l'Europe*, iii, pp. 279 ff., and the literature cited there.

[314] Cf. pp. 110 f.

with her help, the voices demanding a break with the existing policy and an open union with the Western Powers grew more numerous. Every step taken by the Austro-Hungarian government in Albania was watched with jealousy and distrust. Politicians and journalists warned the government not to allow itself to be hoodwinked by promises or agreements, and kept endlessly repeating that the Dual Monarchy intended to swallow up Albania, just as it had engulfed Bosnia and Herzegovina. Then, too, there was the Macedonian question, which was continually giving rise to fresh complaints and recriminations. Especially since the convention of Mürzsteg, in the fall of 1903, when Russia and Austria-Hungary had agreed jointly to undertake administrative reform and the restoration of order in Macedonia, the fear of coming away empty-handed from the division of spoils had driven the Italian politicians and publicists to attack their Danubian ally with ever increasing violence.[315] At the same time the chorus of demands for the liberation of the 'unredeemed' territory kept swelling. This Irredentist movement received fresh impetus from the clashes between German and Italian students at the University of Innsbruck. In 1905, Marcora, President of the Italian Chamber, spoke of "our Tyrol."[316]

In all these Austro-Italian conflicts Germany had assumed the rôle of mediator, usually with success. She had been able to do so because no particular points of friction existed between her and Italy, although the efforts of the latter to ingratiate herself with France were watched with increasing displeasure in Berlin, where there was no lack of censure of the restless and rapacious Italian policy. Hitherto, the leading German statesmen had not given up hope that in the event of war between France and Germany, Italy would be mindful of her obligations and align herself with her ally; but when Italy supported Germany's adversaries in the Moroccan affair and during the course of the Algeciras conference, many were shaken in this belief. The question then arose whether all efforts had not been in vain, whether it was still de-

---

[315] Cf. L. Chlumecky, *Österreich-Ungarn und Italien*, 2d ed., pp. 55 ff.; Sosnosky, pp. 135 ff.

[316] Cf. Singer, p. 154.

sirable to cling to the alliance. Statesmen there were of no mean influence who urged a dissolution of the alliance with Italy and a new orientation of German policy in the direction of a revival of the League of the Three Emperors, in which they saw the surest safeguard against the perils threatening Germany from the West. The German ministers, however, with Bülow in the lead,[317] adhered firmly to the policy of the Triple Alliance. They had no desire to drive Italy into the arms of their opponents, knowing as they did that by so doing the moral influence of the Central European Alliance would be weakened and the aggressive tendencies in France correspondingly strengthened.[318] Similar considerations prevailed with the government of Vienna, which still regarded the security of its southern and southwestern frontiers against Italian invasion as indispensable in the event of a war with Russia, and for this reason preferred the continuance of treaty relations with its undependable ally to an open break.

Italy's leading statesmen were also convinced that the moment had not arrived for a radical change in their foreign policy. They realized that Germany's support could not as yet be dispensed with in carrying out their colonial schemes in North Africa, and that any solution of the Balkan problem in a manner satisfactory to Italy could not be hoped for if opposed by Austria-Hungary — so long at least as Austria kept on good terms with Russia. As Count Nigra once remarked, Italy had to be either the enemy or the ally of Austria-Hungary.[319] Since she did not feel strong enough at that time to seek a decision by trial of arms, her responsible statesmen, defying the radical element of public opinion, found it best to adhere to the treaty of the Triple Alliance, and to that devious policy, thanks to which they had obtained

[317] In *Deutsche Politik*, p. 69, Bülow later expressed the opinion that Italy had not sought to part company with her allies "either at Algeciras, or during her Tripolitan expedition, or shortly before this, on the occasion of the interview of Racconigi." "At Algeciras," he declared, "the Italian representatives took their stand in certain secondary matters with the Western Powers, and against us. . . . In other more important questions, Italy supported and furthered our point of view."

[318] Cf. G. von Jagow, *Ursachen und Ausbruch des Weltkrieges* (1919), p. 43.

[319] Count Nigra is generally recognized as the originator of this remark. Jagow (p. 27) now asserts that Visconti-Venosta once said to him, "L'Italie ne peut être que l'ennemi ou bien l'allié de l'Autriche."

valuable concessions from their allies as well as from the Western Powers, and hoped to obtain others still more valuable.

It was a good omen for the policy favoring the maintenance of friendly relations with the allies, when, in the course of 1903, Giolitti and Tittoni replaced Zanardelli and Prinetti. Both declared their willingness to hold fast to the Triple Alliance, to settle peacefully the existing difficulties with Austria-Hungary, and to avoid fresh ones. Since Goluchowski was striving toward the same end, they succeeded — after many a struggle, it is true, in which the German diplomats were forced to offer mediation — in reaching an agreement, or at least a modus vivendi. For example, the commercial questions, which for years had violently agitated public opinion in Italy and Austria-Hungary and given rise to interminable negotiations between the two cabinets, were now solved by a series of treaties in a manner acceptable to both parties.[320] This was also the case with the Balkan problems. Both countries kept their eyes fixed on the goal and watched Argus-eyed every step taken by the rival; they avoided any open conflict, however, and sought for means of averting the threatened conflict. The conferences between Goluchowski and Tittoni at Abbazia and Venice in 1904 and 1905 also served this purpose. Agreements were reached in all pending questions, and it was decided to forego any policy of aggression in the Balkans. Austria-Hungary bound herself to take no steps in that region without a previous agreement with her ally, only reserving freedom of action with regard to Bosnia, Herzegovina, and the sanjak of Novi-Bazar.[321] By the end of 1905, therefore, Bülow believed that no danger existed of Italy's alienation from the Triple Alliance. "Italy," he declared, "has cast her lot with the Triple Alliance, not for reasons of mawkish sentimentality, but because she finds

[320] After a succession of provisory measures, the definitive settlement took place through the treaty of commerce and navigation concluded at Rome on February 11, 1906. Cf. Bittner, op. cit., iii, p. 548, no. 5152.
[321] Goluchowski's notes on his conversations with Tittoni (State Archives). Tittoni, in his speech of December 18, 1906, expressed himself at length concerning these agreements. The important passages are given in *Italy's Foreign and Colonial Policy: A Selection from the Speeches delivered in the Italian Parliament by Tommaso Tittoni* (English translation by Baron di San Severino, London, 1914), pp. 43–66.

it to her advantage to do so. The reasons which originally brought the three great states together are still in existence; nothing has happened to work a change in them. .   The Triple Alliance is determined to preserve the peace and the status quo in Europe. That was our point of departure; that was why we renewed the Triple Alliance; that is why we are clinging steadfastly to it." [322]

Early in 1906, however, began that sinister disturbance of the relations between Italy and the Central Powers to which reference has already been made.[323] The attitude of the Italian statesmen at Algeciras caused bitterness in Berlin, where there was much talk of Italy's base ingratitude for the manifold services rendered her. It was at this time that Emperor William, in a conversation with Szögyény, "stigmatized Italy's double-faced attitude in particularly disapproving terms." He declared (Szögyény wrote) "that it was really monstrous for any one to give thought to the possibility of war against an ally; he must assure me, however, that *in case Italy should show hostility to Austria-Hungary*, he would seize with real enthusiasm the opportunity to join us and to turn loose upon her his whole military strength." [324] The Italians, on the other hand, disquieted by Austria-Hungary's military preparations in the southern Tyrol,[325] kept complaining with increasing bitterness of the action of the government of Vienna, which, they claimed, was attempting in collaboration with Russia to limit the participation of the other powers in the new ordering of affairs in Macedonia.

So far the question of the renewal of the Triple Alliance had not been mentioned by either side. It appeared best to the parties

---

[322] Cf. Singer, pp. 156 f.   [323] Cf. pp. 134 ff.

[324] Szögyény's letter to Goluchowski, April 10, 1906. Szögyény's telegram of April 8 reads as follows: "He did not wish to waste many words over Italy, and would only give the assurance that if the opportunity should arise — and this was not impossible in view of the unreliable policy of that kingdom — it would give him great satisfaction to join us in administering a salutary lesson to Italy, perhaps even with arms in hand." The difference between the two communications is self-evident. Although the telegram was sent off while the impression of the conversation was still fresh, the more explicit despatch probably gives the Emperor's words more correctly. That these words were only the expression of momentary excitement is shown by the attitude of William II at the conferences of June, 1906 (cf. p. 140), when he most emphatically expressed the opinion that Italy must be kept in the Triple Alliance.

[325] Cf. Singer, p. 158.

concerned to let matters take their natural course. In April, 1906, Count Lützow, the Austro-Hungarian ambassador to Italy, believed he was justified in characterizing as groundless the rumors circulating in Rome that Barrère was working against a renewal of the Triple Alliance. "In German circles," he wrote, "this matter is considered to lack any foundation in fact; indeed, it has not even been mentioned; and Barrère is not a man to waste his powder for nothing." He believed that in Italy, too, the decisive elements of this question had not yet been closely examined. "If that time were finally to arrive," he said, "I consider it by no means improbable that — thanks to Algeciras — the fear of being drawn into complications with England would manifest itself in some manner." Lützow conjectured that the Italians would express a wish "for a revival of the declaration of 1882," which specified that the provisions of the Triple Alliance should under no circumstance be regarded as directed against England.[326] Soon after this, however — in May, 1906 — Count Monts, who chanced to be in Berlin at that time, confronted the Imperial Chancellor and the Secretary of State with the question whether, in view of Italy's attitude, it would not be better to make use of the right of denunciation and dissolve an alliance which afforded disproportionately greater advantages to Italy than to the Central Powers.[327]

Count Monts, on his return to Rome, declared to Lützow that no rational being could believe that Italy would rush to arms to help Germany in a war against France. In its existing form the treaty laid Germany under heavy obligations to Italy without affording a corresponding equivalent; and this state of affairs could not continue. He then suggested diplomatic support by Italy of German economic policy in Asia Minor. Germany, for her part, could insure Italy, through a stipulation annexed to the treaty of the Triple Alliance, against all complications with Eng-

[326] Lützow to Goluchowski, April 17, 1906. In his despatch of April 26, Lützow repeated this opinion in connection with a passage from a speech by Guicciardini, in which he said that in the first treaty of the Triple Alliance of 1882, Italy "had placed first and foremost her traditional and unswerving relations with England."

[327] Szögyény to Goluchowski, May 22, 1906.

land which might arise from the union with the Central Powers.[328] The responsible ministers, however, were not convinced; they considered any discussion of the question to be premature. In the conferences which took place in Vienna in the middle of June, 1906, between Emperor William, Tschirschky, and Goluchowski, no mention was made of a dissolution or a modification of the Triple Alliance. In view of the general situation, emphasis was laid rather on the necessity of drawing Italy as close as possible to the Central Powers.[329] This policy was maintained by Goluchowski and Bülow, and also by Baron Aehrenthal, who had been guiding Austro-Hungarian foreign policy since October, 1906. On the occasion of a conversation which took place between Aehrenthal and Bülow in November, 1906, at Berlin, the two statesmen agreed that "the only right way is to wait calmly for Italy herself to denounce the treaty or to approach us with new proposals." Bülow expected her to do neither. Furthermore, as Count Monts repeatedly asserted in Rome,[330] he expressed no intention of bringing forward suggestions for changes on his own part.[331] In order to calm the Austro-Hungarian government, which feared something of this nature, he officially informed Count Monts that, "al-

---

[328] Lützow to Goluchowski, May 24, 1906 (telegram), and June 12, 1906 (letter). For Count Monts's appraisal of the questionable value of the Triple Alliance, cf. also his article in the *Berliner Tageblatt* of October 14, 1911, cited by Doerkes-Boppard in *Das Ende des Dreibundes*, p. 38, in which he states, *inter alia*: "Of what use is Italy to us, after all? We know of no instance in which we have enjoyed even the diplomatic support of this power. We have far oftener had to see her in the ranks of our opponents. We know well enough that in an hour of peril she would never give us military assistance; on the contrary, we are forced to suspect that she is ready at any moment to attack our Austrian ally in the rear. And yet we allow the continuance of a sham alliance which gives advantages to the Italians alone, and lays upon us nothing but obligations. . . . Away, therefore, with the Triple Alliance; it has long outlived its usefulness."

[329] Goluchowski to Lützow, June 20, 1906. Impartial observers had no high opinion of Italy's loyalty. At that time the Belgian minister in Berlin wrote to Brussels: "Le désir de l'empereur d'Allemagne d'affirmer l'existence de la triple-alliance se comprend d'autant mieux qu'elle est incessament battue en bréche par les puissances qui n'en font pas partie et que la fidélité de l'Italie est devenue au moins douteuse." *Zur europäischen Politik*, ii, p. 121. Cf. Vol. I, *supra*, pp. 16 ff.

[330] Lützow, October 19, 1906, telegram, and despatch to Aehrenthal, October 30, 1906.

[331] Aehrenthal to Lützow, November 21, 1906. Private letter.

though he well realized the deficiencies and shortcomings of the present treaty," he had given up any idea of revising it.[332] Several weeks previously, Tittoni, referring to the rumors which connected the visit to Rome of Tschirschky, the German Secretary of State, with the renewal of the Triple Alliance, had remarked to Count Lützow, "No one cares to denounce it."[333] Thus matters remained.

The efforts of all influential circles were now exerted towards making possible the prolongation of the treaty, which, it was held, worked for the interests of all three states and the peace of Europe as well. "As long as Italy remains faithful and true to the Triple Alliance," declared Bülow on November 14, 1906, in the Reichstag, "she contributes by this very fact toward the maintenance of peace for herself and for others. If Italy were to break away from the Triple Alliance, or pursue a vacillating and ambiguous policy, she would be contributing materially to the chances of a conflagration."[334] Aehrenthal, too, said in his message to the Delegations in December, 1906, that his conversation with Bülow and his communication with Tittoni had resulted in the "happy fact of the complete harmony of our views," and added that "the good relations existing between our government and that of Italy will make it easier for us to deal in perfect calm with the differences which, unfortunately, have often arisen, and to enlighten public opinion in both countries, which has often been irritable and misguided."[335] Tittoni's speech, delivered in the Italian Chamber on December 18, 1906, was animated by the same spirit. He, too, emphasized his purpose to maintain the Triple Alliance, saying, "May this explicit affirmation serve to show the error of those who, from time to time, upon the slightest ground declare it weakened and predict its early end."[336]

Thanks to the efforts of these men and their followers, the Triple Alliance was also brought safely through the grave crisis which threatened its existence in the first months of 1907, partic-

---

[332] Lützow to Aehrenthal, November 24, 1906. Telegram.
[333] Lützow to Aehrenthal, October 19, 1906. Telegram.
[334] Singer, p. 162.
[335] Singer, p. 165.
[336] Tittoni, *op. cit.*, p. 45.

ularly as the result of the efforts of King Edward VII to hem in Germany. In the course of the negotiations between the leading statesmen of the three powers, the question of the denunciation of the treaty of the Triple Alliance was not touched upon, and July 8, 1907, was allowed to pass by without use being made of the right of denunciation. The prolongation of the treaty for a further period of six years, until July 8, 1914, was thus tacitly accomplished.

CHAPTER VII

THE FIFTH TREATY OF THE TRIPLE ALLIANCE
DECEMBER 5, 1912

WHEN the prolongation of the fourth treaty of the Triple Alliance was assured — July, 1907 — no illusions were cherished in Vienna or in Berlin as to its value. The initiated in both capitals took it for granted that, if an emergency were to arise, Italy would in no case fulfil her obligations promptly and in full measure. They knew that Victor Emmanuel III had assumed obligations toward France and England which were incompatible with those of the Triple Alliance. They were convinced that the majority of Italian statesmen would more or less gladly range themselves with the adversaries of the Central Powers, if these should prove to be the stronger. They were well aware that the Italian government was restrained from yielding to the pressure of public opinion and loosing the unnatural tie which bound it to the Central Powers — especially Austria-Hungary — only by its lack of confidence in the straightforwardness of France and its belief that adherence to the Triple Alliance afforded a sort of guaranty for her loyalty.[337] If the government leaders in Berlin and Vienna advocated the continuance of the Triple Alliance, and persisted in their willingness to make fresh sacrifices for the sake of holding their unreliable ally, they did so because they saw in this alliance the only safeguard against Italy's open defection to the camp of the enemy; and this, for their own interests, they wished to avert as long as possible.

This policy was vigorously defended by Aehrenthal against the party which, under the leadership of Conrad von Hötzendorf, chief of the General Staff, urged a 'timely' settling of accounts with the 'faithless' ally. Italy, as Conrad put it, had been "fol-

[337] The Belgian, Greindl, also expressed the same opinion two years later; cf. his despatch of April 17, 1909, cited by Hashagen, *Umrisse der Weltpolitik*, ii, p. 48.

lowing the tricky policy of keeping two irons continually in the fire — namely, the so-called loyal government with the so-called loyal king, and the so-called National party, difficult of restraint, with its Pan-Italian programme." [338] Aehrenthal was in favor of preparing for every possible emergency, but also of avoiding every step which might be regarded in Italy as a provocation. He would listen to no talk of a preventive war. "A conflict of this nature," he declared as early as April, 1907, "would not only be at variance with the traditions of Austria; it would not be understood in these days when war means the mobilization of the entire nation. The necessary unlimited moral coöperation between army and civil population would be lacking. Moreover, I should be at a loss to know the object of such a war. As history has taught us, further territorial acquisitions in Italy would be a disaster for the monarchy." [339]

This conviction, shared by the majority of the German statesmen, especially Chancellors Bülow and Bethmann-Hollweg, dominated Aehrenthal. Supported by his sovereign, who stood by him through thick and thin, he was engaged to the end of his life (February, 1912) in stormy contests with the war party — the supporters of which were not confined to the army — in defence of the preservation of the Triple Alliance and the maintenance of good relations with Italy. In this he was successful. The breach with Italy was avoided, and the Triple Alliance was brought through the serious crisis which threatened its existence between 1907 and 1912. This had not been easily accomplished. Every step taken by Aehrenthal to strengthen the position of his country was opposed by Italy. He had either to forego his plans or buy the assent of the Italian cabinet with significant concessions. His project for extending to Mitrovitza the railroad leading from Sarajevo to the frontier of the sanjak, thus establishing communication with Salonica and the Aegean, was thwarted by the Italians, who demanded the construction of other Balkan railroads running from the Danube to the Adriatic and from Valona to Monastir. And when Aehrenthal proceeded with the annexation

[338] Memorandum from Conrad von Hötzendorf, September 4, 1909.
[339] Aehrenthal's report to Francis Joseph I, April, 1907.

of Bosnia and Herzegovina, shortly after the meeting of Tsar Nicholas II and King Edward VII at Reval in June, 1908, and the Young Turk revolution of July, 1908, he had the greatest difficulty in obtaining Italy's assent by means of suitable compensations. In September, 1908, he declared his willingness to renounce the rights accruing to the Dual Monarchy in Montenegro through paragraph 29 of the Acts of the Congress of Berlin, as well as the right of garrison in the sanjak of Novi-Bazar, which had been promised it by Article 25 of the Treaty of Berlin. In spite of this, fiery speeches against Austria-Hungary's aggressive policy were delivered in the Italian Chamber after the annexation had taken place. The deputy Fortis declared, amid general applause, "The only state which really threatens us with war is in alliance with us." Barzilai, a veteran Austrophobe, demanded, on the ground of the so-called promises which Austria was alleged to have given in 1882,[340] that the Trentino should be handed over to Italy by way of compensation for the annexation of Bosnia and Herzegovina. In other quarters open union with the Triple Entente was demanded; but to Italy's responsible statesmen the time for such a step did not appear to have arrived.

The firmness of the policy of the Central Powers, the energetic support by Emperor William II of his friend and ally, and the obvious impotence of Russia, who could not venture to try conclusions with the united forces of the Danubian Monarchy and Germany after her defeats in Manchuria—all these made it seem advisable to Tittoni, the controller of Italy's foreign policy, to fall into line with his allies. In a speech before the Chamber in December, 1908, he expressed with great cleverness the opinion that his programme of 1907 — "unshakable fidelity to the Triple Alliance and sincere friendship for England and France"[341] — still served Italy's interests best. He most emphatically refused "to choose between alliance and friendship, or to give up either the one or the other"; "Our alliance with Germany and Austria-Hungary, to which we remain true," he said at the time, "must

---

[340] In his speech of December 3, 1908, Tittoni declared that this assertion had no foundation whatever. Cf. *Italy's Foreign and Colonial Policy*, pp. 121 ff.

[341] Tittoni's speech of May 15, 1907. Cf. *Italy's Foreign and Colonial Policy*, p. 85.

not, to my mind, be an obstacle to our traditional friendship with England, to our renewed friendship with France, and to the recent understanding with Russia." [342] In order to set the Austrian government at rest, he expressly stated in the Chamber that he had ransacked the Italian archives in vain for documents which might give a basis for Italy's claim on the Trentino after the annexation of Bosnia and Herzegovina. At the same time he emphasized the fact that the article of the treaty of the Triple Alliance guaranteeing compensations to Italy presupposed new territorial acquisitions by the Dual Monarchy in the Balkans; and the annexation of Bosnia and Herzegovina could not be thus described.[343]

By his censure of the manner in which Aehrenthal had brought about this annexation, however, and his characterization of Italy's rapprochement with Russia as an accomplished fact, he showed plainly enough to the partisans of the Triple Alliance where his real sympathies lay, and along what paths he intended to guide Italy when the right moment should come. He adhered to this shifty policy even after the crisis over the annexation was past. Tittoni lacked faith in the sincerity of the assurances given by Aehrenthal, who had twice pledged himself — in 1907 at Desio, in 1908 at Salzburg — to joint Austro-Italian action in all Balkan questions; [344] he also feared that Austria-Hungary would come to an understanding with Russia regarding the division of Turkish territory in the Balkans, leaving Italy out in the cold. For this reason, he strove, from the end of 1908 to the fall of 1909, to bring about an understanding between Russia, Austria-Hungary, and Italy,[345] which would determine the spheres of influence of the three powers in the Balkans. And while this plan came to nothing, agreements were reached with the Russian government on the occasion of Nicholas II's visit to Racconigi in October, 1909,

[342] Italy's Foreign and Colonial Policy, p. 147.

[343] Ibid., pp. 121 ff.

[344] This matter will be treated in detail in the introduction to the treaties between Italy and Austria-Hungary.

[345] Documents in the State Archives. This question will be examined in detail in another connection. Cf. the despatches of the Belgian representative at this time. Zur europäischen Politik, iii, pp. 106 f., etc.

which not only averted this danger,[346] but also plainly indicated that Italy stood closer to the Western Powers and Russia than to her own allies. Italy's faith in the former was not yet strong enough, however, and the latter were too powerful, to permit her to drop the mask. Her leading statesmen still felt it desirable to cling to the Triple Alliance. For this reason, and in order to prepare for all eventualities, Tittoni sought in the course of 1909 to reassure the Central Powers, whose distrust of Italy's loyalty to the alliance was being expressed more and more insistently. To an interpellation by Barzilai regarding the alleged premature renewal of the treaty of the Triple Alliance, he replied in June, 1909: "The Triple Alliance not only has not been renewed; I can give the most definite assurances that none of the contracting parties has thought or is thinking of a premature renewal. No reason exists for not calmly awaiting its expiration. The wish to renew it prematurely can originate only in misgivings regarding its future existence. Such misgivings, however, are not justified; for the powers of the Triple Alliance are enjoying the best of relations with one another." [347]

These "best of relations" were, as a matter of fact, wholly imaginary. The governing circles in Vienna and Berlin were facing the reality that the Triple Alliance was in a bad way; but they were still determined to block Italy's open defection to the side of their adversaries as long as possible. For this purpose Aehrenthal decided to make another concession. In December, 1909, he reached an agreement with the new Italian government — Guicciardini had now assumed control of foreign policy — which limited yet more the freedom of action of the Dual Monarchy in the Balkans. In interpreting Article VII of the treaty of the

[346] Compare the information concerning the Russo-Italian treaty of October 24, 1909, in the publication *Deutschland schuldig?*, German White Book regarding the responsibility of the authors of the War (1919), p. 189. According to this publication, the last article of the treaty ran: "Italy and Russia bind themselves to observe a benevolent attitude respectively toward the Russian question of the Straits, and toward Italian interests in Tripoli and Cyrenaica." Also see Bethmann-Hollweg, *Betrachtungen zum Weltkriege* (1919), i, p. 76; B. Molden, *Graf Aehrenthal*, pp. 173 f.

[347] Cf. Tittoni, *Sei anni di politica estera* (Rome, 1912), p. 489. The passage is omitted from the English translation which we have several times cited above.

Triple Alliance, Austria-Hungary now bound herself not to re-occupy the sanjak of Novi-Bazar without having previously come to an agreement with Italy based on a suitable compensation. In accordance with Italy's wishes, it was also specified that neither of the two signatory parties should reach an understanding with a third power about any Balkan question without the participation therein of the other signatory power on a footing of absolute equality. They also promised to inform one another of any plans on the part of a third power running contrary to the principle of non-intervention and tending to a modification of the status quo in the Balkans or the Turkish coasts and islands of the Adriatic or of the Aegean Sea.[348]

This new concession did not attain the end desired by Aehrenthal. Italy's leading statesmen, including Guicciardini's successor, the Marquis San Giuliano, who took office in March, 1910, were past masters of the art of using a favorable situation to their own advantage. They kept making new demands, while public opinion in Italy clamored against a continuation of the alliance with the 'hereditary enemy.' The agreement of December, 1909, however, which indicated that Austria-Hungary had no intention of pressing on to Salonica, served to prevent the development of a crisis, and enabled San Giuliano, who actively supported the Triple Alliance and the maintenance of friendly relations between its members, to score a triumph of his policy over the numerous Italian partisans of the Triple Entente. The accommodating attitude observed by him in his conversations with German and Austro-Hungarian statesmen caused great satisfaction to these latter, and led to declarations which, though only verbal, gave hope of joint action by the powers of the Triple Alliance in matters of world policy, and especially of coöperation between Italy and Austria-Hungary, for the immediate future at least, in the Balkan questions. It was also pleasing to Aehrenthal, who was anxious to avoid any strengthening of Pan-Slavic influence in the Western Balkans, with a consequent Russian penetration to the

---

[348] The agreement was consummated through an exchange of notes. Cf. Vol. I, pp. 240-243. The tedious negotiations which preceded the conclusion will be outlined in a subsequent portion of this work.

Adriatic, when San Giuliano declared in September, 1910, that it was to his country's interest to have a strong Austro-Hungarian monarchy as a neighbor. "This would be far more advantageous to Italy," he said, "than if a purely Slavic group were to be formed in the Balkans and to exercise its influence upon the provinces of the Dual Monarchy that border on Italy." [349]

No less acceptable was it to the Austro-Hungarian Minister of Foreign Affairs when he found that his views harmonized with those of San Giuliano with regard to the Turkish question, and the possibility of fresh changes in the Balkans. Both agreed that the dissolution of Turkey or its reduction to a vassal state of Russia must be prevented. Aehrenthal gained the impression that San Giuliano considered the "policy of coquetting with Russia, as pursued by Tittoni, was somewhat objectionable and out of harmony with the spirit of the Alliance." [350] At the close of his negotiations with San Giuliano, Aehrenthal believed that he was justified in alluding to the vigorous efforts of the Italian statesmen "to effect a closer union with the two allies." [351]

The events following immediately after appeared to bear out this view. During the second half of 1910 the relations of the powers of the Triple Alliance were more friendly than at any time since Algeciras. San Giuliano, speaking in the Chamber, bestowed praise in full measure on the Triple Alliance, recommended a policy which would take account of the just demands of the Central Powers, and energetically denounced the Irredentist movement, declaring that "the originators of Irredentist agitation did not represent the true feelings of the great majority of the Italian people, who desired not only peace, but confidence and cordiality in their relations with their neighbors and allies." In his negotiations with the government of Vienna he also avoided bringing up the ticklish question of compensations for the event of an active Austro-Hungarian policy in the Balkans, "for in so

[349] Aehrenthal's notes on the conversations between himself and San Giuliano at Salzburg and Ischl, September, 1910.

[350] Ibid.

[351] As a reason for this, Aehrenthal gives the fact that the ties between Austria-Hungary and Germany were continually growing closer, while the Triple Entente showed "a lack of cohesion."

doing an irreconcilable difference might arise between the two cabinets." He was the more anxious to avoid such an eventuality, because he saw the moment approaching for the realization of a plan with which Italian statesmen had been busied for over a generation: a plan which, for its successful consummation, depended in no small degree upon the attitude of the Central Powers.

The increasingly visible decay of Turkey, as well as France's progress in Morocco, induced the Italian government in the course of 1911 to plan for the occupation of Tripolitania. Italy had been assured a free hand in this region by the agreements concluded with the Western Powers at the beginning of the century. The only question was whether France would hold to the promises she had given; and San Giuliano appears to have had doubts on this score. He knew that French and English in their treaties had encroached on the southern borders of Tripolitania, and he may have feared that as soon as France had subdued Morocco she would take possession of all Tripolitania as well.[352] For this reason he proceeded to take action as soon as the incorporation of Morocco into France's colonial possessions became certain. "We have no other choice," he said, "unless we wish to let slip the last moment when the occupation of Tripoli is possible for us." [353]

This resolution also determined his attitude toward the Central Powers. Italy, in order to make certain of attaining her purpose, had to be sure that her allies, who were both keenly interested in the preservation of Turkey, should not thwart her. The provisions of the Triple Alliance guarded against this. Germany had

[352] In September, 1911, Avarna expressed this fear to Aehrenthal as follows: "France is on the verge of making a very important acquisition of territory, and is also bound by treaty to place no obstacles in the way of Italian activity in Tripoli. No one can tell whether at some later time a fresh grouping of European powers might not cause the favorable attitude of France to become less certain." Aehrenthal to Baron Ambrózy, September 26, 1911. Cf. the Red Book of 1915, p. 201. Reventlow, in his *Politische Vorgeschichte des grossen Krieges* (1919), pp. 78 f., describes Italy's relations with the Western Powers in a different way. According to him, the leading statesmen of England were the decisive element in the affair of Tripoli.

[353] Bülow, *Deutsche Politik*, p. 107.

even assumed the obligation to intervene in Italy's behalf if the last-named power should find herself compelled by French aggression to defend her interests in Tripoli. Austria-Hungary, too, had promised that if the dissolution of Turkey became inevitable, Tripoli should fall to the lot of Italy. It was obviously to Italy's interest to avoid anything which might give her allies just cause for new complaints at this particular moment. When, therefore, in June, 1911, the former Minister of Foreign Affairs, Guicciardini, complained that Italy had fallen into a position tantamount to isolation through the lack of confidence characterizing her relations toward her allies, San Giuliano emphasized with the utmost warmth the necessity of a good understanding with Germany and Austria and vowed fidelity to the Triple Alliance.[354] He believed that he could count on the loyalty of the allies of his sovereign; but Francis Joseph was over eighty years old, and his health was failing. It was generally known throughout Italy that the heir to the throne, Francis Ferdinand, did not favor maintaining the Triple Alliance at any cost.[355] For this reason, it may have appeared desirable to San Giuliano to make certain beyond possibility of doubt, even as early as this, that the treaty, which expired in July, 1914, should be prolonged beyond this period. To attain this end he followed the example often set by his predecessors in office and turned first of all to Germany.

Towards the end of July, 1911, Kiderlen-Wächter informed Count Aehrenthal that he had learned from reliable Roman sources that the Italian premier, Giolitti, and still more King Victor Emmanuel III, were in favor of an immediate renewal of the treaty of the Triple Alliance with no alteration whatever of its provisions, but that they hesitated to take the initiative. Going on the assumption that, in view of the general situation, Aehrenthal, like himself, was in favor of a "quiet renewal of the Treaty, as expeditious as possible and without changes," Kiderlen-

---

[354] Cf. Singer, pp. 219 f.

[355] In his latest work, *Politische Vorgeschichte des grossen Krieges* (1919), p. 3, Reventlow characterizes Francis Ferdinand's policy toward Italy in the following words: "It is most improbable . . . that the heir to the [Austro-Hungarian] throne was planning aggression against Italy. He distrusted Italy, however, and saw in her the enemy of the future."

Wächter recommended a joint action of the Central Powers in Rome as soon as the report received in Berlin had been verified. Emperor William, he said, looked upon the idea with favor.[356] Aehrenthal was quite ready to take up the suggestion of the German cabinet; he hoped that if Italy were kept occupied in Africa she would be diverted from the Adriatic. "I cannot conceal the fact," he wrote to Kiderlen-Wächter, "that Italy's activity in North Africa suits me for obvious reasons. It must indeed come hard to the Italian statesmen to remain virtuous at this particular moment, when a new division of clothes — or rather of petticoats — is going on in Africa." [357] He therefore advised his sovereign to accept the proposal of the cabinet of Berlin, emphasizing the fact that for five years past he had been struggling with might and main to preserve cordial relations with Italy, and pointing out that since the Central Powers were the stronger, they could take the initiative without loss of prestige.[358]

Emperor Francis Joseph was at this time at Ischl. As Mérey, the Austro-Hungarian ambassador in Rome, was also sojourning there, the monarch commanded him to give his views on this question. Mérey declared that the Italian government had never mentioned the renewal of the Triple Alliance to him, but that the Italian ambassador in Vienna, the Duke of Avarna, had done so in March, 1911. Herr von Jagow, the German ambassador in Rome, had also brought up the subject in June. Both these diplomats — particularly Jagow — had recommended that the initiative be assumed by the Central Powers. In a letter to Aehrenthal, Mérey even expressed the opinion that the recent hint dropped by Italy had perhaps originated in Germany; he said he had never doubted that Victor Emmanuel and the Italian government would stand by the Triple Alliance, but that he expected them to express a desire for the revision of certain treaty stipulations. For his own part, he would "rather keep the Italians in suspense until the last moment"; he recognized, however, the

---

[356] Kiderlen-Wächter to Aehrenthal, July 31, 1911.

[357] Aehrenthal to Kiderlen-Wächter, August 10, 1911.

[358] Aehrenthal's report to Francis Joseph I, Mendel, August 3, 1911. Original and draft.

validity of the arguments in favor of a quick settlement of affairs.[359] Emperor Francis Joseph gave his assent to opening negotiations,[360] after it had been ascertained that the information which reached Berlin at the end of July was correct. At the end of September — just as war was beginning between Turkey and Italy [361] — the Duke of Avarna notified Vienna that he had spoken with the king and his ministers on the occasion of his visit to Rome, and was now empowered to express officially the willingness of the Italian government immediately to renew the treaty of the Triple Alliance "in strict secrecy, and without any modifications whatsoever." [362] "If the question of Tripolitania," he added, "should be solved favorably to Italy, she would, by virtue of her complete satisfaction, be a contented, and therefore a more dependable member of the Triple Alliance." [363] The guiding statesmen of the Central Powers were not inclined to believe this; they felt, however, that it was expedient to accede to San Giuliano's request, and gave their assent.[364] It was decided to hold the negotiations in Vienna.[365]

An agreement was swiftly reached with regard to certain points. The duration of the treaty was again fixed at twelve years, to date from July 8, 1914, the date of expiration of the existing agreement.[366] All were equally agreed that there should be no alteration of the text; but since a modification of conditions in North Africa had come about through the Turco-Italian conflict, the proposal was made by Germany, presumably at Italy's instigation, that the treaty provisions relating to these regions should be adapted to the existing circumstances. The result was to be embodied in a protocol attached to the new treaty. Aehrenthal had

[359] Mérey to Aehrenthal, Ischl, August 8, 1911.
[360] Aehrenthal to Kiderlen-Wächter, Mendel, August 10 and 18, September 7 and 11, 1911.
[361] Cf. C. Sax, Geschichte des Machtverfalls der Türkei, 2d ed., pp. 592 ff.
[362] Daily report, September 26, 1911, and private letter of Aehrenthal to Kiderlen-Wächter, September 27, 1911.
[363] Red Book, p. 201.
[364] Germany's assent was communicated to the Austrian government through a telegram from Flotow, dated Berlin, September 27, 1911.
[365] Kiderlen-Wächter to Aehrenthal, September 29, 1911.
[366] Aehrenthal to Kiderlen-Wächter, October 3, 1911.

no objections to make on principle to Kiderlen-Wächter's proposals; he informed Rome that he would come to an agreement with Germany as soon as possible and transmit the protocol as decided upon by both powers to the Italian government.[367] The haste shown by Aehrenthal, and even more by Kiderlen-Wächter, caused Mérey, the Austro-Hungarian ambassador in Rome, to express his doubts as to the advisability of forcing matters to such an extent. He feared that the premature renewal of the Triple Alliance would be regarded in Italy as the price exacted by the Central Powers for their support of Italian projects in Tripolitania, and pointed to the bad impression which the agreement with Italy was bound to make upon the Turkish government. For this reason he recommended postponing the negotiations until a more favorable moment.[368] The statesmen of Vienna and Berlin, however, adhered to their purpose.

Kiderlen-Wächter in particular kept pressing for a conclusion; he told Szögyény that the German government was satisfied with the renewal of the treaty of the Triple Alliance and the date set for its entrance into force — July 8, 1914. Since San Giuliano had declared his willingness to renew the treaty as it stood, he — Kiderlen-Wächter — believed that Articles VII, IX, and X should retain the existing wording; this would prevent the Italian government from bringing up the question of alterations. The provisions of Article VII were to be interpreted in a supplementary protocol between Italy and Austria-Hungary; those of Articles IX and X would be similarly dealt with in a second supplementary protocol between Germany and Italy. In the case of the latter, emphasis was to be laid on the fact "that the 'status quo territorial' should be regarded as that established by the conclusion of peace between Italy and Turkey." Since it was further to be expected that France would extend her protectorate over Morocco after the ratification of the Franco-German agreement as to that country,[369] special mention was to be made of this cir-

[367] Aehrenthal to Mérey, October 20, 1911.

[368] Mérey to Aehrenthal, October 27, 1911.

[369] The treaty of November 4, 1911; printed, e. g., in Debidour, *Histoire diplomatique de l'Europe*, iv, pp. 331 ff.

cumstance in the supplementary protocol. The decision regarding Article VII, Kiderlen-Wächter said, lay with Aehrenthal; Germany would assent to any wording selected by Austria-Hungary. As regards the statement made to him by Aehrenthal, that the value of Article VII would be questionable in case Italy "should take action in the European waters of the Aegean Sea and proceed to an occupation of the coasts or islands of that region without our " (Austria-Hungary's) " assent," Kiderlen-Wächter felt empowered to say that no action in the Aegean contrary to Article VII was to be feared on the part of Italy. This article, he believed, should naturally be retained, because, to a certain extent, it gave Austria-Hungary a "better hold" upon Italy.[370] A few days later Tschirschky, the German ambassador to the court of Vienna, transmitted the German draft of the supplementary protocol, according to which the status quo referred to in Articles IX and X of the treaty should in future "be based upon the recent events in Tripolitania and upon the agreements reached between the signatories of this treaty and France with regard to Morocco."[371]

Count Aehrenthal found that this wording was not definite enough regarding Tripoli. Although this agreement, he said, primarily concerned only Germany and Italy, Austria-Hungary, as a signatory power, would also be assuming the obligation to respect all Italy's rights as recognized by the treaty. From this point of view it appeared necessary to him to replace the indefinite wording, "sur la base des dernières événements en Tripolitaine," by something more precise. He proposed that the status quo for Tripolitania and Cyrenaica should be that established by the future agreement between Italy and Turkey.[372] As for Article

[370] Szögyény to Aehrenthal, November 26, 1911. Telegram.

[371] ". . . qu'il est entendu que le statu quo visé par les articles IX et X du présent traité serait celui fixé sur la base des derniers événements en Tripolitaine et des arrangements survenus entre les puissances signataires de ce traité et la France au sujet du Maroc."

[372] His version ran as follows: "Qu'il est entendu que le statu quo visé par les articles IX and X du présent traité serait pour la Tripolitaine et la Cyrénaïque celui qui sera fixé d'aprés l'accord futur entre l'Italie et la Turquie et pour le Maroc celui établi par les arrangements survenus entre les puissances signataires de ce traité et la France au sujet de ce pays." Aehrenthal to Szögyény, December 6, 1911.

VII, Aehrenthal was resolved to adhere to it in its existing form. "The present conflict," he said, "has shown us that Article VII provides us with a weapon against possible Italian activities which we cannot give up and which cannot be turned against us; for we have no territorial aspirations which might justify Italy in demanding compensations." Only the declaration of June 30, 1902, regarding Tripolitania, which had been rendered superfluous by recent events, would have to be eliminated.[373]

Kiderlen-Wächter gave his assent. It was decided to submit Aehrenthal's project to Rome,[374] but at the same time to demand the elimination of the first protocol, relating to the commercial questions and the relations of the allies to England, since it was no longer adapted to the circumstances of the case.[375] Now, however, the efforts of the German and Austro-Hungarian statesmen quickly and quietly to consummate the renewal of the treaty, as Italy had expressly requested, failed to receive the expected support of the Italian government. Mérey, who was still opposed to hasty action, reported as early as the middle of December that San Giuliano did not consider it 'expedient' to proceed with the renewal of the treaty at this particular moment, when matters in Tripoli were so uncertain. He also pointed to the violent attacks of the Austro-Hungarian press against Italy's policy, which had in turn superinduced a dangerous irritation of Italian public opinion, and advised waiting for the restoration of calm before taking steps toward the renewal of the Triple Alliance.[376] Once more, however, his words of warning made no impression on Aehrenthal.[377]

Aehrenthal had at that time just won a hard-fought battle with the party which clamored insistently for preparation against Italy in view of a possible settling of scores by armed force. "I main-

[373] Aehrenthal to Szögyény, December 6, 1911.

[374] Szögyény to Aehrenthal, December 8, 1911 (telegram), and Aehrenthal to Mérey, December 9, 1911.

[375] Szögyény to Aehrenthal, December 9, 1911, and Aehrenthal to Szögyény, December 11, 1911.

[376] Mérey to Aehrenthal, December 12, 1911.

[377] Aehrenthal to Szögyény, December 15, 1911, and Szögyény's reply, December 16, 1911.

tain" — Conrad von Hötzendorf, leader of this faction, had written shortly before — "I maintain that Italy, with her political aspirations, her economic prosperity, her ceaseless military development, and her great nationalistic schemes, is determined to win the Italian territory of the Dual Monarchy, to obtain the mastery of the Adriatic, to hinder the development of Austro-Hungarian power in the Balkans, and to replace it by her own influence, just as she is striving to obtain a position in Tripoli similar to that of France in Algeria and Tunis. In her clever pursuit of this great purpose, she turns every circumstance to account in attaining the particular objective most in evidence at a given moment. Her other schemes she apparently lets wait; but she stands ready to go on with them when the first has been attained. It is quite in harmony with this plan that Italy, realizing that the moment has come for Tripoli, seemingly renounces all other aims, and makes every effort to buy the friendly neutrality, or even the support, of those powers which would oppose her in the pursuit of those other purposes. This applies above all to the Dual Monarchy. Austria is now confronted with the urgent question whether or not she intends to checkmate Italy's policy, a policy directed toward the progressive attainment of far-reaching aims. She must decide, in the present instance, whether to take a hostile position toward Italy's aspirations in Tripoli, and block them in this manner, or to settle accounts with Italy after that state has become involved in Tripoli, thus frustrating for a long time to come her designs on the Italian territory of the Dual Monarchy, her plans for the mastery of the Adriatic, and her activities in the Balkans." [378] Regarding the measures which, in his opinion, should be taken by Austria-Hungary, Conrad said "that the Dual Monarchy should take a position decidedly unfavorable to Italy's move in Tripoli, assure for herself a complete freedom of action, and, in case Italy opens hostilities in Tripoli, either attack Italy, or secure at least equivalent indemnification in some other region."

Count Aehrenthal answered this with a decided negative. "We are bound to the treaty," he asserted in a memorandum to Francis

[378] Conrad von Hötzendorf to Aehrenthal, September 24, 1911.

Joseph, "and we must not make a move against Italy in Tripoli. These sinister plans against us are not, as a matter of fact, entertained by the Italians. They wish to prolong the Triple Alliance with us until 1920." [379] He then proceeded energetically to defend the maintenance of the Dual Monarchy's policy of conciliation, as he had often done before. Once more the Emperor let him have his way, and Aehrenthal continued to make every effort to hold Italy to the Triple Alliance, attempting to eliminate the friction which had arisen during the course of the Turco-Italian war through the shifting of the scene of action to the heart of Turkey, and making no attempt to prevent the Italians from extending the contest to the Aegean Sea, although this caused severe losses to Austria-Hungary's Levantine trade. And although he demanded suitable compensation for the Dual Monarchy, according to the terms of Article VII of the treaty of the Triple Alliance, after Italy had occupied the twelve islands ('Dodecanesus') off the southwestern coast of Asia Minor, a declaration was simultaneously made deferring these claims until the close of the war.[380]

In Albania, too, where there was the greatest clash of interests between the allies, Aehrenthal's conciliatory activity succeeded in finding a modus vivendi. It was part of his plan to keep Italy in the Triple Alliance by consideration of her susceptibilities and her special interests when he announced in Rome,[380a] for the sake of pacifying San Giuliano, that in case the Triple Alliance was renewed, he should be willing to accede to Italy's wishes and keep the fact secret until a definitely specified time. He also consented to influence the Austro-Hungarian press in favor of a friendly attitude toward Italy — provided, of course, that San Giuliano took similar measures with the Italian press.

At the same time he confided to Mérey his great displeasure at the ambiguous policy of Rome. "The Italian government," he wrote on December 19, 1911, "should value more highly the advantages which the alliance with us has secured it, and should

---

[379] Aehrenthal's memorandum to the Emperor, October 22, 1911.

[380] Cf. *Diplomatische Aktenstücke betreffend die Beziehungen Österreich-Ungarns zu Italien, in der Zeit vom 20. Juli 1914 bis 23. Mai 1915* (Red Book of 1915), pp. 205 ff.

[380a] In the middle of December, 1911.

show its gratitude by abandoning its see-saw policy between the Triple Alliance and the powers of the Entente. Since their notorious escapade, the Italians have been counting overmuch on the indulgence of their allies, and attempting to protect themselves on all sides by all sorts of liaisons. They depend on the Triple Alliance, and realize that they are protected to the rear; they would also like to use the alliance to help them out of their momentary embarrassment by means of Austro-Hungarian and German pressure on Constantinople, and to bait us into exerting such pressure by pretending that they will undertake naval operations as a last resort. On the other hand, the Italians are afraid of France and England; they also feel, and with justice, that an attack on the Dardanelles might break up the agreement they reached with Russia at Racconigi. From these diverse considerations arises a state of mind which makes a clear policy impossible, and which calls forth small confidence on the part of Italy's allies. If Italy wishes to enjoy still further advantages from the Triple Alliance, she must give proof of the fact not only in words, but in the attitude of her government. The more clearly and coherently she expresses this desire, the more intimate and cordial will be our relations with her. In a word, she must put an end to this flirting in all directions, with its consequent vacillation of Italian policy, which awakes distrust in us and has encouraged nationalistic aspirations to lift their heads once more in Italy. Will there be an Italian government with sufficient clearness of vision and courage of its convictions to do this?" [381]

San Giuliano, however, was not satisfied with the offers made by the governments of Berlin and Vienna. At the end of December, indeed, he expressed his approval of a renewal of the treaty as it stood, with a six or twelve year term of validity, beginning on the day of expiration of the existing agreement; but he declared that he could not regard the present moment as suitable for taking this step, owing to the difficulty of preserving secrecy as proposed by the Central Powers, and to the territorial changes which might still come about as a result of the war. In connection with this matter of territorial changes, San Giuliano said that he could not

[381] Aehrenthal to Mérey, December 19, 1911. Draft and copy.

accept the wording of the protocol as proposed by the Central Powers, since this wording carried the implication that some other solution beside the annexation of Tripolitania and Cyrenaica might be possible. It also bound Italy to maintain the existing status quo in Morocco — a pledge which she had not previously assumed.[382] Kiderlen-Wächter, who visited Rome in January, 1912, declared that he was ready immediately to take Italy's wishes into account, and suggested a new version of the supplementary protocol, according to which the status quo was defined as that condition "existing at the moment (July, 1914) when the new treaty shall come into effect." [383] In order to calm San Giuliano's fears of a premature announcement of the renewal of the Triple Alliance, Kiderlen-Wächter proposed a written agreement specifying that the fact of renewal should be given publicity only upon the consent of all three powers.[384] The Austro-Hungarian government gave its assent to these two concessions; [385] but the only result of its complaisance was to bring forth another demand from San Giuliano. This demand, made through the German government, called for the incorporation in the new treaty of the agreement regarding Albania which had been concluded between Austria-Hungary and Italy in December, 1909.[386]

But Count Berchtold, who had taken charge of foreign affairs after Aehrenthal's death on February 17, showed no inclination to consider San Giuliano's ever-increasing importunities. Especially in his first months of office he expressed the opinion that Italy's 'questionable' alliance was not worth the price of further concessions. He therefore declared that he would not consent to any demands which ran contrary to the wishes repeatedly expressed by all parties for a renewal of the treaty as it stood. "If

[382] Mérey to Aehrenthal. Telegram of December 23, 1911, and despatches of December 25, 1911, and January 2, 1912.

[383] Mérey to Aehrenthal, January 23, 1912. Telegram.

[384] Szögyény to Aehrenthal, January 23, 1912 (telegram), and daily report of February 5, 1912.

[385] Telegram to Mérey, March 14, 1912. The wording of the new version regarding Tripoli was as follows: "Il est entendu que le statu quo visé par les articles IX et X du présent traité serait pour la Tripolitaine et la Cyrénaïque celui existant à la date de l'entrée en vigueur du traité."

[386] Szögyény's telegram, March 14, 1912.

once they begin to meddle with the text of the treaty," he remarked to Tschirschky, the German ambassador in Vienna,
"there will be no end to the negotiations; and we might also be
tempted to put that text to a closer examination from the point of
view of our own interests." He went on to say that the Triple
Alliance undeniably contained provisions which were not advantageous to Austria-Hungary, and pointed in particular to Article
II, which bound the Dual Monarchy to participate in a war
launched by France against Italy without provocation on the part
of the latter. "For this no visible equivalent is provided," he
said. He also laid stress on the fact that the wish expressed by
Italy appeared all the more superfluous because the agreement of
December 19, 1909, regarding Albania, particularly specified that
its duration was coterminous with that of the Triple Alliance; its
renewal was therefore implied in the renewal of the main treaty.
Tschirschky observed that the justification for San Giuliano's demands probably lay in his belief that he could better defend the
renewal of the Triple Alliance before the Italian Chamber if he
were able to say that this renewal had not taken place without
changes, thus implying that he had been able to secure certain advantages not provided by the existing stipulations. To this
Berchtold replied that 'this was only one more reason for preserving the existing treaty, since Austria-Hungary obviously had no
interest in letting it appear that the treaty contained new and
one-sided alterations made in favor of Italy.' [387]

Berchtold also championed this view to Emperor William while
the latter was stopping in Vienna on his way to Venice, where a
meeting of the rulers of Germany and Italy was to take place. In
his conversation of March 23, 1912, with Berchtold, Emperor
William declared that every effort must be made to bind Italy as
closely as possible to the Central Powers. The Turco-Italian war,
he said, had been the result of a lamentable blunder of Italian
policy; King Victor Emmanuel would never willingly have taken
the initiative in annexing Tripolitania and Cyrenaica.[388] On the

[387] Daily report of March 16, and telegram to Mérey, March 18, 1912.
[388] This view is also expressed by Jagow in his book *Ursachen und Ausbruch des
Weltkrieges* (1919), p. 47.

contrary, he had expressly stated that he would not lend himself to this project. He had subsequently been driven into the adventure by popular enthusiasm, and had not been strong enough to resist the current. Now Italy was in the midst of a costly struggle, the end of which was not yet in sight. Such a situation could not be disadvantageous either to Germany or to Austria-Hungary. Italy had got into difficulties in North Africa; this drew her into a conflict of interests with France, in the Mediterranean as well as on the African continent, which promised to divert her permanently from the Adriatic. The cooling of Italy's relations with France — those relations which for ten years Barrère had used every legitimate and illegitimate means to strengthen, only to see his efforts come to nothing — must inevitably result in Italy's closer attachment to Austria-Hungary and Germany. As a matter of fact, Victor Emmanuel had told the German Secretary of State that he adhered unreservedly to the Triple Alliance and earnestly desired its renewal.

Berchtold's rejoinder that Italy would be only temporarily diverted from the Adriatic by the annexation of Tripolitania appears to have been "not altogether to the Emperor's liking." The latter did not share Berchtold's doubts, which were based on new despatches from Mérey, as to Italy's inclination immediately to renew the Triple Alliance without alteration. He insisted that Italy must be made sure of as quickly and as completely as possible.[389] Subsequent events showed, however, that the Austro-Hungarian minister had appraised the situation more correctly than the German Emperor. At the conference in Venice, indeed, Victor Emmanuel emphatically expressed his wish to see the Triple Alliance renewed, adding the significant words: "as soon as the question of Tripoli is settled — and it must find a satisfactory solution in the treaty for all time — there can be no obstacle to prevent the Triple Alliance from taking firm root in the consciousness and the feelings of the great masses of the Italian people "[390]

[389] Berchtold's notes on his conversation with Emperor William at Schönbrunn, March 23, 1912.
[390] Mérey to Berchtold, April 4, 1912.

Shortly after, however, on April 14, San Giuliano transmitted an aide-mémoire to Mérey declaring that the revision of the supplementary article, as proposed by the Central Powers, had been rendered inexpedient by the decree of annexation of November 5, 1911, which had become law on February 27, 1912. At that same time he proposed a new version, according to which the status quo established in Articles IX and X, in so far as it concerned Tripolitania and Cyrenaica, should be regarded as that created by the royal law of February 27, 1912, extending the sovereignty of Italy over these two provinces.[391] Furthermore, San Giuliano demanded of Austria-Hungary the insertion of a supplementary protocol in the treaty of the Triple Alliance containing the agreements respectively concluded in 1901 with regard to Albania, and in 1909 with regard to the interpretation of Article VII of the Triple Alliance. Mérey had no objection to make to the latter demand; he held, however, that "as long as Italy's position in both provinces was uncertain, from a military, political, and diplomatic point of view," the former was so impossible of fulfilment that it brought up the question whether "it was not intended to serve the purpose of deferring the renewal of the Triple Alliance until the end of the war, as I have conjectured for months in my despatches." [392] However, since he assumed from the instructions which had previously reached him that an expeditious renewal of the Triple Alliance was desired in Vienna, he forwarded to Berchtold a new version of the passage in the supplementary protocol relating to Tripolitania and Cyrenaica. This version ran: "it is understood that the status quo contemplated by Articles IX and X of the treaty of the Triple Alliance as regards Tripoli and Cyrenaica shall be that expressly recognized by the cabinets of Berlin, Vienna, London, Paris, and St. Petersburg." [393]

[391] Mérey's telegram of April 15, and despatch of April 18, 1912. An aide-mémoire is annexed to the latter. The wording of the supplementary protocol regarding Tripolitania here runs as follows: "Il est entendu que le statu quo visé par les articles 9 et 10 du présent traité en ce qui concerne la Tripolitaine et la Cyrénaïque est celui qui a été créé par la loi du royaume du 27 février 1912 étendant la souveraineté de l'Italie sur les deux provinces."

[392] Ibid.

[393] "Il est entendu que le statu quo visé par les articles 9 et 10 du présent traité en ce qui concerne la Tripolitaine et la Cyrénaïque est celui que les cabinets de Berlin,

Mérey's draft was rejected in Vienna. Berchtold, who was being urged to the utmost complaisance by Germany, was trying to find a solution which should take account of Italy's wishes, and at the same time enable him to maintain the stand, which he had taken on principle, 'that it was not proper to refer in an international treaty to a national Italian law in the making of which the other contracting parties had taken no part.' For this reason the project evolved by him, with the assent of the German government, provided that "the status quo contemplated in Articles IX and X of the treaty of the Triple Alliance shall be, so far as Tripolitania and Cyrenaica are concerned, that created by the fact that Italy has extended her sovereignty over these two provinces." [394] Berchtold had Turkey in mind when he stipulated that this concession should be made conditional on the preservation of the strictest secrecy. [395] As for Italy's wish to add to the treaty a supplementary protocol containing the two agreements of 1901 and 1909, he definitely refused this, "because it runs counter to the idea of renewing the treaty without change, which has been approved by all concerned; because, in view of Italy's activities in the present war, it does not seem suitable for us to limit our freedom of action in Albania by treaty for a number of years; and, finally, because the convention regarding the sanjak stands in organic connection with the treaty of the Triple Alliance, since, according to its wording, it will likewise be implicitly renewed upon the prolongation of the Triple Alliance." [396]

Berchtold's refusal to meet San Giuliano's wishes in this matter was less unacceptable to the Italians, who were not sorry to have the renewal of the Triple Alliance delayed, than in Berlin, where the greatest importance was laid on securing Italy's accession as speedily as possible [397] Since the beginning of April the German

de Vienne, de Londres, de Paris, et de St. Pétersbourg auront expressément reconnu."

[394] "Il est entendu que le statu quo visé par les articles IX et X du présent traité est en ce qui concerne la Tripolitaine et la Cyrénaïque celui créé par le fait que l'Italie a étendu sa souveraineté sur ces deux provinces."

[395] Instruction of May 22, 1912.

[396] Ibid.

[397] In his *Politische Vorgeschichte des grossen Krieges*, p. 81, Reventlow gives the new situation in the Mediterranean as Germany's reason for pressing for a prema-

statesmen, in accordance with a promise given the king of Italy at Venice by Emperor William, had been exerting pressure on the Austro-Hungarian government to secure a revocation of the protest made by Aehrenthal, in the winter of 1911,[398] against the naval demonstration planned by the Italians against Turkey.[399] When Berchtold firmly refused to meet their wishes,[400] they again brought forward the urgent necessity of holding Italy to the Triple Alliance.

"If there should some day be a war with France," Kiderlen-Wächter said, "Austria-Hungary must have no worries regarding her southwestern frontier. She will invade Serbia and array the bulk of her troops against Russia. Germany will likewise march against Russia with a portion of her fighting forces; her main army, however, will fall upon France with its full strength. I do not now believe that Italy will simply tear up the treaty of the Triple Alli-

ture renewal of the Triple Alliance. There was also the consideration "that Italy, puffed up by her success, would clamor for war against Austria-Hungary. Such a war would also, in a measure, be forced on Italy if several more years were to pass before the normal period of renewal of the treaty of the Triple Alliance and the influences hostile to the Triple Alliance in and out of Italy were to have time to do their work."

[398] The two instructions from Aehrenthal, to Mérey and Szögyény respectively, are printed in the Red Book, pp. 203 f.

[399] Berchtold to Mérey, April 6, 13, and 15, 1912. Cf. Red Book, pp. 17 ff. and 206 f. Bethmann-Hollweg (op. cit., pp. 73 f.) throws light on Germany's efforts to prevent the differences between Italy and Austria-Hungary "from becoming a serious menace."

[400] The decisive conference between the Duke of Avarna and Berchtold took place on April 15. The former laid the greatest stress on the fact that Italy's enterprise would involve an island of Turkey in Asia, and not the coasts and islands of Turkey in Europe. Berchtold thereupon pointed to Article VII of the treaty of the Triple Alliance, which drew no distinction between European and Asiatic islands, but referred only in very general terms to "coasts and islands of the Aegean Sea." Berchtold to Mérey, April 16, 1912. Shortly after this Berchtold learned that Italian war vessels had appeared before the entrance of the Dardanelles and had fired upon the fortifications on the European shore. He instructed Mérey to inform the Italian government that since these naval activities had so far caused no reaction in the Balkans, and as "there can be no question of a change of the status quo on the coasts and islands of the Aegean Sea," he would make no protests to Italy. He was obliged, however, to call San Giuliano's attention to the fact that he was unable to recede from the position taken by his predecessor (Aehrenthal), and must let Italy assume the entire responsibility for the possible consequences of her action. Berchtold to Mérey, April 20, 1912. Cf. Fraknói, pp. 75 f.

ance; the personality of the king offers security against that. I believe, rather, that Italy will slowly mobilize and play the waiting game, so to speak. If the first decisive battle with France should turn out favorably to Germany, Italy will coöperate against France. If, however, France should score a great initial victory, Italy's attitude toward us might possibly become alarming. If we assume an initial victory for the German arms, I consider it highly probable that Russia, whose mobilization will take place very slowly, will inform France that she feels it wiser to declare her neutrality. When the time for peace arrives, she will thus be able to back up her words with an unimpaired military strength. It is of the greatest importance that France should declare war, not Germany. In such an event England, to my thinking, will not participate directly in the war, but will send a fleet to Antwerp, her watchword being the preservation of Belgian neutrality, and also possibly land troops there. This would, of course, be an impediment to Germany, for her army would consequently be exposed on the flank. If the war should turn out unfavorably for France, England will observe this sort of neutrality to the end." He believed, however, that France would not desire war; conditions in the French army and fleet were appalling. He held, nevertheless, that it was of the greatest importance to renew the Triple Alliance as quickly as possible; and to bring this about it would be necessary to give Italy full liberty of military action against the Dardanelles.[401]

Count Berchtold's unwillingness to yield this point, together with his rejection of some of the stipulations upon which Italy had conditioned her assent to the renewal of the Triple Alliance, evoked a fresh storm of complaints and entreaties in Berlin. Berchtold remained unshaken. He justified his attitude in detail in a private letter to Szögyény. "In Berlin," he wrote, "this drama of the Turco-Italian conflict appears to be regarded only from the point of view of the renewal of the Triple Alliance. In this they are guided by the fixed idea of Italy's defection to the Western Powers, although they point out at the same time that a

[401] Private letter of the Austro-Hungarian chargé d'affaires in Berlin, Count Flotow, to Berchtold, April 23, 1912.

divergence of interests between Italy on one side, and England and France on the other, has been brought about by the expedition to Tripolitania. By putting forward this latter consideration, they hope to make more palatable for us the view held in Berlin that Italy will thus be driven to a closer and more sincere connection with us, and diverted from the further pursuit of an Austrophobe Adriatic policy. If this view is correct, we may ask whether the fear of Italy's desertion of the Triple Alliance at this present moment has any logical foundation. This continual allusion to public opinion in Italy, which would use intimations of our opposition to a naval demonstration against the Dardanelles to attack the policy of the Triple Alliance, makes one involuntarily doubt the practical value of an alliance in which one party seeks to set aside its obligations whenever it finds it convenient to do so, and the other party is expected to give its approval merely for the sake of holding its unreliable partner in the alliance. Germany herself appears to have misgivings regarding Italy's pledges, since only recently Kiderlen-Wächter, while impressing on our chargé d'affaires the necessity of giving free scope to Italy's wishes, aired the opinion that in the event of a Franco-German war Italy might make her final decision only when the outcome of the conflict was decided. In the treaty of the Triple Alliance of 1882 Italy fared so well that she would probably think twice before recklessly jeopardizing these advantages." Berchtold therefore denied the necessity of making fresh concessions to the undependable ally. "From all reports which reach us from Constantinople," he continued, "it would appear that the occupation of an island near the entrance of the Dardanelles — even Mitylene — would be regarded by Bulgaria as a signal to trespass beyond her frontiers. And yet in spite of this we are bidden to give Italy carte blanche. The occupation of islands farther to the south would serve only as the cause of unpleasant, not to say serious, difficulties between ourselves and Italy with regard to the interpretation of Article VII of the Triple Alliance." [402]

Berchtold held that further concessions in the matter of the supplementary protocol were as undesirable as in the question of

[402] Berchtold to Szögyény, May 8, 1912. Draft and copy.

the naval demonstration, and firmly persisted in his refusal to accept the latest Italian demands. The negotiations were deferred. The Turco-Italian war proceeded on its course. Italy did not succeed in the conquest of Tripolitania; her victories by land and sea were insignificant, especially after the Arabs and Turks had begun to fight under the leadership of Enver Bey. History now repeated itself, however, and an Italian victory was brought about by the intervention of other powers. In October, 1912, the First Balkan War broke out. The Turks, hard pressed by new adversaries, were forced to bow to circumstance and give up Tripoli. On October 18, 1912, the peace of Lausanne delivered into the hands of the Italians this long and ardently coveted land: a success which was due in no small measure to Germany's benevolent neutrality, and to the correct and conciliatory bearing of the Austro-Hungarian government.

It was not gratitude for these services which determined the attitude of the Italian statesmen, but cold calculation of their own interests: and these unmistakably demanded adherence to the policy which had been so profitably pursued in the past. Relations with the Triple Entente must continually be made more cordial; but first and foremost came the maintenance of the Triple Alliance. At the time when the peace of Lausanne was being signed, the Slavic peoples of the Balkans were winning their first great military victories over the Turks. No one could predict how far their successes would lead them. Italy's interests in the Adriatic, which had never been lost sight of and which emerged from obscurity after the struggle for Tripoli had come to an end, could not but be touched in a sensitive spot by the turn of events in the Balkans. Nothing had been left undone by the Italian government to prevent an extension of the Austro-Hungarian sphere of influence on the Adriatic, and to make sure by numerous written agreements that the Dual Monarchy would keep its hands off Albania. Should Italy then stand calmly by and watch an aggressive Slavic Balkan state gain a foothold on the Adriatic in place of conservative Austria-Hungary? Divergent though the interests and plans of the cabinets of Vienna and Rome might be with regard to the Balkans, they had in common the wish to avert a

Slavic domination of the Adriatic. The Italian statesmen were therefore eager to conclude the renewal of the Triple Alliance for a lengthy term of years, and thus make sure of Austria-Hungary's assistance in the event that this should be needed to check the over-ambitious claims of the Greeks or Serbs.

A further and no less important consideration lay in the fact that the prolongation of the alliance afforded Italy the one sure guaranty that Austria-Hungary, pledged as she was to the provisions of Article VII, would take no independent steps frustrating Italy's plans in the Balkans. Finally, there was one more reason determining Italy to accelerate the renewal of the alliance. Tripolitania had been promised her by the treaty of Lausanne, but as yet only a portion of the country was subdued. No one could tell how long it would take her to gain control of the whole territory. In view of this, it must have been acceptable to the Italians when the Central Powers showed an inclination during the negotiations of the winter of 1911–1912 to assume a guaranty of the status quo in this newly acquired region. In the summer of 1912, too, concern was caused in Italy by the considerable strengthening of the French Mediterranean fleet.[403] All these factors taken together decided San Giuliano in favor of a resumption of the negotiations which had been suspended since May, 1912. On the occasion of his meeting with Count Berchtold at Pisa and San Rossore (October 21–23, 1912), he proposed that the matter be settled as quickly as possible.[404] At the same time he handed over the draft of a supplementary protocol which indicated that the Italian government had not only retained all the demands made by it in the spring, but had sought to express them in the manner best suited to its own interests. For instance, San Giuliano's draft contained the stipulation that the two separate agreements con-

[403] Baron Ambrózy informed Berchtold on September 24, 1912, of the great excitement caused in Italy by this action of France. "Especially certain circles, which (as they pretend) wished to make the renewal of the Triple Alliance conditional upon satisfactory guaranties of the preservation of Italy's interests in the Mediterranean, appear to have gone wild over the fact that France takes this particular time to act in a way which makes it impossible for Italy to choose which group of powers is to safeguard her position in the Mediterranean."

[404] Baron Ambrózy to Berchtold, Rome, September 24, 1912.

cluded between Austria-Hungary and Italy in 1900–01 and 1909, with particular reference to Albania, "should be regarded as an integral part of the existing treaty." [405]

The situation was a most difficult one for Berchtold. The complications in the Balkans which seemed to threaten the peace of the world; the tension between the courts of Vienna and St. Petersburg; Serbia's claims on the Adriatic coast — all these forced him to treat with the utmost consideration the wishes of the Italians, who at that particular moment appeared inclined to take joint action with Austria-Hungary in the Balkans. On the other hand, however, he wished to avoid everything which might arouse further Italian aspirations in the Balkans and particularly in Albania. He therefore replied to San Giuliano's declaration with the assurance that he realized of what value the Triple Alliance had been in maintaining the world's peace, and that he was ready to assent to its prolongation; but that he was obliged to make a stand against the incorporation in the treaty of the two separate agreements already alluded to. If this were done, it would be no longer a question of the renewal of the treaty as it was. Since the Triple Alliance had so far served Italy's interests far more than those of Austria-Hungary, he should be obliged to demand consideration of the wishes of the Dual Monarchy in the event of any alterations in the treaty. San Giuliano contradicted this, and an exhaustive debate followed. Both defended their posi-

[405] The wording of this draft is as follows:

"Au moment de procéder à la signature du traité de ce jour entre l'Italie, l'Allemagne, et l'Autriche-Hongrie, les plénipotentiaires soussignés de ces trois puissances, à ce dûment autorisés, se déclarent mutuellement ce qui suit:

"Il est entendu que le statu quo visé par les articles 9 et 10 du présent traité en ce qui concerne la Tripolitaine et la Cyrénaïque est celui qui a été créé par la loi du royaume du 25 février 1912, étendant la souveraineté de l'Italie sur ces deux provinces et reconnu par les gouvernements d'Allemagne et d'Autriche-Hongrie.

"Les accords secrets spéciaux existant actuellement entre l'Italie et l'Autriche-Hongrie et dont communication a été donnée en son temps au gouvernement Allemand, à savoir:

"1°. L'accord concernant l'Albanie, consigné dans l'échange de notes Visconti-Venosta-Goluchowski du 20 décembre 1900–9 février 1901;

"2°. L'accord concernant le sandjak de Novibazar et l'interprétation de l'article VII du traité, consigné dans l'échange de notes Guicciardini-Aehrenthal 30 novembre–15 décembre 1909, sont considérés comme partie intégrante du présent traité."

tions with equal obstinacy; San Giuliano finally quoted Premier Giolitti, "who, as a lawyer, placed the greatest value on the inclusion in one treaty instrument of all agreements existing between Austria-Hungary and Italy." [406] The ministers separated without having reached any agreement. No more successful were the negotiations which took place at the beginning of November in Vienna and Rome. Berchtold took it upon himself to win over the Duke of Avarna; [407] Mérey, San Giuliano. [408] Berchtold's efforts were quite fruitless; Mérey succeeded only in getting San Giuliano to admit that he recognized the justice of Berchtold's objection to the incorporation of the two separate agreements in the treaty. He made no mention, however, of any intention to forego his demands.

Berchtold, who in the meanwhile had been informed from Berlin that Kiderlen-Wächter appreciated the objections made by him, believed that he could now attain his purpose by exerting fresh pressure on the Italian statesmen. On November 8 he telegraphed to Mérey that he had no intention of accepting the Italian demand for the incorporation of the two agreements in the treaty of the Triple Alliance. [409] On the same day, however, a despatch from Berlin showed that he had made a miscalculation. Kiderlen-Wächter, with Szögyény's coöperation, had conducted negotiations with San Giuliano, who had arrived in Berlin on November 4, resulting in a complete unanimity of their views on all important questions of European policy. The future of Albania was also discussed in detail, and it was decided that the autonomous development of that region would best harmonize with the interests of Austria-Hungary and Italy and with the agreements existing between the two countries. The chief feature of the conference was the renewal of the Triple Alliance, which was urgently demanded by public opinion in Germany and Austria-Hungary, and which San Giuliano advocated with the greatest energy. There still existed the difficulty, however, which

---

[406] Daily report of October 26, 1912, regarding Berchtold's conversations with San Giuliano at Pisa and Florence; also instruction to Szögyény, November 1, 1912.

[407] Berchtold to Szögyény, October 30 and November 3, 1912. Telegram.

[408] Mérey to Berchtold, November 5, 1912.

[409] Berchtold to Mérey, November 8, 1912. Telegram.

had arisen between the Italian and Austro-Hungarian governments with regard to the manner of including the agreements of
1900–01 and 1909 in the new treaty. In order to overcome these,
Kiderlen-Wächter and San Giuliano drew up a new supplementary
protocol. In substance, this satisfied Italy's demands; in form,
Berchtold's wishes.

It was decided that the territorial status quo in the North
African regions of the Mediterranean, referred to in Article IX of
the treaty of the Triple Alliance of June 28, 1902, should include
the sovereignty of Italy over Tripolitania and Cyrenaica, and that
in future the status quo existing in the North African territories
at the time of the signature of the new treaty should serve as a
basis for the provisions of Article X of the same treaty. Emphasis
was also laid on the fact that the special agreements concluded in
1900–01 and 1909 between Austria-Hungary and Italy had undergone no modifications by reason of this renewal of the treaty. Any
reference to the law of February, 1912, regarding the annexation
of Tripolitania and Cyrenaica was thus abandoned, together with
San Giuliano's earlier idea that the two agreements of 1900–01
and 1909 should be expressly designated as an integral part of the
treaty of the Triple Alliance.[410] Giolitti immediately gave his approval to this new version. Kiderlen-Wächter informed Berchtold of this, and urgently recommended him to accept this new
and (as he thought) unobjectionably worded supplementary protocol. His admonition had its effect; Berchtold agreed to the new
project. The defeats of the Turks and the great danger to Austria-
Hungary growing out of the advance of the Serbs against Albania
gave him no alternative. On November 14 he instructed Mérey
to inform San Giuliano that he would lay aside his previous objections and assent to the latest version of the supplementary protocol, on the condition that as soon as the treaty was signed Italy
would publicly proclaim the renewal of the Triple Alliance without change.[411] San Giuliano was quite ready to meet Berchtold's

---

[410] Szögyény to Berchtold, November 8, 1912. Telegram. Cf. Bethmann-
Hollweg, p. 75. See the text in Vol. I, pp. 256, 258.

[411] Berchtold to Mérey, November 14, 1912. Telegram.

wish. He gave a written promise to this effect,[412] and added orally that "even later he would allow no intimation to be made that any change had taken place in the supplementary protocol." [413] In return for this, the Central Powers were to grant San Giuliano's request and reinstate in the new treaty the supplementary protocol of June 30, 1902, thus modified, and changed in form from a declaration by Austria-Hungary alone to a regular second final protocol signed by the three powers.[414] The signature of the treaty took place at Vienna on December 5, 1912; the ratifications were exchanged on December 19, 1912. The new treaty, instead of going immediately into effect, was to await the expiration of the existing agreement on July 8, 1914. Its term of validity was to last until 1920, or, in case it were not denounced one year before this, until July 8, 1926.

[412] Mérey to Berchtold, November 20, 1912. Telegram and despatch. The letter of San Giuliano to Mérey runs as follows: "En me rapportant à nos derniers entretiens et aprés avoir pris les ordres de S.M. le roi j'ai l'honneur de faire connaître à V.E. que nous sommes prêts à procéder à la signature du renouvellement du traité de la Triple Alliance et du protocole additionnel dans la rédaction concordée. Nous sommes également prêts à faire publier de notre côté que le traité de la Triple Alliance a été renouvelé tel quel sans aucune modification. La date et la forme sous lesquelles cette publication aura lieu de la part des trois gouvernements devront étre concertées ultérieurement entre eux."

[413] Mérey to Berchtold, November 20, 1912.

[414] Tschirschky to Berchtold, December 2, 1912. Cf. Vol. I, pp. 232 f., 256–259.

CONCLUSION

It hardly lies within the province of this work to describe the last days of the Triple Alliance down to the time of its disruption by Italy in May, 1915.[415] The break, when it came, was earlier and more complete than had been foreseen by any of the statesmen who participated in the renewal of the treaty in December, 1912; for it seemed at first that this renewal would be followed by a new blossoming of friendly relations between the allies. Italy's diplomatic intercourse with Germany became steadily more friendly. While strictly safeguarding Italy's special interests, San Giuliano was able not only to preserve correct relations with Austria-Hungary, but also to provide a basis for common action in important political questions. During the Balkan troubles which filled 1913, he repeatedly joined Berchtold in defending, before the council of great European powers, the policy of checking the advance of the Slavic peoples toward the Adriatic, and won many a success which was to the advantage of the Dual Monarchy as well.

Italy participated with great zeal in the military measures which were designed to ward off a possible aggressive move on the part of the Triple Entente. The Italian General Staff had, it is true, informed the German and Austro-Hungarian governments, toward the end of 1912, that in view of the existing political situation Italy could not fulfil the agreements previously made with Germany, and that the third Italian army could not serve as the left wing of the German army and engage France beyond the Rhine.[416] However, as Berlin was promised at the same time that

[415] Cf. Fraknói, pp. 86 ff.; Doerkes-Boppard, pp. 45 ff.

[416] By order of the General Staff of the Italian army, the following communication was transmitted in Vienna on December 18, 1912, by the Italian military attaché, Major A. Albricci: "Par loyauté d'allié on fait connaître, que jusqu'à nouvelle décision on est obligé de supprimer l'envoi de la 3ième armée italienne sur le Rhin, parceque l'Italie dans les conditions actuelles ne pourrait se priver de telle partie des forces. L'état major I. et R. pourrait cependant, le cas échéant, disposer de ses lignes de chemin de fer et du matériel qui seraient actuellement destinés aux transports italiens." According to the information supplied by the Chief of the German

in the interest of her allies Italy's entire fighting force would be disposed south of the Alps along the coast, no great importance was attached, at least by the Germans,[417] to Italy's withdrawal from her obligations; in fact, new agreements were concluded in the course of 1913 regarding the employment of the land forces in case of war.[418] At the same time a new agreement providing for the disposition of the naval forces of the allies was reached as the result of the naval conventions [419] concluded between France and Russia, in July, and between France and England in the autumn of 1912. The three fleets were no longer to operate separately, as stipulated by the naval convention of December, 1900, but were to take joint action, in order to attain as expeditiously as possible their goal, the naval supremacy of the Mediterranean. The protection of the Adriatic and the prevention of the transport of French colonial troops from Africa to Europe were also provided for in the convention.[420]

In spite of all these agreements, in spite of San Giuliano's constantly repeated assurances that the Triple Alliance must remain the corner stone of Italian foreign policy, the fact could not long

Admiralty Staff, Vice-Admiral von Heeringen, to the Austro-Hungarian naval attaché at Berlin, Count Colloredo-Mannsfeld (despatch dated Berlin, January 11, 1913), the communication made to Berlin stated that the Italian General Staff had renounced its original plan of taking a portion of the Italian army over the Brenner Pass into South Germany in the event of a joint war, and employing it against France as the left wing of the German army. Its intention now was to dispose the entire Italian army south of the Alps along the coast.

[417] In Austria-Hungary this declaration was characterized by the opponents of Italy as fresh proof of her faithlessness. On December 19 Conrad wrote to Berchtold that he was transmitting Albricci's communication, "which permits me to declare with satisfaction that I was not deceived in my appraisal of Italy's friendship. I can only regret that we did not come to a reckoning with this unreliable neighbor years ago, as I repeatedly pointed out the necessity of doing."

[418] Documents in the State Archives.

[419] The text of the Franco-Russian naval agreement of July 16, 1912, appears, among others, in *Deutschland Schuldig?*, the German White Book regarding the responsibility of the authors of the war (1919), p. 145. For the Anglo-French agreements, see E. von Reventlow, *Politische Vorgeschichte des grossen Krieges* (1919), pp. 265 ff.; Helfferich, *op. cit.*, i, pp. 23 ff.

[420] The agreement received legal force on November 1, after having been prepared in draft on June 23 and completed on August 2. Cf. the text, Vol. I, pp. 282–305. The conclusion was reached only after long negotiations, regarding which there is abundant material in the State Archives.

be kept hidden that the Triple Alliance was never again to acquire its old-time power. "The obligations assumed by Rome were too numerous," declared Bethmann-Hollweg after the break had come. "All sorts of ties bound Italy not only to the Western Powers, but to Russia as well." [421]

ʃ So it happened that in spite of San Giuliano's efforts and the accommodating spirit of the cabinet of Vienna, the insurmountable divergence of interests existing between the two powers in all Balkan matters kept asserting itself and blighting every attempt at conciliation. Italy kept company with the Dual Monarchy as long as it was a question of checking the Slavic onrush to the Adriatic; but whenever the Austro-Hungarian statesmen made a move meant to enlarge the sphere of influence of their country in the Balkans, the Italian government opposed them most energetically and frustrated their plans. This was the case in the spring of 1913, when Berchtold announced the intention of using armed force, if necessary, to compel the evacuation of Scutari. This city had been occupied on April 23 by the Montenegrin troops of King Nikita, who refused to hand it over to Albania, constituted a state by the Conference of London. San Giuliano immediately protested against any independent action of the cabinet of Vienna, on the ground that this would be contrary to Article VII of the treaty of the Triple Alliance, while Tittoni, the Italian ambassador in Paris, declared that the Triple Alliance would cease to exist on the day when Austria-Hungary took it upon herself to disturb the balance of power in the Adriatic in any manner whatsoever. [422] At the beginning of July, 1913, [423] this conviction was repeated by San Giuliano in a still more pointed form, when Berchtold, realizing the perils that threatened Bulgaria

---

[421] Bethmann-Hollweg, *Betrachtungen zum Weltkriege*, i, pp. 75 f.

[422] Cf. Fraknói, pp. 97 ff.; Doerkes-Boppard, pp. 22 f.

[423] In a speech before the Chamber in December, 1914, Giolitti read the telegrams exchanged between him and San Giuliano in this matter, and designated August 9 as the day on which this took place. This, however, is an error. The telegraphic exchange of views between Premier Giolitti and San Giuliano, Minister of Foreign Affairs, took place on July 9. (Mérey's despatch of July 12, 1913.) Cf. Fraknói, pp. 104 ff.; Reventlow, pp. 277 ff. Since both authors assume that Berchtold first planned the move against Serbia at the beginning of August, their inferences stand in need of correction.

from the combined armies of Serbia, Greece, and Rumania, announced in Rome and in Berlin that Austria-Hungary could not witness any further large territorial acquisitions by Serbia with composure, "since this would not only imply a considerable moral and material strengthening of a neighbor which has been traditionally hostile towards us, but would also necessarily result in encouraging to no small degree the idea of a Greater Serbia and its propaganda." [424] San Giuliano protested energetically against this imperilling of the peace of the world by the Austrian government. This was all the less justified, he declared, "because there is no question of any imminent peril — certainly not of any serious threat against the existence of the Dual Monarchy — but rather of fancied future dangers which can easily be averted by other means than by war." [425] "On vous retiendra," he said to Mérey, "par les pans de votre redingote, si c'est nécessaire." [426]

At that time a breach was avoided. Germany seemed inclined to back up Italy, and Berchtold beat a retreat. Serbia was thus enabled by the peace of Bucharest to add materially to her possessions in Macedonia. Austria-Hungary waited in vain for Italy to make some returns for her compliance. San Giuliano, it is true, supported Berchtold when, in the autumn of 1913, he demanded that the Serbs evacuate the Albanian territory occupied by them in violation of the agreements of London; but this was simply because Italy's special interests called for a checkmate of Serbia's

[424] Berchtold to Mérey (in Rome) and to Szögyény (in Berlin), July 4, 1913.
[425] Mérey to Berchtold, July 12, 1913. Mérey reported that in a conversation with San Giuliano, the Italian Minister of Foreign Affairs had alluded to his impressions of the meeting of the sovereigns of Italy and Germany at Kiel early in July, 1913, and to a visit which he had received shortly before from the Rumanian ambassador, and had then stated "that we (Austria-Hungary) would alienate ourselves from our two other allies, Germany and Rumania, by the attitude we had taken." (Berchtold noted here, "Rumania has staked her existence on the possibility of a European conflagration.") "Both, indeed, are pursuing a policy diametrically opposed to ours — namely, the weakening of Bulgaria and no hostility in any event toward Serbia." (Berchtold noted here, "This was not formerly the German policy.") "Is it possible that these states will reverse this policy for our sake, and, in addition, bring upon themselves a European conflagration?" (Berchtold noted here, "But we are expected to do so for the sake of Germany and Rumania.")
[426] Ibid. Berchtold noted here, "Tschirschky declares the contrary."

schemes.[427] Germany, acting as intermediary, also succeeded in obtaining Italy's assent to the choice of Prince William of Wied as prince of Albania. The divergence of Austro-Hungarian and Italian interests in Albania, however, kept cropping out again and again, undermining the understanding laboriously built up in 1912 and 1913 between the two Adriatic powers. Although San Giuliano [428] told Berchtold at Abbazia that 'every Italian statesman acknowledged the justice of the idea of an independent Albania, and would give it his support,' and although he again expressed his belief that without the aid of Austria-Hungary, Italy would he overwhelmed by the onrushing Slavic tide, the attitude of the Italian press and the Italian agents, especially during the second Albanian revolt, which began in May, 1914, showed how little control San Giuliano exercised over public opinion in his country. While he was again presenting to the Chamber on May 26, 1914,[429] a comprehensive programme of conciliation based on the principle of an independent Albania under the Prince of Wied, Italy's diplomatic representatives in Albania were doing everything in their power to undermine the power of the new ruler, and the Italian press was assuming a progressively harsher attitude toward Austria-Hungary's Albanian policy.

It was the Serbian question, however, and not that of Albania, which decided the fate of the Triple Alliance. On June 28, 1914, a few days before the new treaty of the Triple Alliance was to go into force, Archduke Francis Ferdinand, the heir to the Austro-Hungarian throne, was murdered by conspirators of Serbian nationality. The difficulties arising between Austria-Hungary and Serbia as the result of this deed led several weeks later to the hostilities which brought the World War in their train. Of no avail were the efforts of the Central Powers to induce Italy, as an ally, to join them in the conflict. The Italian statesmen asserted that the casus foederis provided for in the treaty had not been established. They promised benevolent neutrality toward their allies, indeed,

[427] Frakn6i, p. 109.

[428] Berchtold's notes on his conversations with San Giuliano at Abbazia, April 14 to 18, 1914.

[429] Hashagen, *Umrisse der Weltpolitik*, ii, p. 131.

but at the same time they put forward claims to the compensation which, they asserted, was due them in accordance with Article VII of the treaty. After a prolonged resistance Count Berchtold yielded to German pressure and accepted in principle the justice of these claims. The negotiations begun forthwith led, however, to no result, since the Italian demands became greater with the failure of the expected decisive victories of the Central Powers to materialize. Toward the end of 1914 they were extended by Sonnino, the new Italian Foreign Minister, to include portions of old Austrian territory. The statesmen of Austria-Hungary, yielding step by step to Italian pressure and urged by Germany to make the greatest possible concessions, reluctantly acceded in principle to these demands. All to no purpose. Italy raised her price from month to month, until it had reached a height transcending all measure. At the same time she was continuing extensive negotiations with the Triple Entente, and preparing for battle against her allies. By the end of April, 1915, she had concluded binding agreements with the adversaries of the Central Powers. Soon after this, on May 4, Sonnino informed Vienna that he was forced to give up hope of coming to an agreement with Austria-Hungary, although the Dual Monarchy had proclaimed its willingness to make new and far-reaching concessions. Italy then declared the existing alliance void, and reserved for herself all freedom of action in the future. On May 20, thirty-three years to a day after the signature of the first treaty of the Triple Alliance, the Italian Chamber gave its sanction to the action of the government and empowered the Salandra-Sonnino cabinet to proceed as it thought best. Three days later Victor Emmanuel III declared war on Austria-Hungary, and Italy openly ranged herself with the enemies of the Central Powers, a step for which she had been preparing for many years.

Without decisive victories in the field, Italy brought the war to a conclusion satisfactory to herself. By authority of the victors she has been promised not only the 'unredeemed provinces,' but also large districts inhabited almost exclusively by Germans, and great territories with an overwhelmingly Slavic population. Austria-Hungary, her old rival in the contest for mastery of the

Adriatic, no longer exists as a national entity. But the danger of French domination in the Mediterranean, through fear of which Italy had allied herself with the Central Powers, exists as much today as ever before; and in place of Austria-Hungary, weakened as she was by grave internal difficulties and incapable of an energetic policy of action, the Slavic peoples have secured a firm foothold on the Adriatic, and are showing a determination to continue the struggle for the mastery of this sea with all their power.

One can not deny that the men who guided Italian foreign policy during the generation which has passed since the conclusion of the first treaty of the Triple Alliance proved themselves to be clever diplomats. Whether they were far-seeing statesmen, whether they secured lasting advantages for their country, only the future can disclose.

APPENDICES

APPENDIX A

THE AGREEMENTS OF SCHÖNBRUNN, REICHSTADT, AND BUDAPEST

In September, 1872, on the occasion of the meeting at Berlin of the German, Russian, and Austrian emperors, accompanied by their foreign ministers, questions of policy were confidentially discussed. No written agreements were entered into; but a general understanding was reached, and an informal league of the Three Emperors was concluded, a league which may be regarded as the precursor of the secret formal one created by the treaty of 1881.[1] These oral agreements of 1872 were supplemented in the following year by two written ones. In May, 1873, during a return visit to St. Petersburg, a convention was signed by Emperor William I with Tsar Alexander II. This, however, Bismarck later refused to regard as binding because it was not countersigned by himself.[2] Soon afterwards, during a stay of Alexander II in Vienna, a convention was signed at the palace of Schönbrunn between Austria and Russia, which may be regarded as the complement of the German-Russian one. It was, indeed, even more noteworthy, because Austria and Russia had aspirations and interests difficult to reconcile with one another, whereas Germany had no questions pending with either. This convention of Schönbrunn, whose terms are now first published, was conservative in its nature, and did not look forward to changes in the political map of Europe. It was intended to avert possible difficulties between the two empires, and it succeeded in doing so during the next three years. Even in the early days of a new crisis in the Eastern Question Russia and Austria worked together. Both subscribed to the Andrássy note of January, 1876, and the memorandum of Berlin of May, 1876, demanding reforms on the part of the Turks; but as the situation became more acute, and hostilities spread in the

[1] For the text of the treaty, see Vol. I, p. 36.
[2] The general purport of this convention has long been known, but the exact terms have not yet been published.

Balkan Peninsula, the need was felt of a further understanding. This was reached at a brief meeting between Francis Joseph and Alexander and their foreign ministers at Reichstadt in Bohemia, and the result was noted down in a memorandum by Andrássy. By this new agreement, whose text we at last have, Russia gave her provisional assent to the Austrian occupation of Bosnia and Herzegovina. In return Austria assented to the recovery by Russia of the part of Bessarabia of which she had been deprived after the Crimean war.

But the agreement of Reichstadt was not explicit and comprehensive enough to meet the necessities of a difficult and changing situation. As the months passed and as the probability of war between Russia and Turkey increased, the relations between Russia and Austria became strained. Convinced that they could

1. THE CONVENTION OF SCHÖNBRUNN. 1873.

(a)

Agreement between the Emperor-King of Austria-Hungary and the Emperor of Russia.

S.M. l'empereur d'Autriche et roi de Hongrie et S. M. l'empeur [sic] de toutes les Russies: désirant donner une forme pratique à la pensée qui préside à leur entente intime, dans le but de consolider l'état de paix qui existe actuellement en Europe, et ayant à coeur d'éloigner les chances de guerre qui pourraient la troubler, — convaincus que ce but ne saurait être mieux atteint que par une entente directe et personnelle entre les souverains, entente indépendante des changemens qui pourraient se faire dans leurs administrations, sont tombés d'accord sur les points suivans:

1°. L. L. M. M. se promettent mutuellement, lors même que les intérêts de leurs états présenteraient quelques divergences à propos de questions spéciales, de se concerter afin que ces divergences ne puissent pas prévaloir sur les considérations d'un ordre plus élevé qui les préoccupent. L. L. M. M. sont décidés à empêcher qu'on ne puisse réussir à les séparer sur le terrain des principes qu'elles considèrent comme seuls capables d'assurer et s'il le

not safely advance against the Turks without first assuring their flank and rear against Austrian hostility, the Russians, after turning in vain to Bismarck for support or even for an assurance of neutrality, saw themselves obliged to come to specific terms with Austria before they could proceed against the Turks. These were reached after some negotiation; and the results were set down in two conventions, concluded, the one in January, the other in March, 1877, but fused together into one document and given the earlier date. It was with this treaty in her pocket that Russia went to war against the Turks; it was this that Austria accused her of violating by the Peace of San Stefano; and it was this that pre vented her at the Congress of Berlin from objecting to the granting of Bosnia and Herzegovina to Austria, little as she liked it.

A. C. C.

1. THE CONVENTION OF SCHÖNBRUNN. 1873.

(a)

Agreement between the Emperor-King of Austria-Hungary and the Emperor of Russia.

His Majesty the Emperor of Austria and King of Hungary and His Majesty the Emperor of All the Russias: desiring to give a practical form to the thought which presides over their intimate understanding, with the object of consolidating the state of peace which exists at present in Europe, and having at heart to reduce the chances of war which might disturb it — convinced that this object could not better be attained than by a direct and personal understanding between the Sovereigns, an understanding independent of the changes which might be made in their administrations, have come into agreement upon the following points:

1. Their Majesties mutually promise, even though the interests of their States should present some divergences respecting special questions, to take counsel together in order that these divergences may not be able to prevail over the considerations of a higher order which preoccupy them. Their Majesties are determined to prevent any one from succeeding in separating them in the field of the principles which they regard as alone capable of

faut d'imposer le maintien de la paix de l'Europe contre tous les bouleversemens de quelque côté qu'ils viennent.

2°. Pour le cas où une agression venant d'une puissance tierce menacerait de compromettre la paix Européenne L. L. M. M. s'engagent mutuellement à s'entendre d'abord entr' elles sans rechercher ni contracter de nouvelles alliances, afin de convenir de la ligne de conduite à suivre en commun.

3°. Si à la suite de cette entente une action militaire devenait nécessaire, elle serait reglée par une convention spéciale à conclure entre L. L. M. M.

4°. Si l'une des hautes parties contractantes, voulant reprendre son indépendance d'action, désirait dénoncer le présent acte, elle serait tenue de le faire deux ans d'avance, afin de donner à l'autre partie le temps de prendre les arrangemens qui seraient dans ses convenances.

Schönbrunn, le 25 Mai 1873.

6 Juin

François Joseph.   Alexandre.

(b)

Accession of the Emperor of Germany.

[*The whole text of the Agreement preceding*]

S. M. l'empereur d'Allemagne ayant pris connaissance de l'entente ci-dessus, rédigée et signée à Schönbrunn par L. L. M. M. l'empereur d'Autriche et roi de Hongrie et l'empereur de toutes les Russies, et trouvant le contenu conforme à la pensée qui a présidé à l'entente signée à St. Pétersbourg entre L. L. M. M. l'empereur Guillaume et l'empereur Alexandre, accède en tout aux stipulations qui s'y trouvent consignées.

L. L. M. M. l'empereur et roi François Joseph et l'empereur et roi Guillaume en approvant et en signant cet acte d'accession, le porteront à la connaissance de S. M. l'empereur Alexandre.

Schoenbrunn, le 22 Octobre 1873.

François Joseph.   Guillaume.

assuring, and, if necessary, of imposing the maintenance of the peace of Europe against all subversions, from whatsoever quarter they may come.

2. In case an aggression coming from a third Power should threaten to compromise the peace of Europe, Their Majesties mutually engage to come to a preliminary understanding between themselves, without seeking or contracting new alliances, in order to agree as to the line of conduct to be followed in common.

3. If, as a result of this understanding, a military action should become necessary, it would be governed by a special convention to be concluded between Their Majesties.

4. If one of the High Contracting Parties, wishing to recover its independence of action, should desire to denounce the present Agreement, it must do so two years in advance, in order to give the other Party time to make whatever arrangements may be suitable.

Schönbrunn, May 25 1873.
June 6

Francis Joseph.   Alexander.

(b)

Accession of the Emperor of Germany.

[*The whole text of the Agreement preceding.*]

His Majesty the Emperor of Germany, having taken cogni zance of the above understanding, drawn up and signed at Schön brunn by Their Majesties the Emperor of Austria and King of Hungary and the Emperor of All the Russias, and finding the contents in conformity with the thought which has presided over the understanding signed at St. Petersburg between Their Majesties the Emperor William and the Emperor Alexander, accedes in every respect to the stipulations which are set forth therein.

Their Majesties the Emperor and King Francis Joseph and the Emperor and King William, in approving and in signing this Act of Accession, will bring it to the knowledge of His Majesty the Emperor Alexander.

Schönbrunn, October 22, 1873.

Francis Joseph.   William.

2. Résumé des pourparlers secrets de Reichstadt du 8 Juillet 1876.[3]

On a raisonné dans deux hypothéses: celle où les Turcs sortiraient victorieux de la lutte et celle où ils seraient vaincus.

Dans le premier cas l'on est convenu de ne pas les laisser aller au delà de certaines garanties qui ne seraient pas exagérées. On s'efforcerait d'empêcher que la guerre ne devienne une lutte d'extermination; on maintiendrait la Serbie et le Monténégro dans les circonscriptions territoriales que ces deux principautés ont actuellement et l'on s'opposerait à l'idée d'un rétablissement des forteresses turques en Serbie.

On ne reconnait pas à cette derniére le caractére d'un état indépendant; mais on est tombé d'accord de le reconnaître au Monténégro quelle que fût interprétation que d'autres puissances voudraient donner à la position politique de la Montagne Noire. Par suite de cette indépendance, le gouvernement austro-hongrois s'est déclaré prêt à fermer les deux ports de Klek et de Cattaro à toute importation d'armes et de munitions pour les parties adverses, bien qu'il prévoie de la part du gouvernement turc, de trés graves objections à la fermeture du premier de ces ports.

Pour ce qui est des insurgés, l'on est convenu, toujours dans le cas d'une victoire des Turcs, de faire des efforts communs pour leur garantir les libertés et les réformes qui ont été demandées à la Porte et promises par elle.

Dans toutes les éventualités susmentionnées il ne serait pas question d'un remaniement territorial quelconque, ni d'un côté ni de l'autre.

En passant à la seconde hypothése, celle d'une défaite des Turcs, voici les idées sur lesquelles on est tombé d'accord:

L'Autriche-Hongrie ayant déclaré ne pouvoir admettre que la Serbie occupe et garde par droit de conquête l'enclave comprise entre la Dalmatie, la Croatie, et la Slavonie, attendu que cela impliquerait un danger pour les provinces de la monarchie, sur-

---

[3] The following remark by Andrássy in his own hand: "Niedergeschrieben gleich nach Reichstadt nach meiner Dictée durch Nowikoff und dem russischen Cabinet mitgetheilt." ("Written down immediately after Reichstadt by Nowikoff at my dictation and communicated to the Russian Cabinet.")

2. RÉSUMÉ OF THE SECRET CONFERENCES OF REICHSTADT OF JULY 8, 1876.[3]

The reasoning has been on two hypotheses: That of the Turks coming out of the struggle victorious and that of their being defeated.

In the event of the first, it was agreed not to let them obtain more than 'certain guaranties, which should not be excessive. Efforts were to be made to prevent the war from becoming a struggle for extermination; Serbia and Montenegro were to be maintained in the territorial limits which now circumscribe these two principalities, and the idea of a reëstablishment of the Turkish fortresses in Serbia was to be opposed.

In the case of Serbia, the character of an independent state was not to be recognized; but agreement was reached to recognize it in the case of Montenegro, whatever might be the interpretation which other Powers might wish to give to the political position of the Black Mountain. As a consequence of this independence, the Austro-Hungarian Government has declared itself ready to close the two ports of Klek and of Cattaro to all importation of arms and of munitions for the opposing parties; although it foresees very grave objections on the part of the Turkish Government to the closing of the first of these ports.

Concerning the insurgents, it was agreed (always in the event of the victory of the Turks) to make common efforts to guarantee to them the liberties and the reforms which have been requested of the Porte and promised by it.

In all the eventualities abovementioned, there was to be no question of any territorial modification, either on one side or on the other.

In passing to the second hypothesis, that of a defeat of the Turks, the following are the ideas on which agreement was reached:

Austria-Hungary having declared that she can not permit that Serbia occupy and keep by right of conquest the enclave comprised between Dalmatia, Croatia, and Slavonia, as this would mean a danger to the provinces of the Monarchy, especially to its

tout pour son littoral dalmate lequel, s'étendant comme un mince ruban, devrait évidemment ou être annexé à la nouvelle Serbie ou placer le gouvernement I. et R. dans la nécessité de s'annexer la Serbie même, ce qui est exclu du programme; l'on est convenu que la Serbie obtiendrait une extension de territoire du côté de la Drina en Bosnie, en même tems que du côté de Novi-Bazar dans l'ancienne Serbie et dans la direction du Lim. De son côté le Monténégro serait arrondi par l'annexion d'une partie de l'Herzégovine adjacente; il obtiendrait le port de Spizza ainsi qu'un agrandissement du côté du Lim, de maniére à ce que la langue de terre, qui s'étend aujourd'hui entre la Serbie et le Monténégro fût partagée entre les deux principautés par le cours de ce fleuve.

Le reste de la Bosnie et de l'Herzégovine serait annexé à l'Autriche-Hongrie. La Russie reprendrait ses frontières naturelles d'avant 1856 et pourrait s'arrondir du côté de la Mer Noir et dans la Turquie d'Asie autant que cela serait nécessaire pour lui constituer de meilleures frontières dans cette direction et pour servir d'équivalent à la partie du territoire à étre annexé à l'Autriche-Hongrie.

La Bulgarie, la Roumélie et l'Albanie pourraient former des états autonomes. La Thessalie, l'île de Créte devraient étre annexées à la Gréce.

Constantinople avec une banlieue à déterminer, deviendrait ville libre.

L'on est également convenu que toutes ces idées seraient gardées secrétes entre les deux empereurs et leurs ministres respectifs: qu'elles ne seraient pas communiquées aux autres puissances et plus spécialement encore aux Serbes et Monténégrins jusqu'à ce que le moment de leur réalisation soit arrivé.[4]

3. THE TREATY OF BUDAPEST. 1877.

S.M. l'empereur d'Autriche etc. et roi apostolique de Hongrie et S.M. l'empereur de Russie, considérant que dans le cours des

---

[4] With the above there is also a "Note by Prince Gorchakov concerning the meeting at Reichstadt": "Les deux empereurs se sont séparés dans le meilleur accord, décidés à proclamer le principe de la non-intervention dans le moment actuel. Ils se reservent une entente ultérieure avec les grandes puissances chrétiennes, si les

Dalmatian littoral, which, extending like a thin ribbon, would evidently have to be annexed to the new Serbia or else place the Imperial and Royal Government under the necessity of annexing Serbia herself, which is excluded from the programme; it was agreed that Serbia should obtain an extension of territory in the Drina region in Bosnia, at the same time as in that of Novi-Bazar in Old Serbia and in the direction of the Lim. On her side Montenegro should be rounded out by the annexation of a part of Herzegovina adjoining her territories; she should obtain the port of Spizza as well as an aggrandizement in the region of the Lim, in such a way that the tongue of land which now stretches between Serbia and Montenegro should be divided between the two principalities by the course of this river.

The rest of Bosnia and Herzegovina should be /annexed to Austria-Hungary. Russia should resume her natural frontiers of before 1856 and might round herself off in the region of the Black Sea and in Turkey in Asia to the extent that this should be necessary for the establishment of better frontiers for herself in this direction and to serve as an equivalent for the slice of territory to be annexed to Austria-Hungary.

Bulgaria, Rumelia, and Albania might form autonomous states. Thessaly and the island of Crete should be annexed to Greece.

Constantinople, with a territory to be determined, should become a free city.

It was equally agreed that all these ideas should be kept secret between the two Emperors and their respective Ministers; that they should not be communicated to the other Powers, and more particularly not to the Serbians and Montenegrins, until the moment of their realization should arrive.[4]

3. THE TREATY OF BUDAPEST. 1877.

His Majesty the Emperor of Austria, etc., and Apostolic King of Hungary, and His Majesty the Emperor of Russia, considering

circonstances en démontrent la nécessité." ("The two Emperors parted in the best of agreement, determined to proclaim the principle of non-intervention at the present time. They reserve a later understanding with the great Christian Powers, if circumstances demonstrate the necessity thereof.") In pencil.

négociations diplomatiques pendantes il pouvait surgir des dissentiments de nature à amener une rupture entre la Russie et l'empire ottoman, ont jugé conforme à l'étroite amitié qui les lie et à l'urgence d'obvier à la possibilité d'une collision des intérêts de leurs états respectifs de s'entendre en prévision de cette éventualité.

A cet effet L.L. dites M^{és} ont nommé pour leurs plénipotentiaires:

S. M. l'empereur d'Autriche, roi de Bohême etc. et roi apostolique de Hongrie le sieur Jules comte Andrássy de Csik-Szent-Király et Kraszna-Horka, grand' croix de son ordre de St. Etienne, chevalier de l'ordre impérial de Russie de St. André, grand d'Espagne etc., etc., son conseiller intime, général dans ses armées, son ministre de la maison et des affaires étrangéres;

et S. M. l'empereur de toutes les Russies son conseiller privé le sieur Eugéne Novikow, son ambassadeur extraordinaire et plénipotentiaire prés S. M. l'empereur d'Autriche, roi de Bohême etc. et roi apostolique de Hongrie, chevalier des ordres de Russie: de St. Alexandre Nevsky, de l'aigle blanc, de St. Wladimir de la 2e classe, de St. Anne de la 1ère classe et de St. Stanislas de la 1ère classe; des ordres de St. Etienne, de Léopold et de la couronne de fer de 1ère classe d'Autriche-Hongrie et de plusieurs autres ordres étrangers:

Lesquels, aprés avoir échangé leurs pleins-pouvoirs trouvés en bonne et due forme, sont convenus des articles suivants.

ART. I. L.H.P.C. considérant que les populations chrétiennes et musulmanes en Bosnie et dans l'Herzégovine sont trop entremêlées pour qu'il soit permis d'attendre d'une organisation autonome seule une amélioration réelle de leur sorte, sont convenues entre elles de ne demander pour ces provinces dans la conférence de Constantinople qu'un régime autonome ne dépassant pas trop la mesure fixée par la dépêche du 30 Décembre 1875 [5] et

---

[5] The so-called Andrássy note is printed in French as Nr. 202, pp. 156–162, in *Actenstücke aus den Correspondenzen des kais. und kön. gemeinsamen Ministeriums des Aeussern über orientalische Angelegenheiten (vom 16. Mai 1873 bis 31. Mai 1877)* (Vienna, 1878); as Nr. 5580 in *Das Staatsarchiv*, xxx, pp. 22–30; and as no. 55, in French with English translation, in "Turkey. No. 2 (1876). Correspondence re-

that in the pending diplomatic negotiations disagreements might arise of a nature to bring about a rupture between Russia and the Ottoman Empire, have decided, in conformity with the close friendship which binds them, and with the urgency of obviating the possibility of a collision between the interests of their respective States, to reach an understanding in contemplation of that eventuality.

For this purpose Their said Majesties have appointed as Their Plenipotentiaries: His Majesty the Emperor of Austria, King of Bohemia, etc., and Apostolic King of Hungary, the Sieur Julius Count Andrássy of Csik-Szent-Király and Kraszna-Horka, Grand Cross of His Order of St. Stephen, Chevalier of the Imperial Russian Order of St. Andrew, Grandee of Spain, etc., etc., His Privy Councillor, General in His Armies, His Minister of the Household and of Foreign Affairs;

and His Majesty the Emperor of All the Russias, His Privy Councillor the Sieur Eugene Novikow, His Ambassador Extraordinary and Plenipotentiary to His Majesty the Emperor of Austria, King of Bohemia, etc., and Apostolic King of Hungary, Chevalier of the Russian Orders of St. Alexander Nevsky, of the White Eagle, of St. Vladimir of the Second Class, of St. Anne of the First Class, and of St. Stanislas of the First Class; of the Austro-Hungarian Orders of St. Stephen, of Leopold, and of the Iron Crown of the First Class; and of several other foreign Orders:

Who, after having exchanged their full powers, found in good and due form, have agreed upon the following Articles:

ARTICLE I. The High Contracting Parties, considering that the Christian and Mohammedan populations in Bosnia and in Herzegovina are too much intermingled for it to be permissible to expect from a mere autonomous organization a real amelioration of their lot, are agreed with one another to ask for these provinces in the conference of Constantinople only an autonomous regime not too greatly exceeding the measure fixed by the despatch of December 30, 1875,[5] and the guaranties of the memorandum of

specting affairs in Bosnia and the Herzegovina" (*Parl. Pap.*, 1876, lxxxiv, p. 137. c. 1475), at pp. 74–83.

les garanties du memorandum de Berlin.⁶ La Bulgarie étant placée dans des conditions plus favorables à l'exercice d'institutions autonomes, elles s'engagent à réclamer pour cette province dans la conférence une autonomie plus large, entourée de sérieuses garanties.

ART. II. Pour le cas où les négociations ne devraient pas aboutir et qu'il dût en résulter une rupture suivie d'une guerre entre la Russie et la Turquie, le gouvernement I. et R. prend l'engagement formel d'observer en présence de l'action isolé de la Russie une attitude de neutralité bienveillante et de paralyser, autant qu'il dépend de lui, par son action diplomatique, les essais d'intervention ou de médiation collective que pourraient tenter d'autres puissances.

ART. III. Si le gouvernement de l'empereur et roi est invité à concourir à la mise en exécution du traité du 15 Avril 1856⁷ il déclinera sa coopération pour le cas prévu dans la présente convention et, sans contester la validité du dit traité, proclamera sa neutralité. De même il ne prêtera pas son concours actif à une action effective qui pourrait être proposée sur la base de l'article VIII⁸ du traité du 30 Mars de la même année.

ART. IV. Considérant que les nécessités du passage du Danube pour les troupes russes et le besoin de protéger ce passage contre les canonnières turques obligeront le gouvernement impérial de Russie à apporter des difficultés temporaires à la navigation du fleuve placé sous la garantie des traités, ce qui peut donner lieu à des protestations, le gouvernement austro-hongrois, comme signataire de ces traités et principal intéressé dans la liberté du fleuve, envisagera cette question comme incident de fait

⁶ The so-called memorandum of Berlin of May 12, 1876, is printed in French as Nr. 326, pp. 221–222, in *Actenstücke aus den Correspondenzen des kais. und kön. gemeinsamen Ministeriums des Aeussern über orientalische Angelegenheiten (vom 16. Mai 1873 bis 31. Mai 1877)* (Vienna, 1878); as Nr. 5683, Beilage, in *Das Staatsarchiv*, xxx, pp. 270–272; and as enclosure 2 in no. 248, in French with English translation, in "Turkey. No. 3 (1876). Correspondence respecting the affairs of Turkey and the insurrection in Bosnia and the Herzegovina" (*Parl. Pap.*, 1876, lxxxiv, p. 255. c. 1531), at pp. 138–141.

⁷ The treaty of April 15, 1856, between Great Britain, Austria, and France, guaranteeing the independence and integrity of the Ottoman Empire, is printed in

Berlin.⁶ As Bulgaria is placed under more favorable conditions for the exercise of autonomous institutions, they mutually engage to demand for this province in the conference a larger autonomy, buttressed by substantial guaranties.

ARTICLE II. In the case that the negotiations should not succeed, and should result in a rupture followed by war between Russia and Turkey, the Imperial and Royal Government formally pledges itself to observe an attitude of benevolent neutrality in the presence of the isolated action of Russia, and by its diplomatic action to paralyze, so far as this lies in its power, efforts at intervention or collective mediation which might be attempted by other Powers.

ARTICLE III. If the Government of the Emperor and King is invited to assist in putting into force the treaty of April 15, 1856,⁷ it will, in the event foreseen by the present convention, refuse its coöperation, and, without contesting the validity of the said Treaty, it will proclaim its neutrality. Likewise it will not lend its active aid to effective action which might be proposed on the basis of Article VIII ⁸ of the Treaty of March 30 of that same year.

ARTICLE IV. Considering that the necessity for the Russian troops of crossing the Danube and the need to protect this crossing against the Turkish gunboats will oblige the Imperial Government of Russia to offer temporary hindrances to the navigation of a river placed under the guaranty of treaties, which may give rise to protests, the Austro-Hungarian Government, as a signatory of these treaties and the one principally interested in the freedom of the river, will regard this question as an incident of a temporary

French in *British and Foreign State Papers*, xlvi, pp. 25–26; *Nouveau recueil général de traités*, xv, pp. 790–791; Leopold Neumann, *Recueil des traités et conventions conclus par l'Autriche*, vi, p. 292; Alexandre de Clercq, *Recueil des traités de la France*, vii, p. 90.

⁸ Article VIII of the Treaty of Paris, March 30, 1856, between Great Britain, Austria, France, Prussia, Sardinia, and Turkey on the one part, and Russia on the other, reads:

"If there should arise between the Sublime Porte and one or more of the other signing Powers, any misunderstanding which might endanger the maintenance of their relations, the Sublime Porte, and each of such Powers, before having recourse to the use of force, shall afford the other contracting parties the opportunity of preventing such an extremity by means of their mediation."

temporaire, inévitable en cas de guerre, mais ne touchant pas aux grands principes dont le maintien intéresse l'Europe. De son côté le gouvernement russe prend l'engagement formel de respecter les principes de la liberté de navigation et de la neutralité du Danube et de se mettre d'accord avec le gouvernement de S. M. l'empereur et roi pour rétablir aussitôt que faire se pourra. ,

Art. V. Le gouvernement austro-hongrois prêtera, dans les limites de la convention de Genéve, un concours bienveillant à l'organisation des ambulances provisoires russes sur les lignes de chemins-de-fer Cracovie-Léopol-Csernowitz (entre Granicza et Suczava) avec les embranchements de Woloczysk et Brody, ainsi qu'un mouvement sur les lignes susmentionnées du matériel roulant nécessaire à ces ambulances. Il admettra dans ses hôpitaux civils et militaires sur le parcours des lignes susmentionnées les malades et blessés russes contre paiement d'aprés le tarif militaire autrichien en vigueur.

Art. VI. Le gouvernement austro-hongrois ne mettra aucun obstacle à ce que les commissionnaires et agents du gouvernement russe effectuent dans les limites des états austro-hongrois les achats et commandes d'objets indispensables à l'armée russe à l'exclusion des articles de contrebande de guerre prohibés par les lois internationales. Toutefois le gouvernement de S. M. I. et R. s'engage à user dans l'application et dans l'interprétation de ces lois de la plus large bienveillance à l'égard de la Russie.

Art. VII. S. M. l'empereur d'Autriche etc. et roi apostolique de Hongrie se réserve le choix du moment et du mode de l'occupation de la Bosnie et de l'Herzégovine par ses troupes. Il demeure entendu que cette mesure, sans assumer un caractére de solidarité avec l'occupation de la Bulgarie par l'armée russe, ne devra présenter, ni dans son interprétation par le gouvernement de S. M. I. et R., ni dans son exécution, un caractére d'hostilité à l'égard de la Russie. De même l'intervention de l'armée russe en Turquie ne devra présenter, ni dans son interprétation par le gouvernement impérial de Russie, ni dans son exécution un caractère d'hostilité à l'égard de l'Autriche-Hongrie.

nature, inevitable in case of war, but not affecting the great principles whose maintenance is of interest to Europe. On its side, the Russian Government formally pledges itself to respect the principles of the freedom of navigation and of the neutrality of the Danube, and to put itself into agreement with the Government of His Majesty the Emperor and King to reëstablish them as soon as may be.

ARTICLE V. The Austro-Hungarian Government will lend, within the limits of the Convention of Geneva, its benevolent assistance to the organization of temporary Russian ambulances on the Cracow-Lemberg-Czernowitz lines of railroad (between Granicza and Suczava) with the Woloczysk and Brody branches, as well as to the movement on the abovementioned lines of the rolling stock necessary for these ambulances. It will admit into its civil and military hospitals along the abovementioned lines Russian sick and wounded, in return for payment according to the existing Austrian military tariff.

ARTICLE VI. The Austro-Hungarian Government will not obstruct the commissioners and agents of the Russian Government in making in the limits of the Austro-Hungarian States purchases and contracts for objects indispensable to the Russian Army, with the exception of articles contraband of war prohibited by international laws. The Government of His Imperial and Royal Majesty, however, engages in the application and in the interpretation of these laws to show the broadest good will towards Russia.

ARTICLE VII. His Majesty the Emperor of Austria, etc., and Apostolic King of Hungary reserves to himself the choice of the moment and of the mode of the occupation of Bosnia and of Herzegovina by his troops. It remains understood that this measure, without assuming a character of solidarity with the occupation of Bulgaria by the Russian Army, shall not present, either in its interpretation by the Government of His Imperial and Royal Majesty or in its execution, a character of hostility towards Russia. Likewise the intervention of the Russian Army in Turkey shall not present, either in its interpretation by the Imperial Government of Russia or in its execution, a character of hostility towards Austria-Hungary.

Art. VIII. L. H. P. C. s'engagent réciproquement à ne pas étendre le rayon de leur action militaire respective: S.M. l'empereur d'Autriche etc. et roi apostolique de Hongrie, à la Roumanie, la Serbie, la Bulgarie et le Monténégro;

et S.M. l'empereur de toutes les Russies à la Bosnie, l'Herzégovine, la Serbie et le Monténégro. La Serbie, le Monténégro et la partie de Herzégovine qui sépare ces deux principautés formeront une zone neutre continue que les armées des deux empires ne pourront pas franchir, et destinée à préserver ces dernières de tout contact immédiat. Toutefois il demeure entendu, que le gouvernement I. et R. ne s'opposera pas à l'action combinée des forces serbes et monténégrines hors de leurs pays avec les troupes russes.

Art. IX. Les conséquences de la guerre et les remaniements territoriaux qui résulteraient d'une dissolution éventuelle de l'empire ottoman seront réglés par une convention spéciale et simultanée.

Art. X. L.H.P.C. s'engagent à tenir secrétes les stipulations de la présente convention. Elle sera ratifiée et les ratifications en seront échangées dans l'espace de quatre semaines, ou plus tôt si faire se peut.

En foi de quoi les plénipotentiaires respectifs l'ont signée et y ont apposé le sceau de leurs armes.

Fait à Budapest, le quinziéme jour du mois de Janvier de l'an mil huit cent soixante dix sept.

L.S.   Andrássy.
L.S.   Novikow.

Convention additionnelle.

S.M. l'empereur d'Autriche etc. et roi de Hongrie d'une part et S.M. l'empereur de toutes les Russies de l'autre, en exécution de l'article IX de la convention secréte signée en date d'aujourd'hui ont jugé conforme à l'étroite amitié qui les lie et à l'urgence d'obvier à la possibilité d'une collision des intérêts de leurs états respectifs; de s'entendre sur les conséquences de la guerre et de conclure à cet

ARTICLE VIII. The High Contracting Parties reciprocally engage not to extend the radius of their respective military action: His Majesty the Emperor of Austria, etc., and Apostolic King of Hungary, to Rumania, Serbia, Bulgaria, and Montenegro;

and His Majesty the Emperor of All the Russias to Bosnia, Herzegovina, Serbia, and Montenegro. Serbia, Montenegro, and the portion of Herzegovina which separates these two principalities are to form a continuous neutral zone, which the armies of the two Empires may not cross, and intended to preserve these latter from all immediate contact. It remains understood, however, that the Imperial and Royal Government will not oppose the combined action of Serbian and Montenegrin forces outside of their own countries with the Russian troops.

ARTICLE IX. The consequences of war and the territorial modifications which would result from an eventual dissolution of the Ottoman Empire shall be reguläted by a special and simultaneous convention.

ARTICLE X. The High Contracting Parties mutually engage to keep secret the stipulations of the present Convention. It shall be ratified and ratifications thereof shall be exchanged within the period of four weeks, or sooner if may be.

In witness whereof the respective Plenipotentiaries have signed it and have affixed the seal of their arms.

Done at Budapest, the fifteenth day of the month of January in the year one thousand eight hundred and seventy-seven.

L. S.   Andrássy.

L. S.   Novikow.

Additional Convention.

His Majesty the Emperor of Austria, etc., and King of Hungary on the one part, and His Majesty the Emperor of All the Russias on the other, in execution of Article IX of the secret Convention signed under today's date, have deemed it in conformity with the close friendship which binds them and with the urgency of obviating the possibility of a collision between the interests of their respective States, to reach an understanding respecting the

effet une convention additionnelle destinée à régler d'avance les remaniements territoriaux que la guerre ou la dissolution de l'empire ottoman pourrait avoir pour résultat. A cet effet L. L. dites M^és ont nommé pour leurs plénipotentiaires, savoir:

S.M. l'empereur d'Autriche roi de Bohéme etc. et roi apostolique de Hongrie le sieur Jules comte Andrássy de Csik-Szent Királyi, grand d'Espagne, son conseiller intime actuel et ministre des affaires étrangéres etc., etc.

et S. M. l'empereur de toutes les Russies le sieur Eugéne Novikow, son ambassadeur extraordinaire etc., etc.

lesquels aprés avoir échangé leurs plein-pouvoirs, trouvés en bonne et due forme, sont convenus des articles suivants:

Art. 1. Les deux H.P.C. ayant pour but final l'amélioration du sort des chrétiens et voulant écarter tout projet d'annexions d'une étendue qui pourrait compromettre la paix ou l'équilibre européen, ce qui n'est ni dans leurs intentions, ni dans les intérêts des deux empires, sont tombées d'accord de limiter leurs annexions éventuelles aux territoires suivants:

L'empereur d'Autriche etc. et roi de Hongrie: à la Bosnie et l'Herzégovine à l'exclusion de la partie comprise entre la Serbie et le Monténégro, au sujet de laquelle les deux gouvernements se réservent de se mettre d'accord lorsque le moment d'en disposer serait venu;

L'empereur de toutes les Russies: en Europe aux contrées de la Bessarabie qui rétabliraient les anciennes frontières de l'empire avant 1856.

Art. 2. L.H.P.C. s'engagent à se prêter un mutuel concours sur le terrain diplomatique, si les remaniements territoriaux résultant d'une guerre ou de la dissolution de l'empire ottoman devaient donner lieu à une délibération collective des grandes puissances.

Art. 3. S.M. l'empereur d'Autriche etc. et le roi de Hongrie et S.M. l'empereur de toutes les Russies sont tombés d'accord en principe dans l'entrevue qui a eu lieu entre elles à Reichstadt sur les points suivants: En cas d'un remaniement territorial ou

consequences of the war, and to conclude for this purpose an Additional Convention designed to regulate in advance the territorial modifications which might result from the war or the dissolution of the Ottoman Empire. To this end Their said Majesties have appointed as Their Plenipotentiaries, to wit:

His Majesty the Emperor of Austria, King of Bohemia, etc., and Apostolic King of Hungary, the Sieur Julius Count Andrássy of Czik-Szent-Királyi, Grandee of Spain, His Actual Privy Councillor and Minister of Foreign Affairs, etc., etc.;

and His Majesty the Emperor of All the Russias, the Sieur Eugene Novikow, His Ambassador Extraordinary, etc., etc.:

Who, after having exchanged their full powers, found in good and due form, have agreed upon the following Articles:

ARTICLE 1. The two High Contracting Parties, having as their ultimate aim the amelioration of the lot of the Christians, and wishing to eliminate any project of annexation of a magnitude that might compromise peace or the European equilibrium, which is neither in their intentions nor in the interests of the two Empires, have come to an agreement to limit their eventual annexations to the following territories:

The Emperor of Austria, etc., and King of Hungary: to Bosnia and Herzegovina, with the exception of the portion comprised between Serbia and Montenegro, on the subject of which the two Governments reserve the right to reach an agreement when the moment for disposing of it arrives;

The Emperor of All the Russias: in Europe to the regions of Bessarabia which would reëstablish the old frontiers of the Empire before 1856.

ARTICLE 2. The High Contracting Parties engage to lend each other mutual assistance in the diplomatic field, if the territorial modifications resulting from a war or from the dissolution of the Ottoman Empire should give rise to a collective deliberation of the Great Powers.

ARTICLE 3. His Majesty the Emperor of Austria, etc., and King of Hungary, and His Majesty the Emperor of All the Russias, in the interview which took place between them at Reichstadt, came to an agreement in principle on the following

d'une dissolution de l'empire ottoman, l'établissement d'un grand état compact slave ou autre est exclu; en revanche la Bulgarie, l'Albanie et le reste de la Roumélie pourraient être constituées en états indépendants; la Thessalie, une partie de l'Epire et l'île de Créte, pourraient être annexées à la Gréce; Constantinople avec une banlieue, dont la circonscription reste à déterminer, pourrait devenir ville libre. Leurs dites M^{és} constatent n'avoir rien à changer à ces vues et déclarent de nouveau vouloir les maintenir comme bases de leur action politique ultérieure.

Art. 4. L.H.P.C. s'engagent à tenir secrétes les stipulations de la présente convention qui sera ratifiée et dont les ratifications seront échangées à Vienne dans l'espace de quatre semaines ou plus tôt si faire se peut.

En foi de quoi les plénipotentiaires respectifs l'ont signée et y ont apposé le sceau de leurs armes.

Fait à Budapest, le quinziéme jour du mois de Janvier de l'an mil huit cent soixante dix sept.

L.S.   **Andrássy.**   **L.S.**   **Novikow.**

points: In case of a territorial modification or of a dissolution of the Ottoman Empire, the establishment of a great compact Slavic or other state is excluded; in compensation, Bulgaria, Albania, and the rest of Rumelia might be constituted into independent states; Thessaly, part of Epirus, and the island of Crete might be annexed to Greece; Constantinople, with a territory of which the limit remains to be determined, might become a free city. Their said Majesties record that they have nothing to change in these views, and declare anew that they wish to maintain them as bases of their subsequent political action.

ARTICLE 4. The High Contracting Parties engage to keep secret the stipulations of the present Convention, which shall be ratified and whose ratifications shall be exchanged at Vienna within the space of four weeks, or sooner if may be.

In witness whereof the respective Plenipotentiaries have signed it and have affixed thereto the seal of their arms.

Done at Budapest, the fifteenth day of the month of January in the year one thousand eight hundred and seventy-seven.

L. S.   Andrássy.   L. S.   Novikow.

APPENDIX B

THE DUAL ALLIANCE [1]

It was always asserted by the states which formed the Triple Alliance, and by the partisans of that alliance everywhere, that it was of a purely defensive nature and was first and foremost a league of peace. Now that we have at last the full text of the documents, we may freely admit that this assertion was justified, at least as far as the first treaty was concerned. By the second, that of 1887, we find in Articles III and IV of the separate treaty between Germany and Italy provisions looking forward to an Italian occupation of Tripoli and to possible Italian acquisitions

[1] Ministère des affaires étrangéres. *Documents diplomatiques. L'alliance franco-russe: Origines de l'alliance, 1890–1893; Convention militaire, 1892–1899; et Convention navale, 1912.* Paris, Imprimerie nationale, 1918. This entire Yellow Book was republished in *Pages d'histoire*, no. 159. The best single account of the negotiations resulting in this alliance is Pierre Albin's *La paix armée, L'Allemagne et la France en Europe (1885–1894)* (Paris, Alcan, 1913). The *Souvenirs, 1878–1893*, of C. de S. de Freycinet (Paris, Delagrave, 1913) contain a chapter of value upon the alliance, by the premier active in promoting its first stage. See also *Revanche-Idee und Panslawismus: Belgische Gesandtschaftsberichte zur Entstehungsgeschichte des Zweibundes*, edited by Wilhelm Kohler (Berlin, Hobbing, 1919), the fifth volume of the series *Zur europäischen Politik*; Jens Julius Hansen's *L'Alliance franco-russe* (Paris, 1897) and *Ambassade à Paris du Baron de Mohrenheim* (Paris, Flammarion, 1907); André Tardieu's *La France et les Alliances* (Paris, Alcan, 1904; London and New York; Macmillan, 1908); Ernest Daudet's *Souvenirs et révélations: Histoire diplomatique de l'alliance franco-russe, 1873–1893* (Paris, Ollendorff, 1894); Élie de Cyon's *Histoire de l'entente franco-russe, 1886–1894; documents et souvenirs* (Paris, Charles, 1895); V. de Gorloff's *Origines et bases de l'alliance franco-russe* (Paris, Grasset, 1913); and Laurence B. Packard's "Russia and the Dual Alliance," in *American Historical Review*, xxv, pp. 391–410 (April, 1920).

Speeches of Baron de Mohrenheim on August 31, 1891, of Premier de Freycinet on September 10, and of M. Ribot on September 29 respecting the conclusion of the alliance are printed in *Archives diplomatiques*, xl, pp. 212–214.

The alliance was officially announced by M. Ribot, then Premier, to the French Chamber of Deputies on June 10, 1895. *Journal officiel*, Chambre des députés, June 10, 1895, pp. 1647–1654. It was again discussed authoritatively with respect to its scope by M. Ribot in the French Senate on April 6, 1911. *Annales du Sénat. Débats parlementaires*, lxxviii, p. 461.

of territory at the expense of France. Of course these were provisions stated to be operative only under necessities of self-defence, but they were at bottom primarily of an offensive, not of a defensive, character. But granting that the Triple Alliance was merely one for mutual defence, it conferred on its members great advantages in their dealings with other states, especially with those against whom the alliance was directed.

On the other hand, in the nature of things Germany, Austria, and Italy could not by their various combinations hold Russia in check on the one side and overawe France on the other without tending to·bring about, sooner or later, some sort of a counter agreement between these two. Isolated, France and Russia were comparatively powerless; by uniting they at once obtained greater security and freedom of action and formed in their turn a combination which even the Triple Alliance must treat as an equal. This danger was clear to Bismarck, who always did his utmost to avert it. Conservative as he was, he favored a republican form of government for France, because he believed that this would hamper her in making an alliance with any monarchical state, and particularly with the most monarchical of all, the Russian one. He also assiduously cultivated good relations with Russia, when they could be maintained without the sacrifice of more important interests. The conclusion of the Austro-German alliance in 1879 did not prevent the formation of the League of the Three Emperors in 1881, which was renewed three years later, although the Triple Alliance had come into existence in the meantime. Even in 1887, after the renewal of the Triple Alliance and the definite estrangement between Austria and Russia, Bismarck by his secret Reinsurance treaty still kept his wire to St. Petersburg; it was only severed after his fall in 1890.

But even before that date, relations between Paris and St. Petersburg had become increasingly cordial. Little interchanges of politeness and good offices grew frequent. A more serious sign of the times lay in the fact that the closing of the Berlin market to Russian securities was soon followed by the formal opening of the Paris one. The termination of the Boulanger episode and the success of the Paris exhibition of 1889 appear to have given the

Tsar a higher opinion of the steadiness, as well as of the firmness, of the French Republic, while the understanding between England, Austria, and Italy, which checkmated any Russian action in Bulgaria, emphasized the disadvantages of his isolation. When, therefore, William II and Count Caprivi refused to renew the Reinsurance treaty and entered upon a policy of cultivating intimate relations with England, the Tsar proceeded to draw closer to France. The second renewal of the Triple Alliance in March, 1891, was answered on July 18 of the same year by the visit of the French fleet to Kronstadt.

Although the idea of a demonstration of this kind was not a new one, yet, carried out at this time and in the way that it was, it served as a notification to the world that France and Russia were henceforth practically allies. The terms of their alliance were not yet settled, and it was not until a later date that the negotiations led to a final exchange of signatures. Like the Triple, the Dual

I. DEFINITION OF THE RUSSO-FRENCH UNDERSTANDING.

(a)

M. de Mohrenheim, Ambassador of Russia at Paris, to M. Ribot, Minister of Foreign Affairs of France, communicating the instructions of M. de Giers, Russian Minister of Foreign Affairs.[2]

Paris, le 15/27 août 1891.

Durant mon récent séjour à Saint-Pétersbourg, où j'ai été mandé d'ordre de mon Auguste Souverain, il a plu à l'Empereur de me munir d'instructions spéciales, consignées dans la lettre ci-jointe en copie que m'a adressée Son Excellence M. de Giers, Ministre des Affaires étrangéres, et dont Sa Majesté a daigné me prescrire de donner communication au Gouvernement de la République.

En exécution de cet ordre suprême, je me fais un devoir empressé de porter cette piéce à la connaissance de Votre Excellence, dans le ferme espoir que son contenu, préalablement concerté et formulé d'un commun accord entre nos deux Cabinets, rencon-

Alliance remained secret; and there were many surmises as to its exact contents, which were only revealed to the public after the outbreak of the World War and the downfall of the Russian Empire. It also was strictly defensive in its terms and in its nature. It did not countenance aggressive policies, but it did give the greater security which the two signatories desired. During the twenty and more years of friendship, the policies of France and Russia did not always agree with one another, and the enthusiasm of the first moments was followed by a calmer appreciation of the merits of the compact; but it remained unbroken. When the supreme test came in 1914, on a question in which France had no direct interest, none the less, as unhesitatingly as Germany supported Austria, France remained loyal to her bond, and accepted without flinching all the terrible risks and sacrifices of the World War.

A. C. C.

1. DEFINITION OF THE RUSSO-FRENCH UNDERSTANDING.

(a)

M. de Mohrenheim, Ambassador of Russia at Paris, to M. Ribot, Minister of Foreign Affairs of France, communicating the instructions of M. de Giers, Russian Minister of Foreign Affairs.[2]

Paris, August 15/27, 1891.

During my recent sojourn in St. Petersburg, whither I was ordered by my August Sovereign, it pleased the Emperor to provide me with special instructions, set forth in the letter, subjoined in copy, which His Excellency, M. de Giers, Minister of Foreign Affairs, addressed to me, and which His Majesty has deigned to direct me to communicate to the Government of the Republic.

In execution of this Supreme order, I am making it my pressing duty to bring this document to the knowledge of Your Excellency, in the firm hope that its contents, previously concerted and formulated by common agreement between our two Cabinets, will

---

[2] *Documents diplomatiques. L'alliance franco-russe,* no. 17.

trera le plein suffrage du Gouvernement français, et que vous
voudrez bien, Monsieur le Ministre, conformément au voeu exprimé par M. de Giers, m'honorer d'une réponse témoignant du
parfait accord heureusement établi désormais entre nos deux
Gouvernements.

Les développements ultérieurs dont les deux points ainsi convenus sont non seulement susceptibles, mais qui en formeront le
complément nécessaire, pourront faire l'objet de pourparlers con-
fidentiels et intimes à tel moment jugé opportun par l'un ou
l'autre Cabinet, où ils estimeront pouvoir y procéder en temps
utile.

Me tenant, à cet effet, à l'entière disposition de Votre Excellence, je suis heureux de pouvoir me prévaloir d'une occasion
pareille pour la prier de vouloir bien agréer l'hommage renouvelé
de ma plus haute considération et de mon plus inaltérable dé-·
vouement.

　　　　　　　　　　　　　　　　　　　　Mohrenheim.

ANNEX.

*Letter of M. de Giers, Minister of Foreign Affairs of Russia,
to M. de Mohrenheim, Ambassador of Russia at Paris.*

　　　　　　　　　Pétersbourg, le 9/21 août 1891.

La situation créée en Europe par le renouvellement manifeste
de la triple alliance et l'adhésion plus ou moins probable de la
Grande-Bretagne aux visées politiques que cette alliance pour-
suit, a motivé, lors du récent séjour ici de M. de Laboulaye, entre
l'ancien Ambassadeur de France et moi, un échange d'idées ten-
dant à définir l'attitude qui, dans les conjonctures actuelles et en
présence de certaines éventualités, pourrait le mieux convenir à
nos Gouvernements respectifs, lesquels, restés en dehors de toute
ligue, n'en sont pas moins sincèrement désireux d'entourer le
maintien de la paix des garanties les plus efficaces.

C'est ainsi que nous avons été amenés à formuler les deux
points ci-dessous:

1°. Afin de définir et de consacrer l'entente cordiale qui les
unit et désireux de contribuer d'un commun accord au maintien
de la paix qui forme l'objet de leurs voeux les plus sincéres, les

meet with the full approbation of the French Government; and that you will be kind enough, Mr. Minister, in conformity with the wish expressed by M. de Giers, to honor me with a reply testifying to the perfect agreement fortunately established from this time on between our two Governments.

The ulterior developments, of which the two points thus agreed upon not only are susceptible, but which will form their necessary complement, may be made the subject of confidential and intimate conferences at the moment judged opportune by either Cabinet, when they believe they can proceed to it at a good time.

Holding myself for this purpose at the entire disposition of Your Excellency, I am happy to be able to take advantage of such an occasion to ask you to be kind enough to accept the renewed homage of my highest consideration and of my most unalterable devotion.

Mohrenheim.

ANNEX.

Letter of M. de Giers, Minister of Foreign Affairs of Russia, to M. de Mohrenheim, Ambassador of Russia at Paris.

Petersburg, August 9/21, 1891.

The situation created in Europe by the open renewal of the Triple Alliance and the more or less probable adhesion of Great Britain to the political aims which that alliance pursues, has, during the recent sojourn here of M. de Laboulaye, prompted an exchange of ideas between the former Ambassador of France and myself, tending to define the attitude which, as things now stand and in the presence of certain eventualities, might best suit our respective Governments, which, having kept out of any league, are none the less sincerely desirous of surrounding the maintenance of peace with the most efficacious guaranties.

It is thus that we have been led to formulate the two points below:

1. In order to define and consecrate the cordial understanding which unites them, and desirous of contributing in common agreement to the maintenance of the peace which forms the ob-

deux Gouvernements déclarent qu'ils se concerteront sur toute question de nature à mettre la paix générale en cause;[3]

2°. Pour le cas où cette paix serait effectivement en danger et spécialement pour celui où l'une des deux parties serait menacée d'une agression, les deux parties conviennent de s'entendre sur les mesures dont la réalisation de cette éventualité imposerait l'adoption immédiate et simultanée aux deux Gouvernements.[4]

Ayant soumis à l'Empereur le fait de cet échange d'idées ainsi que le texte des conclusions qui en étaient résultées, j'ai l'honneur de vous informer aujourd'hui que Sa Majesté a daigné approuver entièrement ces principes d'entente et verrait avec faveur leur adoption par les deux Gouvernements.

En vous faisant part de ces dispositions Souveraines, je vous prie de vouloir bien les porter à la connaissance du Gouvernement français et de me communiquer les résolutions auxquelles, pour sa part, il pourrait s'arrêter.

Giers.

(b)

M. Ribot, French Minister of Foreign Affairs, to M. de Mohrenheim, Russian Ambassador at Paris, in reply to the preceding.[5]

Paris, le 27 août 1891.

Vous avez bien voulu, d'ordre de votre Gouvernement, me communiquer le texte de la lettre du Ministre des Affaires étrangéres de l'Empire, où sont consignées les instructions spéciales dont l'Empereur Alexandre a décidé de vous munir, à la suite du dernier échange d'idées auquel la situation générale de l'Europe a donné lieu entre M. de Giers et l'Ambassadeur de la République française à Saint-Pétersbourg.

Votre Excellence était chargée d'exprimer en même temps l'espoir que le contenu de cette piéce, préalablement concerté et formulé d'un commun accord entre les deux Cabinets, rencontrerait le plein suffrage du Gouvernement français.

---

[3] Cf. Article V, par. 1, of the treaty of the Triple Alliance of May 20, 1882. Vol. I, p. 67, *supra.*

[4] Cf. Article III of the treaty of the Triple Alliance of May 20, 1882. Vol. I, p. 67, *supra.*

ject of their sincerest aspirations, the two Governments declare that they will take counsel together upon every question of a nature to jeopardize the general peace;[3]

2. In case that peace should be actually in danger, and especially if one of the two parties should be threatened with an aggression, the two parties undertake to reach an understanding on the measures whose immediate and simultaneous adoption would be imposed upon the two Governments by the realization of this eventuality.[4]

Having submitted to the Emperor the fact of this exchange of ideas as well as the text of the conclusions resulting therefrom, I have the honor to inform you today that His Majesty has deigned to approve completely these principles of agreement, and would view with favor their adoption by the two Governments.

In informing you of these Sovereign dispositions, I beg that you be kind enough to bring them to the knowledge of the French Government and to communicate to me the decisions which it may take on its side.

Giers.

(b)

M. Ribot, French Minister of Foreign Affairs, to M. de Mohrenheim, Russian Ambassador at Paris, in reply to the preceding.[5]

Paris, August 27, 1891.

You have been kind enough, by order of your Government, to communicate to me the text of the letter of the Minister of Foreign Affairs of the Empire, wherein are set forth the special instructions with which the Emperor Alexander decided to provide you in pursuance of the last exchange of ideas to which the general situation of Europe had given rise between M. de Giers and the Ambassador of the French Republic at St. Petersburg.

Your Excellency was instructed to express at the same time the hope that the contents of this document, previously concerted and formulated in common agreement between the two Cabinets, would meet with the full assent of the French Government.

---

[5] *Documents diplomatiques. L'alliance franco-russe*, no. 18.

Je m'empresse de remercier Votre Excellence de cette communication.

Le Gouvernement de la République ne pouvait qu'envisager comme le Gouvernement Impérial la situation créée en Europe par les conditions dans lesquelles s'est produit le renouvellement de la triple alliance et il estime avec lui que le moment est venu de définir l'attitude qui, dans les conjonctures actuelles et en présence de certaines éventualités, pourrait le mieux convenir aux deux Gouvernements, également désireux d'assurer au maintien de la paix les garanties qui résultent de l'équilibre entre les forces européennes.

Je suis heureux en conséquence de faire savoir à Votre Excellence que le Gouvernement de la République donne son entière adhésion aux deux points qui font l'objet de la communication de M. de Giers et qui sont ainsi formulés:

1°. Afin de définir et de consacrer l'entente cordiale qui les unit et désireux de contribuer d'un commun accord au maintien de la paix qui forme l'objet de leurs voeux les plus sincéres, les deux Gouvernements déclarent qu'ils se concerteront sur toute question de nature à mettre la paix générale en cause;

2°. Pour le cas où cette paix serait effectivement en danger et spécialement pour celui où l'une des deux parties serait menacée d'une agression, les deux parties conviennent de s'entendre sur les mesures dont la réalisation de cette éventualité imposerait l'adoption immédiate et simultanée aux deux Gouvernements.

Je me tiens d'ailleurs à votre disposition pour examiner toutes les questions qui, dans l'état actuel de la politique générale, s'imposent plus particulièrement à l'attention des deux Gouvernements.

D'autre part, le Gouvernement impérial se rendra compte sans doute comme nous de l'intérêt qu'il y aurait à confier à des délégués spéciaux, qui seraient désignés le plus tôt possible, l'étude pratique des mesures destinées à parer aux éventualités prévues par le second point de l'accord.

En vous priant de porter à la connaissance du Gouvernement de Sa Majesté la réponse du Gouvernement français, je tiens à

I hasten to thank Your Excellency for this communication. The Government of the Republic can only take the same view as does the Imperial Government of the situation created in Europe by the conditions under which the renewal of the Triple Alliance has come to pass, and believes with it that the moment has arrived to define the attitude which, as things now stand and in the presence of certain eventualities, might seem best to the two Governments, equally desirous of assuring the guaranties for the maintenance of peace which result from the European balance of power.

I am, therefore, happy to inform Your Excellency that the Government of the Republic gives its entire adhesion to the two points which form the subject of the communication of M. de Giers and which are formulated as follows:

1. In order to define and consecrate the cordial understanding which unites them, and desirous of contributing in common agreement to the maintenance of the peace which forms the object of their sincerest aspirations, the two Governments declare that they will take counsel together upon every question of a nature to jeopardize the general peace;

2. In case that peace should be actually in danger, and especially if one of the two parties should be threatened with an aggression, the two parties undertake to reach an understanding on the measures whose immediate and simultaneous adoption would be imposed upon the two Governments by the realization of this eventuality.

I furthermore hold myself at your disposal for the examination of all questions which, under present political conditions, make more particular demand upon the attention of the two Governments.

Conversely, the Imperial Government will doubtless appreciate, as do we, the importance of confiding to special delegates, who should be designated as soon as possible, the practical study of measures designed to meet the eventualities foreseen by the second point of the agreement.

In begging you to bring the reply of the French Government to the knowledge of the Government of His Majesty, I wish to em-

marquer combien il m'a été précieux de pouvoir concourir, en ce qui me concerne, à la consécration d'une entente qui a été constamment l'objet de nos communs efforts.

Ribot.

2. THE MILITARY CONVENTION.

(a)

Draft of Military Convention.[6]

La France et la Russie, étant animées d'un égal désir de conserver la paix, et n'ayant d'autre but que de parer aux nécessités d'une guerre défensive, provoquée par une attaque des forces de la Triple Alliance contre l'une ou l'autre d'entre elles, sont convenues des dispositions suivantes:

1°. Si la France est attaquée par l'Allemagne, ou par l'Italie soutenue par l'Allemagne, la Russie emploiera toutes ses forces disponibles pour attaquer l'Allemagne.[7]

Si la Russie est attaquée par l'Allemagne, ou par l'Autriche soutenue par l'Allemagne, la France emploiera toutes ses forces disponibles pour combattre l'Allemagne.

2°. Dans le cas où les forces de la Triple Alliance, ou d'une des Puissances qui en font partie, viendraient à se mobiliser, la France et la Russie, à la premiére annonce de l'événement, et sans qu'il soit besoin d'un concert préalable, mobiliseront immédiatement et simultanément la totalité de leurs forces, et les porteront le plus prés possible de leurs frontières.

3°. Les forces disponibles qui doivent être employées contre l'Allemagne seront, du côté de la France, de 1,300,000 hommes, du côté de la Russie, de 700,000 à 800,000 hommes.

Ces forces s'engageront à fond, en toute diligence, de maniére que l'Allemagne ait à lutter, à la fois, à l'Est et à l'Ouest.

[6] *Ibid.*, no. 71, Report, containing the definitive draft of the military convention, from General de Boisdeffre to the Minister of War, dated at St. Petersburg, August 18, 1892. The report is in the form of a diary. The draft was signed on August 17. The following note is attached to the draft:

"This document is preserved in an envelope bearing this autographic annota-

phasize how much I cherish the opportunity to participate in the consecration of an understanding which has been the constant object of our common efforts.

Ribot.

2. THE MILITARY CONVENTION.

(a)
Draft of Military Convention.[6]

France and Russia, being animated by an equal desire to pre-serve peace, and having no other object than to meet the necessi ties of a defensive war, provoked by an attack of the forces of the Triple Alliance against the one or the other of them, have agreed upon the following provisions:

1. If France is attacked by Germany, or by Italy supported by Germany, Russia shall employ all her available forces to attack Germany.[7]

If Russia is attacked by Germany, or by Austria supported by Germany, France shall employ all her available forces to fight Germany.

2. In case the forces of the Triple Alliance, or of one of the Powers composing it, should mobilize, France and Russia, at the first news of the event and without the necessity of any previous concert, shall mobilize immediately and simultaneously the whole of their forces and shall move them as close as possible to their frontiers.

3. The available forces to be employed against Germany shall be, on the part of France, 1,300,000 men, on the part of Russia, 700,000 or 800,000 men.

These forces shall engage to the full, with all speed, in order that Germany may have to fight at the same time on the East and on the West.

tion: 'The military convention is accepted by the letter of M. de Giers to M. de Montebello giving treaty force to this convention. (Signed) Félix Faure. October 15.' See Document no. 91."

[7] Cf. Articles II, X, and XI of the treaty of the Triple Alliance of May 6, 1891. Vol. I, pp. 153, 157, 159, *supra*.

4°. Les États-Majors des Armées des deux pays se concerteront en tout temps pour préparer et faciliter l'exécution des mesures prévues ci-dessus.

Ils se communiqueront, dés le temps de paix, tous les renseignements relatifs aux armées de la Triple Alliance qui sont ou par viendront à leur connaissance.

Les voies et moyens de correspondre en temps de guerre seront étudiés et prévus d'avance.

5°. La France et la Russie ne concluront pas la paix séparé ment.[8]

6°. La présente Convention aura la méme durée que la Triple Alliance.[9]

7°. Toutes les clauses énumérées ci-dessus seront tenues rigoureusement secrétes.[10]

Signature du Ministre:

Signature du Ministre:

L'Aide de Camp général,   Le Général de Division,
    Chef de l'État-Major général,   Conseiller d'État,
    Signé: Obroutcheff.   Sous-Chef d'État-Major de
                     l'Armée,
                     Signé: Boisdeffre.

(b)

Approval of the Convention.

M. de Giers, Russian Minister of Foreign Affairs, to M. de Montebello, French Ambassador at St. Petersburg.[11]

Saint-Pétersbourg, le 15/27 décembre 1893.

TRÈS-SECRÈTE,

Aprés avoir examiné, d'ordre Supréme, le projet de Convention militaire élaboré par les États-majors russe et français en août 1892, et en avoir soumis mon appréciation à l'Empereur, je me fais un devoir d'informer Votre Excellence, que le texte de cet arrangement, tel qu'il a été approuvé en principe par Sa Majesté

---

[8] Cf. Article V, par. 2, of the treaty of the Triple Alliance of May 6, 1891. Vol. I, p. 155, *supra.*

The third treaty of the Triple Alliance was signed May 6, 1891, to remain in force for a period of six years from the exchange of ratifications, which took place at Berlin on May 17. Vol. I, p. 159, *supra.*

4. The General Staffs of the Armies of the two countries shall coöperate with each other at all times in the preparation and facilitation of the execution of the measures above foreseen. They shall communicate to each other, while there is still peace, all information relative to the armies of the Triple Alliance which is or shall be within their knowledge. Ways and means of corresponding in times of war shall be studied and arranged in advance.

5. France and Russia shall not conclude peace separately.[8]

6. The present Convention shall have the same duration as the Triple Alliance.[9]

7. All the clauses above enumerated shall be kept rigorously secret.[10]

Signature of the Minister:
Signature of the Minister:

General Aide-de-Camp,
   Chief of the General Staff,
Signed: Obrucheff.

General of Division,
   Councillor of State,
Sub-Chief of the General
   Staff of the Army,
Signed: Boisdeffre.

(b)

Approval of the Convention.

M. de Giers, Russian Minister of Foreign Affairs, to M. de Montebello, French Ambassador at St. Petersburg.[11]

St. Petersburg, December 15/27, 1893.

Very secret.

After having examined, by Supreme order, the draft of a military convention drawn up by the Russian and French General Staffs in August, 1892, and after having submitted my estimate thereof to the Emperor, I esteem it my duty to inform Your Excellency that the text of this arrangement, as approved in prin-

---

[10] Cf. Article XII of the third treaty of the Triple Alliance, May 6, 1891. Vol. I, p. 159, *supra.*

[11] Annex to the despatch of M. de Montebello, French Ambassador at St. Petersburg, to M. Casimir Périer, President of the Council, Minister of Foreign Affairs, dated St. Petersburg, December 30, 1893. *Documents diplomatiques. L'alliance franco-russe,* no. 91.

et signé par MM. l'Aide de Camp général Obroutcheff et le général de division de Boisdeffre, peut être considéré désormais comme ayant été définitivement adopté dans sa forme actuelle. — Les deux États-Majors auront ainsi la faculté de se concerter en tout temps et de se communiquer réciproquement tous les renseignements qui pourraient leur étre utiles.[12]

Giers.

3. Exchange of Letters Modifying the Convention of 1893.

(a)

Count Mouravieff, Russian Minister of Foreign Affairs, to M. Delcassé, French Minister of Foreign Affairs.[13]

Saint-Pétersbourg, le 28 juillet/9 août 1899.

Les quelques jours que Votre Excellence vient de passer parmi nous Lui auront permis, je l'espére, de constater une fois de plus la solidité des liens de vive et invariable amitié qui unissent la Russie à la France.

Afin de dormer une nouvelle expression à ces sentiments et de répondre au désir que Vous avez exprimé à Sa Majesté, l'Empereur a daigné m'autoriser, Monsieur le Ministre, à Vous proposer, entre nous, un échange de lettres destinées à établir que:

Le Gouvernement Impérial de Russie et le Gouvernement de la République Française, toujours soucieux du maintien de la paix générale et de l'équilibre entre les forces européennes,

Confirment l'arrangement diplomatique formulé dans la lettre du 9/21 août 1891 de M. de Giers, celle du 15/27 août 1891 du Baron Mohrenheim et la lettre responsive de M. Ribot, portant également la date du 15/27 août 1891.

Ils décident que le projet de convention militaire, qui en a été le complément et qui se trouve mentionné dans la lettre de M. de Giers du 15/27 décembre 1893 et celle de M. le Comte de Montebello du 23 décembre 1893/4 janvier 1894, demeurera en vigueur

---

[12] A note of the same purport, dated at St. Petersburg, December 23, 1893/ January 4, 1894 (*ibid.*, no. 92), from M. de Montebello, French Ambassador at St. Petersburg, to M. de Giers, Russian Minister of Foreign Affairs, announced to the

ciple by His Majesty and signed by Aide-de-Camp General Obrucheff and General of Division de Boisdeffre, may be regarded henceforth as having been definitively adopted in its existing form. — The two General Staffs will thus have the faculty of taking counsel together at any time and of reciprocally communicating any information which might be useful to them.[12]

Giers.

3. EXCHANGE OF LETTERS MODIFYING THE CONVENTION OF 1893.

(a)

Count Mouravieff, Russian Minister of Foreign Affairs, to M. Delcassé, French Minister of Foreign Affairs.[13]

St. Petersburg, July 28/August 9, 1899.

The few days that Your Excellency has just spent among us will, I hope, have permitted you to note once more the solidity of the bonds of lively and unchanging friendship which unite Russia to France.

In order to give fresh expression to these sentiments and to respond to the desire that you have expressed to His Majesty, the Emperor has deigned to authorize me, Mr. Minister, to propose to you an exchange of letters between us which shall establish that:

The Imperial Government of Russia and the Government of the French Republic, ever solicitous for the maintenance of the general peace and of the European balance of power,

Confirm the diplomatic arrangement formulated in the letter of August 9/21, 1891, of M. de Giers, that of August 15/27, 1891, of Baron Mohrenheim, and the letter in reply of M. Ribot, likewise bearing the date of August 15/27, 1891.

They decide that the draft of a military convention which was the complement thereof and which is mentioned in the letter of M. de Giers of December 15/27, 1893, and that of Count de Montebello of December 23, 1893/January 4, 1894, shall remain in force

latter the approval of the Military Convention by the President of the French Republic and by the Ministry.

[13] *Ibid.*, no. 93.

autant que l'accord diplomatique conclu pour la sauvegarde des intérêts communs et permanents des deux pays.

Le secret le plus absolu quant à la teneur et à l'existence méme desdits arrangements devra étre scrupuleusement observé de part et d'autre.

En Vous adressant cette communication, Monsieur le Ministre, je profite de l'occasion qu'elle m'offre pour Vous renouveler l'assurance de ma haute considération.

Comte Mouravieff.

(b)

M. Delcassé, Minister of Foreign Affairs of the French Republic, to Count Mouravieff, Minister of Foreign Affairs of Russia.[14]

Saint-Pétersbourg, 28 juillet–9 août 1899.

Monsieur le Ministre,

Dimanche dernier, quand, avec son agrément, j'eus exposé à Sa Majesté l'Empereur mon opinion sur l'utilité de confirmer notre arrangement diplomatique du mois d'août 1891 et de fixer à la Convention militaire qui le suivit la même durée qu'à cet arrangement, Sa Majesté voulut bien me déclarer que ses propres sentiments répondaient parfaitement aux vues du Gouvernement de la République.

Par votre lettre de ce matin, vous me faites l'honneur de m'informer qu'il a plu à Sa Majesté l'Empereur d'approuver la formule suivante qui a, d'autre part, l'entière adhésion du Président de la République et du Gouvernement français et sur laquelle l'entente s'était préalablement établie entre Votre Excellence et moi:

[*Here follow the third to the sixth paragraphs, inclusive, of the preceding note.*]

Je me félicite, M. le Ministre, que ces quelques jours passés à Saint-Pétersbourg m'aient permis de constater une fois de plus la solidité des liens de vive et invariable amitié qui unissent la France et la Russie, et je vous prie d'agréer la nouvelle assurance de ma haute considération.

Delcassé.

[14] *Documents diplomatiques. L'alliance franco-russe*, no. 94.

as long as the diplomatic agreement concluded for the safeguarding of the common and permanent interests of the two countries.

The most absolute secrecy as to the tenor and even as to the existence of the said arrangements must be scrupulously observed on either side.

In addressing this communication to you, Mr. Minister, I avail myself of the opportunity it offers me to renew to you the assurance of my high consideration.

Count Mouravieff.

(b)

M. Delcassé, Minister of Foreign Affairs of the French Republic, to Count Mouravieff, Minister of Foreign Affairs of Russia.[14]

St. Petersburg, July 28–August 9, 1899.

Mr. Minister,

Last Sunday, when, with his consent, I had expressed to His Majesty the Emperor my opinion upon the utility of confirming our diplomatic arrangement of August, 1891, and of assigning to the military Convention which followed it the same duration as to the arrangement itself, His Majesty was kind enough to tell me that his own sentiments were in complete accord with the views of the Government of the Republic.

By your letter of this morning, you have done me the honor to inform me that it has pleased His Majesty the Emperor to approve the following formula: which has, moreover, the entire adherence of the President of the Republic and of the French Government, and on which the understanding was previously established between Your Excellency and myself:

[*Here follow the third to the sixth paragraphs, inclusive, of the preceding note.*]

I congratulate myself, Minister, that these few days spent at St. Petersburg have permitted me to note once more the solidity of the bonds of lively and unchanging friendship which unite France and Russia; and I beg you to accept the fresh assurance of my high regard.

Delcassé.

4. Naval Convention of July 16, 1912.

(a)

Draft of Naval Convention.[15]

ARTICLE PREMIER. — Les forces navales de la France et de la Russie coopéreront dans toutes les éventualités où l'alliance prévoit et stipule l'action combinée des armées de terre.

ART. 2.—La coopération des forces navales sera préparée dès le temps de paix.

A cet effet, les Chefs d'État-Major de l'une et l'autre Marines sont dés maintenant autorisés à correspondre directement, à échanger tous renseignements, à étudier toutes hypothéses de guerre, à concerter tous programmes stratégiques.

ART. 3.—Les Chefs d'État-Major de l'une et l'autre Marines conféreront en personne, une fois l'an au moins; ils dresseront procès-verbal de leurs conférences.

ART. 4.—Pour la durée, l'efficience et le secret, la présente Convention est assimilée à la Convention militaire du 17 août 1892 et aux accords subséquents.

Paris, le 16 juillet 1912.

Le Chef d'État-Major général de la Marine française,	Le Chef d'État-Major de la Marine impériale russe,
Signé: Aubert.	Signé: Prince Lieven.
Le Ministre de la Marine,	Le Ministre de la Marine,
Signé: M. Delcassé.	Signé: J. Grigorovitch.

(b)

Convention for the Exchange of Information between the Russian Navy and the French Navy.[16]

A la suite d'un échange de vues survenu dans le courant du mois de juillet 1912, entre M. le Vice-Amiral, Prince Lieven, Chef d'État-Major général de la Marine impériale russe, et M. le Vice-Amiral Aubert, Chef d'État-Major général de la Marine française,

---

[15] L'alliance franco-russe, no. 102. An official note appended says: "The original of this document is at the Ministry of Marine."

4. NAVAL CONVENTION OF JULY 16, 1912.

(a)

Draft of Naval Convention.[15]

ARTICLE 1. The naval forces of France and Russia shall co-operate in every eventuality where the alliance contemplates and stipulates combined action of the land armies.

ARTICLE 2. The coöperation of the naval forces shall be prepared while there is still peace.

To this end the Chiefs of General Staff of the two Navies are authorized from now on to correspond directly, to exchange any information, to study all hypotheses of war, to counsel together on all strategic problems.

ARTICLE 3. The Chiefs of General Staff of the two Navies shall confer in person at least once a year; they will draw up minutes of their conferences.

ARTICLE 4. As to duration, effectiveness, and secrecy, the present Convention is to run parallel to the Military Convention of August 17, 1892, and to the subsequent Agreements.

Paris, July 16, 1912.

Chief of the General Staff of the French Navy,
Signed: Aubert.
Minister of Marine,
Signed: M. Delcassé.

Chief of the General Staff of the Imperial Russian Navy,
Signed: Prince Lieven.
Minister of Marine,
Signed: J. Grigorovitch.

(b)

Convention for the Exchange of Information between the Russian Navy and the French Navy.[16]

Following an exchange of views that occurred during the month of July, 1912, between Vice Admiral Prince Lieven, Chief of the General Staff of the Imperial Russian Navy, and Vice Admiral Aubert, Chief of the General Staff of the French Navy,

[16] *L'alliance franco-russe*, no. 103. An official note appended says: "The original of this document is at the Ministry of Marine."

les décisions de principe qui suivent ont été arrêtées entre les deux conférents:

1°. A partir du 1/14 septembre 1912, le Chef d'État-Major général de la Marine impériale russe et le Chef d'État-Major général de la Marine française échangeront tous renseignements sur leurs marines respectives et, régulièrement tous les mois, par écrit, les renseignements que ces deux pays pourront se procurer; le télégraphe chiffré pourra être employé en certains cas urgents;

2°. Pour éviter toute indiscrétion ou toute divulgation relative à ces renseignements, il est indispensable d'adopter le procédé de transmission suivant:

Toute demande de renseignements sur la Marine française, intéressant la Marine russe, sera adressée par l'Attaché naval russe à Paris au Chef d'État-Major général de la Marine française; et, réciproquement, toute demande de renseignements sur la Marine russe, intéressant la Marine française, sera adressée par l'Attaché naval français à Saint-Pétersbourg au Chef d'État-Major général de la Marine russe.

Ce procédé sera exclusif de tout autre: on ne pourra donc pas, en principe, demander directement aux Attachés navals des renseignements sur leur propre Marine.[17]

Paris, le 16 juillet 1912.

Le Chef d'État-Major général   Le Chef d'État-Major général
   de la Marine française,   de la Marine russe,
   Signé: Aubert.   Signé: Prince Lieven.

[17] M. Sazonoff, Minister of Foreign Affairs of Russia, in a note to M. Raymond Poincaré, Minister of Foreign Affairs of France, dated at St. Petersburg, August 2/15, 1912, stated that the draft of the convention "has been examined by the Imperial Government and submitted with a favorable opinion to His Majesty the Emperor, who has deigned to give it his approval." The next day M. Poincaré replied to the effect that "the Government of the Republic gives it its approval." *L'alliance franco-russe*, nos. 106, 107.

the following decisions of principle have been reached between the two conferees:

1. Dating from September 1/14, 1912, the Chief of the General Staff of the Imperial Russian Navy and the Chief of the General Staff of the French Navy shall exchange all information as to their respective navies, and regularly every month, in writing, any information which these two countries may obtain; telegraphic cipher may be used in certain urgent cases;

2. In order to avoid any indiscretion or any disclosure relative to this information, it is indispensable to adopt the following procedure in transmission:

Any request for information about the French Navy of interest to the Russian Navy shall be addressed by the Russian Naval Attaché at Paris to the Chief of the General Staff of the French Navy; and, reciprocally, any request for information about the Russian Navy of interest to the French Navy shall be addressed by the French Naval Attaché at St. Petersburg to the Chief of the General Staff of the Russian Navy.

This procedure will be exclusive of all other. In principle, therefore, a direct request is not to be made to the Naval Attachés for information respecting their own Navies.[17]

Paris, July 16, 1912.

Chief of the General Staff	Chief of the General Staff of the
of the French Navy,	Imperial Russian Navy,
Signed: Aubert.	Signed: Prince Lieven.

APPENDIX C

THE FRANCO–ITALIAN AGREEMENTS (1900–02)[1]

THROUGHOUT the history of the Triple Alliance, the states which composed it indulged, sometimes with and sometimes without the knowledge and consent of their partners, in flirtations with other powers. At the outset one reason why Italy was obliged to sue for admission almost *in forma pauperis* was that, thanks to the recently formed League of the Three Emperors, of which she knew nothing, neither Germany or Austria felt pressing need of her friendship. By 1887, however, when the question of the renewal of the Alliance came up, this League had dissolved; Italy was therefore able to obtain better terms for herself. As for the various subsidiary agreements concluded by individual members of the Alliance with such humbler friends as Serbia or with neutral states like England and Spain, they were agreeable to all, for they represented a continuation of the same policy, and none of them were with powers regarded as possible enemies. But Bismarck's famous 'Reinsurance' treaty with Russia was a different matter. Not only its terms but its very existence were kept carefully secret from Germany's closest ally. When some years after its expiration the fact that there had been such a treaty was revealed to the world, the disclosure created an uncomfortable impression in Germany and a painful one in Austria.

[1] Ministère des affaires étrangéres. *Documents diplomatiques. Les accords franco-italiens de 1900–1902.* Paris, Imprimerie nationale, 1920. The essential texts of this Yellow Book were published in *Le Temps* of December 29, 1919.

An Italian Green Book, *Accordi italo-francesi (1900–1902)* (Rome, 1920), contains several of the texts; as does also Professor Edgard Rouard de Card's *Accords secrets entre la France et l'Italie concernant le Maroc et la Lybie* (Paris, 1921). The latter work includes further (P. 50) the exchange of notes respecting Libya and Morocco in 1912 (see p. 256, *infra*, and note 18), and (p. 51) "Déclaration signée le 9 mars 1916, entre la France et l'Italie, relative à la suppression des Capitulations dans la zone française de l'Empire chérifien."

In the quieter times that followed after the Dual Alliance had been formed and a balance of power established, conventions concerning particular subjects between separate members of the two great leagues were not uncommon; but though legitimate in themselves, they sometimes affected the relations of the partners to one another. The agreement reached in 1897 [2] between Austria and Russia in regard to Balkan affairs, supplemented by that of Mürzsteg in 1903, was an instance of the sort. Valuable as it might be to the peace of Europe by diminishing Austrian and Russian rivalry, it was looked at askance by Italy, who feared that Austria, secure on the side of Russia if not actually co-operating with her, might push with greater vigor interests and ambitions conflicting with Italian ones.

Meanwhile Italy herself, after years of estrangement from France, was drawing closer again. She was within her rights in so doing. Her allies could raise no objections to her bringing to an end in 1898 the tariff war between the two, which had done much harm to both countries, nor could they in 1900 object to her making a pact according to which she agreed not to oppose French aims in Morocco, in return for a similar promise by France in regard to Italian projects in Tripoli. Germany and Austria had already virtually approved of these projects in the existing treaty of the Triple Alliance. The terms of this Franco-Italian agreement were not published, and could not well be as long as either country remained on friendly terms with Turkey, the then legitimate possessor of Tripoli; but there was little concealment as to the fact of its existence, and none at all as to the reëstablishment of good relations between France and Italy, a reëstablishment which was welcomed by public opinion in both countries.

Displeasing as this new friendship might be to the allies of Italy and especially to Germany, they still were anxious to maintain the Triple Alliance. As the Italian government likewise desired to maintain it, it was renewed on June 28, 1902. But both sides had taken their precautions. On June 1 the Austro-German Alliance of 1879 had been indefinitely prolonged;[3] and on June 4 the Italian foreign minister, Prinetti, had informed the French that "in the

[2] Vol. I, *supra*, pp. 184–195.   [3] Vol. I, pp. 216–219.

renewal of the Triple Alliance, there is nothing directly or indirectly aggressive toward France, no engagement in any eventuality binding us to take part in an aggression against her, finally no stipulation which menaces the security and tranquillity of France." They were also told that "the protocols or additional conventions to the Triple Alliance, of which there has been much talk of late, and which would alter its completely defensive character, and which would even have an aggressive character against France, do not exist."

The "talk" of additional protocols may have owed its origin to the provisions, inserted in the treaty of 1887 as a separate document, by which Germany bound herself not only to support the territorial status quo in North Africa, but in case of war to favor Italian annexation of French territory. Since 1891 these provisions were safely imbedded in Articles IX–XI of the main treaty.

More important, however, than Prinetti's statement of June 4 was the exchange between him and the French ambassador to Rome, Barrére, on November 1, of notes in which, after repeating their promises in regard to Tripolitania and Morocco, they declared, among other things:

"In case France [Italy] should be the object of a direct or indirect aggression on the part of one or more powers, Italy [France] will maintain a strict neutrality.

"The same shall hold good in case France [Italy], as the result of a direct provocation, should find herself compelled, in the defence of her honor or of her security, to take the initiative of a declaration of war   I am authorized further to confirm to you that on the part of Italy [France] no protocol or military provision in the nature of an international contract which would be in disagreement with the present declarations exists or will be concluded by her."

With the recent publication of these papers, we are now for the first time able to appreciate the full difficulty of the position in which Italy found herself three years later, during the Moroccan dispute of 1905–06, and especially at the Conference of Algeciras. When matters there came to a vote, she took the side of France,

to the great anger of the Germans, who, however, did not think it politic to display their resentment. In spite, too, of a later cooling off of Franco-Italian friendship, and in spite of the renewal of the Triple Alliance in 1912, the promises exchanged in 1902 continued to be regarded as binding. This is shown by the reference to them in the exchange of notes in October, 1912, by which Italy and France, now that they were in possession of the coveted territories in Morocco and Tripolitania, undertook to refrain from "putting any obstacle in the way of the realization of all measures they shall deem it opportune to enact." This promise may still be useful some day, at least to France. It is perhaps difficult to reconcile the clause about "no protocol or military provision" in the notes of December, 1902, with the German-Austrian-Italian naval agreement of 1913 and its specific provisions as to just how and where the French Mediterranean fleet was to be attacked in the event of hostilities.

Finally, we can see that the clause about "direct or indirect aggression" furnished France with a strong claim for Italian neutrality in 1914, when Germany, without waiting for a hostile act or declaration on her part, launched an ultimatum at her as well as at Russia and precipitated the World War.

A. C. C.

1. Recapitulation of the Negotiations.

*M. Barrère, Ambassador of the French Republic at Rome,
to M. Poincaré, President of the Council, Minister
of Foreign Affairs.*[4]

Rome, le 10 mars 1912.

Les incidents récents qui se sont produits entre la France et l'Italie, les polémiques de presse auxquelles ils ont donné lieu, ont rappelé l'attention sur les rapports franco-italiens et réveillé certaines curiosités à l'égard des accords qui en sont la base et dont l'existence seule est connue avec précision du public. J'ai eu l'occasion d'indiquer à Votre Excellence, sur une question qu'elle a bien voulu me poser, dans quelle mesure on pouvait, selon moi, expliquer publiquement la valeur et la portée de ces accords, et plus particulièrement de celui qui porte les dates des 1 et 2 novembre 1902.

Il m'a paru qu'il était opportun de rappeler les conditions dans lesquelles ce dernier accord a été conçu, négocié et conclu par la Diplomatie française. Cet examen, qui résumera des pourparlers longs et souvent délicats, donnera au Département l'occasion d'embrasser par une vue d'ensemble le but poursuivi; il lui permettra en outre, en replaçant l'instrument diplomatique dont il s'agit dans les circonstances qui l'ont fait naître, de lui attribuer son sens exact, tant en ce qui nous concerne qu'en ce qui touche la position qu'il a faite au Royaume dans la Triple alliance et par conséquent dans la situation politique internationale.

Sans remonter trop loin dans le passé, on peut assigner pour point de départ aux pourparlers qui devaient aboutir en 1902 à l'accord secret la situation créée entre la France et l'Italie par la visite que fit à Toulon, au printemps de 1901, l'escadre italienne commandée par le Duc de Gênes. A ce moment, le rapprochement franco-italien était un fait accompli. Les négociations relatives à la Tunisie, l'arrangement commercial, la délimitation des possessions des deux pays dans la Mer Rouge, enfin l'accord

---

[4] *Les accords franco-italiens de 1900–1902*, no. 11, pp. 11–14.

1. RECAPITULATION OF THE NEGOTIATIONS.

M. Barrère, Ambassador of the French Republic at Rome,
to M. Poincaré, President of the Council, Minister
of Foreign Affairs.[4]

Rome, March 10, 1912.

The recent incidents which have occurred between France and Italy, the press polemics to which they have given rise, have called attention to Franco-Italian relations and have awakened certain curiosities in regard to the understandings upon which they are based and of which the existence only is definitely known to the public. I have had occasion to indicate to Your Excellency, in reply to a question which you were kind enough to put to me, in what measure, in my opinion, the value and scope of these understandings, and more particularly of the one which bears the dates of November 1 and 2, 1902, could be publicly explained.

It seemed to me that it was opportune to recall the conditions under which this last agreement was conceived, negotiated, and concluded by French diplomacy. This examination, which will summarize long and often delicate conferences, will give the Department the opportunity to comprehend in a single survey the object pursued; it will moreover permit it, by placing the diplomatic instrument in question back in the circumstances which gave it birth, to assign to it its exact sense both as respects ourselves and as regards the position into which it has put the Kingdom in the Triple Alliance and consequently in the international political situation.

Without going too far back into the past, we may assign, as the point of departure for the conferences which were to result in 1902 in the secret agreement, the situation created between France and Italy by the visit which the Italian squadron commanded by the Duke of Genoa paid to Toulon in the spring of 1901. At that time the Franco-Italian rapprochement was an accomplished fact. The negotiations relative to Tunisia, the settlement in commercial matters, the delimitation of the possessions of the two countries on the Red Sea, and finally the agreement relative to

relatif à la Tripolitaine et au Maroc, intervenu en décembre 1900, en avaient marqué les étapes. Ce dernier protocole était secret. Mais si on en ignorait le texte, on en connaissait l'existence. Il était désormais avéré que la France et l'Italie avaient dissipé entre elles les causes de trouble et de malaise, mis fin à la rivalité méditerranéenne en définissant leurs intérêts respectifs. Il leur restait, sur ce dernier point, un pas de plus à faire en précisant leurs intérêts à Tripoli et au Maroc, et en affirmant, d'une façon plus nette, leur désintéressement mutuel dans le sens indiqué par l'accord négocié avec le Marquis Visconti Venosta. C'était un des légitimes désirs de la politique italienne que d'arriver à cette entente complémentaire. La diplomatie française, qui le désirait de son côté, pour ce qui concerne le Maroc, jugeait qu'au moment d'engager la conversation, il y avait lieu de s'expliquer en toute amitié concernant l'avenir des relations des deux pays. Le présent était satisfaisant. Toutefois, l'existence de la Triple alliance lui donnait un caractére précaire. Pour assurer aux bons rapports rétablis une stabilité qui leur conférât tout leur prix, il fallait éclaircir le point de savoir si la Triplice était, sous la forme qu'elle possédait alors, compatible avec l'amitié franco-italienne.

En 1901, la Triple Alliance n'était plus ce qu'elle fut à ses débuts. Le texte méme du traité portant la signature de l'Italie n'avait pas été modifié. L'alliance demeurait défensive. Mais elle permettait une interprétation trés large des devoirs des Alliés: si la France, ouvertement provoquée, déclarait la guerre, l'Italie pouvait-elle considérer cette déclaration comme un acte défensif de notre part? C'était douteux. Bien plus, rien ne l'empêchait de dépasser le texte méme du traité, si elle jugeait que son intérêt politique le lui commandait.

C'est la connaissance de cet état de choses qui amenait le Dé-'partement et cette ambassade à conclure que, sous des dehors défensifs, la Triple alliance comportait un caractére éventuellement offensif qu'il convenait de faire disparaître dans l'intérêt de notre sécurité et des rapports d'amitié entre les deux pays. C'est dans cette voie que s'engagèrent les conversations, poursuivies

Tripolitania and Morocco reached in December, 1900, had marked its stages. This last protocol was secret. But if its text was unrevealed, its existence was known. It was henceforth established that France and Italy had dispelled from between them the causes of trouble and uneasiness, and put an end to Mediterranean rivalry by defining their respective interests. On this last point there remained a further step for them to take by defining their interests in Tripoli and in Morocco, and by affirming more clearly their mutual disinterestedness in the sense indicated in the agreement negotiated with Marquis Visconti-Venosta. It was one of the legitimate desires of Italian policy to arrive at this complementary understanding. French diplomacy, which on its part desired this so far as concerned Morocco, deemed that at the moment of beginning the conversation there was need of making in all friendliness mutual explanations concerning the future of the relations between the two countries. The present was satisfactory. The existence, however, of the Triple Alliance made its character precarious. In order to assure to the reëstablished good relations a stability which should confer upon them their full value, it was necessary to clear up the point of knowing whether the Triple Alliance was, under the form which it then possessed, compatible with Franco-Italian friendship.

In 1901, the Triple Alliance was no longer what it was at its beginning. The actual text of the Treaty bearing the signature of Italy had not been modified. The Alliance remained defensive. But it permitted a very broad interpretation of the duties of the Allies: if France, openly provoked, should declare war, could Italy regard this declaration as a defensive step on our part? It was doubtful. What is more, nothing prevented her from going beyond the actual text of the Treaty, if she should judge that her political interests demanded it of her.

It is the knowledge of this state of affairs which led the Department and this Embassy to conclude that, under defensive appearances, the Triple Alliance implied an eventually offensive character, which ought to be got rid of in the interest of our security and of the relations of friendship between the two countries. It is along this line that conversations, pursued in

parallèlement, à Paris par M. Delcassé avec l'ambassadeur d'Italie, et à Rome par moi-même avec M. Prinetti. Celui-ci, en butte d'ailleurs à des attaques allemandes, en vue de l'expiration prochaine du traité, était néanmoins porté à prendre une orientation définitive du côté de la France où le poussaient ses sympathies personnelles et une conception trés haute de l'avenir de son pays. Encouragé par des partisans déclarés de l'amitié franco-italienne, tels que MM. Luzzatti et Rattazzi, aussi par les sentiments bien connus de M. Zanardelli, président du conseil, par l'appui qu'il recevait de M. Giolitti, ministre de l'intérieur, par les exhortations du Marquis di Rudini, trés pénétré de la nécessité d'établir sur une base solide les rapports politiques généraux des deux pays en les consacrant par un accord mutuel, et par l'attitude du Baron Sonnino qui, des rangs de l'opposition, conseillait la consolidation des bons rapports avec la France, le Ministre des Affaires étrangéres affermit sa position et fut en mesure de causer avec moi de ce qui restait à faire pour établir une confiance mutuelle.

Le moment approchait d'ailleurs où la question allait devenir brûlante. Un an s'était écoulé depuis nos premiers entretiens. M. Prinetti devait se rencontrer à Venise avec M. de Bülow, ils parleraient certainement du renouvellement de l'alliance. Dans une conversation que j'eus avec lui au mois de mars 1902, il aborda nettement le sujet. M. Prinetti ne croyait pas possible de modifier le texte même du traité. Il se déclarait par contre prêt à nous donner des assurances de nature à ne laisser aucun doute dans notre esprit sur le caractére et sur la portée de cet acte. Il voudrait, disait-il; pouvoir nous le communiquer, mais cela lui sera impossible parce que la Triple Alliance porte sur d'autres points qui ne nous intéressent ni ne nous touchent. D'ailleurs ce n'est pas expressément dans le texte proprement dit du traité que figurait ce dont la France avait le droit de se préoccuper; c'était dans les actes annexes: "Ceux-là, ajoutait-il, devaient tomber et disparaître, car ils visaient des conjonctures qui ne pouvaient plus se produire."

parallel fashion, were entered into at Paris by M. Delcassé with the Ambassador of Italy, and at Rome by myself with M. Prinetti. The latter, exposed from the other side to German attacks in view of the expiration of the Treaty, was nevertheless inclined to take the side of France, to which his personal sympathies and a very high conception of the future of his country impelled him. Encouraged by declared partisans of Franco-Italian friendship, such as MM. Luzzatti and Rattazzi, as also by the well known sentiments of M. Zanardelli, President of the Council, by the support which he received from M. Giolitti, Minister of the Interior, by the exhortations of the Marquis di Rudini, who was strongly imbued with a sense of the necessity of establishing on a solid basis the general political relations of the two countries by consecrating them through a mutual agreement, and by the attitude of Baron Sonnino, who from the ranks of the Opposition counselled the strengthening of good relations with France, the Minister of Foreign Affairs took a stronger stand and was in a position to talk with me of what remained to be done in order to establish mutual confidence.

The moment, moreover, was approaching when the question was going to become a burning one. A year had elapsed since our first conversations. M. Prinetti was to have a meeting at Venice with Herr von Bülow; they would certainly speak of the renewal of the Alliance. In a conversation I had with him in the month of March, 1902, he specifically broached the subject. M. Prinetti did not believe it possible to modify the actual text of the Treaty. He declared himself ready, on the other hand, to give us assurances of a nature to leave no doubt in our mind as to the character and as to the scope of this document. He wished, he said, that he could communicate it to us, but this would be impossible for him, because the Triple Alliance bears upon other points which do not interest or affect us. Moreover, it was not expressly in the text of the Treaty, properly speaking, that the thing figured with which France had a right to be concerned; it was in the documents annexed. "These," he added, "must fall and disappear, for they looked forward to conjunctures which could no longer occur."

En rapportant au Département cette intéressante conversation, j'indiquais qu'elle ouvrait la porte à une négociation et à une entente. De son côté, M. Delcassé saisissait l'occasion d'un entretien avec le Comte Tornielli pour prendre acte des déclarations de M. Prinetti, relatives au renouvellement éventuel de la Triple Alliance, et lui indiquer que seule l'exécution des assurances qu'il nous avait données pouvait assurer aux relations des deux pays un long et fécond avenir.

Sur ces entrefaites eut lieu l'entrevue de Venise, au cours de laquelle M. Prinetti essaya d'amener le Prince de Bülow à modifier le texte du traité. Le Chancelier ne l'ayant pas suivi dans cette voie, M. Prinetti n'insista point.[5] Il lui apparaissait désormais que c'était dans une entente directe avec nous qu'il devait trouver le moyen de fixer à notre endroit l'interprétation que l'Italie entendait donner à ses obligations d'alliée. Eût-il réussi d'ailleurs qu'il ne pouvait nous suffire d'avoir communication du texte ainsi modifié; il était nécessaire qu'un engagement écrit mutuel nous donnât la certitude que le gouvernement italien n'entendrait pas modifier à nouveau la clause ainsi restreinte. Il fut bientôt décidé entre M. Prinetti et moi que le moment était venu d'aborder la discussion sur l'accord à intervenir, et j'allai à Paris m'entendre à ce sujet avec M. Delcassé. Sur ces entrefaites, comme le prochain renouvellement de la Triplice devenait de notoriété publique, M. Prinetti, sans attendre que nos accords éussent été conclus, crut devoir charger le Comte Tornielli de faire au Ministre des Affaires étrangéres de la République une déclaration de nature à rassurer le gouvernement français sur les dispositions de l'Italie envers notre pays. Cette démarche avait pour effet de permettre à M. Delcassé de pouvoir, sans en divulguer le texte qui devait rester secret, éclairer le Parlement sur la portée du renouvellement de l'alliance en faisant allusion à une déclaration spontanée du gouvernement royal ayant pour but de nous rassurer à cet égard.[6] Votre Excellence connaît cet important document qui détermine la valeur purement défensive de la Triplice à notre égard et qui constate "qu'il n'existe point" de protocole ou conventions annexes de nature à altérer ce caractére;

---

[5] Cf. pp. 127 ff., *supra*.   [6] Cf. p. 133, *supra*.

In reporting this interesting conversation to the Department, I indicated that it would open the door to a negotiation and to an understanding. On his side, M. Delcassé seized the occasion of an interview with Count Tornielli to take note of the declarations of M. Prinetti relative to the eventual renewal of the Triple Alliance, and to indicate to him that only the execution of the assurances which he had given us could assure to the relations of the two countries a long and fruitful future.

Hereupon, the interview of Venice took place, in the course of which M. Prinetti tried to bring Prince von Bülow to modify the text of the Treaty. The Chancellor not having followed him in this path, M. Prinetti did not insist.[5] It appeared to him thenceforth that it was in a direct understanding with us that he should find the means of fixing the interpretation with regard to us which Italy intended to give to her obligations as an ally. Moreover, had he succeeded, he could not have satisfied us by having the text thus modified communicated to us; it was necessary that a mutual written engagement should give us the certainty that the Italian Government would not undertake to modify anew the clause thus restricted. It was soon decided between M. Prinetti and myself that the moment had come to take up the discussion of the agreement, which was to come about, and I went to Paris to reach an understanding on this subject with M. Delcassé. Hereupon, as the approaching renewal of the Triple Alliance was becoming a matter of public notoriety, M. Prinetti, without waiting for our agreements to be concluded, felt impelled to instruct Count Tornielli to make to the Minister of Foreign Affairs of the Republic a declaration of a nature to reassure the French Government concerning the dispositions of Italy towards our country. This step had the effect of enabling M. Delcassé, without divulging its text, which must remain secret, to enlighten the Parliament as to the scope of the renewal of the Alliance by alluding to a spontaneous declaration of the Royal Government intended to reassure us in this respect.[6] Your Excellency is acquainted with this important document, which determines the purely defensive value of the Triple Alliance as respects us, and which records "that there does not exist" any protocol or annexed conventions

La déclaration visait le *renouvellement* et non le passé. Si donc des actes annexes inquiétants pour nous avaient existé, ils venaient de disparaître.

A mon retour à Rome, je repris les négociations avec M. Prinetti. Elles devaient aboutir bientôt aprés. La forme de lettres qu'a revêtue cet accord a été choisie pour ne pas donner à cet acte le caractére d'un contre-traité. L'Italie ne prenait, il est vrai, aucun engagement en contradiction avec ses alliances. Nous ne le lui avions jamais demandé. M. Prinetti a toujours affirmé que l'accord franco-italien devait être en harmonie avec les alliances telles qu'il les a renouvelées, et sans protocoles militaires. L'accord ne contredit nullement les devoirs de l'Italie. Il se borne à en préciser le caractère. Ce faisant, le Gouvernement italien n'a pas contrevenu à ses engagements envers ses alliés; il les a définis en ce qui nous concerne, en les interprétant dans l'esprit qui convenait à ses relations d'amitié avec nous; il a éliminé toute équivoque sur le caractére *défensif* de l'alliance par la définition du cas de provocation. En même temps, il s'est interdit de modifier à son gré, d'élargir dans l'avenir cette interprétation dans un sens défavorable à notre égard, sans que nous en fussions avertis et sous les conditions que déterminent les lettres échangées entre M. Prinetti et moi.

D'aprés le texte des deux principales lettres datées du 1er novembre, c'est le Gouvernement italien qui a pris l'initiative de nous interpeller, ma lettre étant une réponse à la sienne. Par contre, dans les lettres interprétatives de la provocation directe, c'est nous qui avons pris l'initiative de demander au Gouvernement italien de la préciser.

Enfin les lettres datées du 1er novembre débutaient par des déclarations relatives au Maroc et à la Tripolitaine. Ce n'était pas sans raison qu'on avait rattaché ces questions à l'interprétation de la Triple Alliance. On avait voulu justifier cette interprétation par l'importance qu'avait pour les deux pays ce règlement de leurs intérêts méditerranéens. Ainsi s'expliquait pour l'Italie le motif qui l'avait amenée à nous donner des assurances sur son attitude en cas de guerre franco-allemande. L'accord n'est pas,

of a nature to alter this character. The declaration looked to the *renewal* and not to the past. If, therefore, there had existed annexed documents disturbing to us, they had just disappeared.

On my return to Rome, I resumed the negotiations with M. Prinetti. They were soon to be concluded. The form of letters which covered this agreement was chosen in order not to give to this document the character of a counter-treaty. Italy took, it is true, no engagement in contradiction with her Alliances. We had never asked it of her. M. Prinetti always asserted that the Franco-Italian agreement must be in harmony with the Alliances, as he renewed them, and without military protocols. The agreement is in no way contradictory to the obligations of Italy. It confines itself to defining their character. In doing this, the Italian Government did not contravene its engagements towards its Allies; it defined them as regards us by interpreting them in a spirit suitable to its relations of friendship with us; it eliminated all ambiguity as to the *défensive* character of the Alliance by its definition of an act of provocation. At the same time, it precluded itself from modifying at will, from enlarging in the future, this interpretation in a sense unfavorable to us, without our being advised thereof under the conditions which the letters exchanged between M. Prinetti and myself determine.

According to the text of the two principal letters dated November 1, it is the Italian Government which took the initiative of putting the question to us, my letter being a reply to its own. On the other hand, in the letters interpretative of a direct provocation, it is we who took the initiative of asking the Italian Government to define it.

Finally, the letters dated November 1 began by declarations relative to Morocco and Tripolitania. It was not without reason that these questions had been brought together with the interpretation of the Triple Alliance. It had been desired to justify this interpretation by the importance which this adjustment of their Mediterranean interests had for the two countries. Thus as regards Italy the motive was explained which had led her to give us assurances about her attitude in case of a Franco-German war.

je l'ai dit, un contre-traité, mais il est une *contre-partie* de la Triplice.

A l'heure actuelle, aprés environ dix ans d'existence, quelle place occupent les accords de 1902 dans la politique franco-italienne? Il résulte de ce qui précéde que leur valeur est plus précieuse pour nous que jamais. Le texte en est si pressant, si formel, qu'il ne laisse place qu'à un minimum d'interprétation. Avant 1902, il pouvait suffire de mésintelligences sérieuses pour faire poser de ce côté-ci des Alpes la question de l'interprétation ou de la modification des Alliances dans un sens périlleux.

Telles sont, Monsieur le Président du Conseil, les considérations qui découlent d'un examen attentif de nos engagements mutuels de 1900–1902.

J'ai à m'excuser d'en avoir rendu l'énonciation un peu longue, mais il m'a semblé qu'elles méritaient d'être mises en lumiére.

Barrère.

2. EXCHANGE OF LETTERS CONCERNING MOROCCO AND TRIPOLITANIA.

(a)

M. Barrère, Ambassador of the French Republic at Rome, to His Excellency the Marquis Visconti-Venosta, Minister of Foreign Affairs of Italy.[7]

Rome, 14 décembre 1900.

A la suite de la conclusion entre la France et la Grande-Bretagne de la Convention du 21 mars 1899,[8] mon Gouvernement, répondant à votre honorable prédécesseur, eut l'occasion de lui donner, par mon intermédiaire, des éclaircissements de nature à dissiper toute équivoque sur la portée de cet instrument.

[7] *Les accords franco-italiens de 1900–1902*, p. 3, annex i to no. 1, which is a despatch from M. Barrére to M. Delcassé, French Minister of Foreign Affairs, dated at Rome, January 10, 1901. Also *Accordi italo-francesi*, p. 1, no. 1; *Accords secrets*, p. 45.

[8] The documents referred to here and subsequently are: Convention between the United Kingdom and France for the delimitation of their respective possessions to the west of the Niger, and of their respective possessions and spheres of influence to the east of that river, signed at Paris, June 14, 1898; together with a declaration

The agreement is not, I have said, a counter-treaty, but it is a *counterpart* of the Triple Alliance.

At the present hour, after about ten years of existence, what place do the agreements of 1902 occupy in Franco-Italian policy? It follows from the above that their value is more precious for us than ever. The text is so cogent, so explicit, that it leaves room only for a minimum of interpretation. Before 1902 it could have produced serious misunderstandings to raise on this side of the Alps the question of the interpretation or of the modification of the Alliance in a dangerous sense.

Such are, Mr. President of the Council, the considerations which spring from a careful examination of our mutual engagements of 1900–1902.

I must excuse myself for having made the exposition of them a little lengthy, but it has seemed to me that they deserve to be elucidated.

Barrére.

2. EXCHANGE OF LETTERS CONCERNING MOROCCO AND TRIPOLITANIA.

(a)

M. Barrère, Ambassador of the French Republic at Rome, to His Excellency the Marquis Visconti-Venosta, Minister of Foreign Affairs of Italy.[7]

Rome, December 14, 1900.

Following the conclusion of the convention of March 21, 1899,[8] between France and Great Britain, my Government, replying to your honorable predecessor, had the opportunity to give him through me explanations of a nature to dissipate all ambiguity as to the scope of that instrument.

completing the same, signed at London, March 21, 1899. They are to be found textually in *Parliamentary Papers*, 1899, cix, p. 837 (c. 9334); de Clercq, *Recueil des Traités de la France*, xxxi, p. 386; *British and Foreign State Papers*, vol. 91, pp. 38, 109, 110; vol. 99, p. 55; *Nouveau Recueil Général de Traités*, 2ᵉ série, xxix, pp. 116, 387; xxx, pp. 249, 264. The conventions of 1898 and 1899 were issued in French Yellow Books in those years.

Depuis, Votre Excellence a exprimé l'avis que ces assurances, réitérées d'une maniére plus explicite, contribueraient à affermir les bons rapports entre nos deux pays.

J'ai été, en conséquence, autorisé par le Ministre des Affaires étrangéres à faire connaître à Votre Excellence, en raison des relations amicales qui ont été établies entre la France et l'Italie, et dans la pensée que cette explication conduira à les améliorer encore, que la Convention du 21 mars 1899, en laissant en dehors du partage d'influence qu'elle sanctionne le vilayet de Tripoli, marque pour la sphére d'influence française, par rapport à la Tripolitaine Cyrénaïque,[9] une limite que le Gouvernement de la République n'a pas l'intention de dépasser et qu'il n'entre pas dans ses projets d'intercepter les communications caravanières de Tripoli avec les régions visées par la susdite convention.

Ces explications, que nous sommes convenus de tenir secrétes, contribueront, je n'en doute pas, à consolider, sur ce point comme sur d'autres, les relations amicales entre nos deux pays.

Barrére.

(b)

Marquis Visconti-Venosta, Minister of Foreign Affairs of Italy, to M. Barrère, Ambassador of the French Republic at Rome.[10]

Rome, le 16 décembre 1900.

La situation actuelle dans la Méditerranée et les éventualités qui s'y pourraient produire ont formé entre nous l'objet d'un échange amical d'idées, nos deux gouvernements étant également animés du désir d'écarter, à cet égard aussi, tout ce qui serait susceptible de compromettre, dans le présent et dans l'avenir, la bonne entente mutuelle.

En ce qui concerne plus particulièrement le Maroc, il est ressorti de nos entretiens que l'action de la France a pour but d'ex-

[9] Cf. Article IX of the third treaty of the Triple Alliance of May 6, 1891, Vol. I, p. 157, and the negotiations on the subject of the territories mentioned, pp. 99 ff., *supra.*

Since then, Your Excellency has expressed the opinion that these assurances, reiterated in a more explicit manner, would contribute to strengthen the good relations between our two countries.

Consequently, I have been authorized by the Minister of Foreign Affairs to inform Your Excellency, in view of the friendly relations which have been established between France and Italy, and in the belief that this explanation will conduce further to improve them, that the Convention of March 21, 1899, while leaving the vilayet of Tripoli outside of the partition of influence which it sanctions, marks for the French sphere of influence, in relation to Tripolitania-Cyrenaica,[9] a limit which the Government of the Republic has not the intention of exceeding; and that it does not enter into its plans to interrupt communications by caravan from Tripoli with the regions contemplated by the aforesaid convention.

These explanations, which we are agreed to keep secret, will contribute, I have no doubt, to strengthen, on this as upon other points, the friendly relations between our two countries.

Barrére.

(b)

Marquis Visconti-Venosta, Minister of Foreign Affairs of Italy, to M. Barrère, Ambassador of the French Republic at Rome.[10]

Rome, December 16, 1900.

The present situation in the Mediterranean and the eventualities which might occur there have been the subject of a friendly interchange of ideas between us, our two Governments being equally animated by the desire to eliminate, in this respect also, everything that would be susceptible of compromising, in the present and in the future, their mutual good understanding.

So far as concerns Morocco more particularly, it appeared from our conversations that the action of France has as its purpose

---

[10] *Les accords franco-italiens de 1900–1902*, pp. 3 f., annex ii to no. 1; *Accordi italo-francesi*, p. 1, no. 2; *Accords secrets*, p. 46.

ercer et de sauvegarder les droits qui résultent pour elle du voisinage de son territoire avec cet Empire.

Ainsi définie, j'ai reconnu qu'une pareille action n'est pas à nos yeux de nature à porter atteinte aux intérêts de l'Italie comme puissance méditerranéenne.

Il a été entendu également que, s'il en devait résulter une modification de l'état politique ou territorial du Maroc, l'Italie se réserverait, par mesure de réciprocité, le droit de développer éventuellement son influence par rapport à la Tripolitaine Cyrénaïque.

Ces explications, que nous sommes convenus de tenir secrétes, contribueront, je n'en doute pas, à consolider les relations amicales entre nos deux pays.

Visconti Venosta.

3. DECLARATION OF ITALY THAT "IN THE RENEWAL OF THE TRIPLE ALLIANCE THERE IS NOTHING DIRECTLY OR INDIRECTLY AGGRESSIVE TOWARD FRANCE." JUNE 4, 1902.[11]

(a)

Count Tornielli, Italian Ambassador at Paris, to M. Prinetti, Minister of Foreign Affairs of Italy.

Parigi, 4 giugno 1902.

Signor Ministro,

Ho l'onore di inviare qui acclusa a Vostra Eccellenza copia della dichiarazione che ho oggi rilasciata a questo signor Ministro degli affari esteri, giusta la istruzione di lei, circa il nessun pericolo che presenta per la Francia il rinnovamento della Triplice Alleanza, perché da essa è escluso quanto direttamente o indirettamente possa essere aggressivo contro la Francia stessa.

Il signor Delcassé mi espresse la più profonda riconoscenza del Governo francese per questa alta prova di lealtà che il Governo del Re dava della sua politica di pace.

G. Tornielli.

---

[11] *Les accords franco-italiens de 1900–1902*, no. 4 (contains (b) and (c)); *Accordi italo-francesi*, p. 2, no. 3 (contains (a) and (c)).

the exercise and the safeguarding of the rights which are the result for her of the proximity of her territory with that Empire.

So defined, I recognized that such action is not in our view of a nature to prejudice the interests of Italy as a Mediterranean power.

It was likewise understood that, if a modification of the political or territorial status of Morocco should result therefrom, Italy would reserve to herself, as a measure of reciprocity, the right eventually to develop her influence with regard to Tripolitania-Cyrenaica.

These explanations, which we are agreed to keep secret, will contribute, I have no doubt, to strengthen the friendly relations between our two countries.

Visconti-Venosta.

3. DECLARATION OF ITALY THAT "IN THE RENEWAL OF THE TRIPLE ALLIANCE THERE IS NOTHING DIRECTLY OR INDIRECTLY AGGRESSIVE TOWARD FRANCE." JUNE 4, 1902.[11]

(a)

Count Tornielli, Italian Ambassador at Paris, to M. Prinetti, Minister of Foreign Affairs of Italy.

Paris, June 4, 1902.

Mr. Minister,

I have the honor to send Your Excellency a copy, enclosed herewith, of the declaration which I have today given, according to your instructions, to the Minister of Foreign Affairs here: that the renewal of the Triple Alliance presents no danger for France, because there is excluded from it whatever could be directly or indirectly aggressive against France.

M. Delcassé expressed to me the deepest gratitude of the French Government for this highly loyal proof which the King's Government had given of its policy of peace.

G. Tornielli.

(b)

Autograph Note of M. Delcassé.

Le 4 juin 1902. :

M. le Comte Tornielli vient de me donner lecture du télégramme suivant, contenant la déclaration annoncée et dont, sur ma demande, il m'a laissé copie.

4 juin 1902, 4 heures du soir.

Delcassé.

(c)

Copy left by Count Tornielli.

J'ai été autorisé par S. E. M. Prinetti à communiquer à Votre Excellence un télégramme dans lequel le Ministre des Affaires étrangéres d'Italie me confirme que, dans le renouvellement de la Triple Alliance,[12] il n'y a rien qui soit directement ou indirectement agressif envers la France, aucun engagement qui puisse nous obliger en aucune éventualité à prendre part à une agression contre elle, enfin aucune stipulation qui menace la sécurité et la tranquillité de la France.

M. Prinetti désire également que je sache que les protocoles ou conventions additionnelles à la Triple Alliance, dont on a beaucoup parlé dans les derniers temps et qui en altéreraient le caractére complétement défensif et qui auraient méme un caractére agressif contre la France, n'existent point.

Le Ministre des Affaires étrangéres d'Italie exprime en méme temps sa ferme confiance que cette communication aura pour effet de consolider de plus en plus les bonnes relations existantes entre les deux pays et d'en assurer le développement fécond.

Cette communication est destinée à rester secréte.

---

[12] The negotiations for the renewal of the Triple Alliance were completed early in May, 1902, though the actual signing of the treaty was postponed until June 28. See p. 131, *supra.*

(b)

Autograph Note of M. Delcassé.

June 4, 1902.

Count Tornielli has just read me the following telegram, containing the declaration stated, and has left a copy with me at my request.

June 4, 1902.   4 P.M.
Delcassé.

(c)

Copy left by Count Tornielli.

I have been authorized by His Excellency, M. Prinetti, to communicate to Your Excellency a telegram in which the Minister of Foreign Affairs of Italy assures me that, in the renewal of the Triple Alliance,[12] there is nothing directly or indirectly aggressive toward France, no engagement binding us in any eventuality to take part in an aggression against her, finally no stipulation which menaces the security and tranquillity of France.

M. Prinetti likewise desires that I should know that the protocols or additional conventions to the Triple Alliance, of which there has been much talk of late, and which would alter its completely defensive character, and which would even have an aggressive character against France, do not exist.

The Minister of Foreign Affairs of Italy expresses at the same time his firm confidence that this communication will have the effect of strengthening more and more the good relations existing between the two countries and of assuring the fruitful development thereof.

This communication is meant to remain secret.

4. EXCHANGE OF LETTERS DECLARING THAT NO DIVERGENCE SUBSISTS BETWEEN THE TWO COUNTRIES AS TO THEIR RESPECTIVE INTERESTS IN THE MEDITERRANEAN.

(a)

M. Prinetti, Minister of Foreign Affairs of Italy, to M. Barrère, Ambassador of the French Republic at Rome.[13]

Rome, le 1er novembre 1902.

A la suite des conversations que nous avons eues touchant la situation réciproque de l'Italie et de la France dans le bassin méditerranéen, et touchant plus spécialement les intérêts respectifs des deux nations en Tripolitaine Cyrénaïque et au Maroc, il nous a paru opportun de préciser les engagements qui résultent des lettres échangées à ce sujet entre Votre Excellence et le Marquis Visconti Venosta, les 14 et 16 décembre 1900, en ce sens que chacune des deux Puissances pourra librement développer sa sphére d'influence dans les régions susmentionnées au moment qu'elle jugera opportun, et sans que l'action de l'une d'elles soit nécessairement subordonnée à celle de l'autre. Il a été expliqué à cette occasion que, par la limite de l'expansion française en Afrique septentrionale, visée dans la lettre précitée de Votre Excellence du 14 décembre 1900, on entend bien la frontiére de la Tripolitaine indiquée par la carte annexée à la déclaration du 21 mars 1899, additionnelle à la Convention franco-anglaise du 14 juin 1898.

Nous avons constaté que cette interprétation ne laissait subsister actuellement entre nos Gouvernements aucune divergence sur leurs intérêts respectifs dans la Méditerranée.

A l'occasion de ces pourparlers, et pour éliminer d'une maniére définitive tout malentendu possible entre nos deux pays, je n'hésite pas, pour préciser leurs rapports généraux, à faire spontanément à Votre Excellence, au nom du Gouvernement de Sa Majesté le Roi, les déclarations suivantes:

[13] *Les accords franco-italiens de 1900–1902*, no. 8; *Accordi italo-francesi*, pp. 2 f., no. 4; *Accords secrets*, pp. 48 f.

4. EXCHANGE OF LETTERS DECLARING THAT NO DIVERGENCE
SUBSISTS BETWEEN THE TWO COUNTRIES AS TO THEIR
RESPECTIVE INTERESTS IN THE MEDITERRANEAN.

(a)

*M. Prinetti, Minister of Foreign Affairs of Italy, to M. Barrère,
Ambassador of the French Republic at Rome.*[13]

Rome, November 1, 1902.

In continuation of the conversations which we have had concerning the reciprocal situation of Italy and of France in the
Mediterranean basin, and concerning more especially the respective interests of the two countries in Tripolitania-Cyrenaica
and in Morocco, it seemed to us opportune to define the engagements which result from the letters exchanged on this subject,
between Your Excellency and Marquis Visconti-Venosta, on
December 14 and 16, 1900, in this sense, that each of the two
Powers can freely develop its sphere of influence in the abovementioned regions at the moment it deems it opportune, and
without the action of one of them being necessarily subordinated
to that of the other. It was explained on that occasion that the
limit of French expansion in Northern Africa contemplated in
the abovementioned letter of Your Excellency of December 14,
1900, was fully understood to be the frontier of Tripolitania
indicated by the map attached to the Declaration of March 21,
1899, additional to the Franco-English Convention of June 14,
1898.

We noted that this interpretation left no divergence still existing between our Governments as to their respective interests in
the Mediterranean.

Profiting by the occasion of these conferences, and in order to
eliminate in a definitive manner any possible misunderstanding
between our two countries, I do not hesitate, in order to define
their general relations, to make of my own accord to Your Excellency, in the name of the Government of His Majesty the King,
the following declarations:

Au cas où la France serait l'objet d'une agression directe ou indirecte de la part d'une ou de plusieurs puissances, l'Italie gardera une stricte neutralité.[14]

Il en sera de même au cas où la France, par suite d'une provocation directe, se trouverait réduite à prendre, pour la défense de son honneur ou de sa sécurité, l'initiative d'une déclaration de guerre. Dans cette éventualité, le Gouvernement de la République devra communiquer préalablement son intention au Gouvernement royal, mis ainsi à même de constater qu'il s'agit bien d'un cas de provocation directe.

Pour rester fidèle à l'esprit d'amitié qui a inspiré les présentes déclarations, je suis autorisé, en outre, à vous confirmer qu'il n'existe de la part de l'Italie, et qu'il ne sera conclu par elle aucun protocole ou disposition militaire d'ordre contractuel international qui serait en désaccord avec les présentes déclarations.

J'ai à ajouter que, sauf en ce qui concerne l'interprétation des intérêts méditerranéens des deux Puissances, laquelle a un caractère définitif, conformément à l'esprit de la correspondance échangée, les 14 et 16 décembre 1900, entre Votre Excellence et le Marquis Visconti Venosta, les déclarations qui précédent étant en harmonie avec les engagements internationaux actuels de l'Italie, le Gouvernement royal entend qu'elles auront leur pleine valeur aussi longtemps qu'il n'aura pas fait savoir au Gouvernement de la République que ces engagements ont été modifiés.

Je serais reconnaissant à Votre Excellence de vouloir bien m'accuser réception de la présente communication, qui devra rester secrète, et m'en donner acte au nom du Gouvernement de la République.

Prinetti.

[14] Cf. Articles II and III of the fourth treaty of the Triple Alliance, Vol. I, p. 223.

In case France should be the object of a direct or indirect aggression on the part of one or more Powers, Italy will maintain a strict neutrality.[14]

The same shall hold good in case France, as the result of a direct provocation, should find herself compelled, in defence of her honor or of her security, to take the initiative of a declaration of war. In that eventuality, the Government of the Republic shall previously communicate its intention to the Royal Government, which will thus be enabled to determine whether there is really a case of direct provocation.

In order to remain faithful to the spirit of friendship which has inspired the present declarations, I am authorized further to confirm to you that on the part of Italy no protocol or military provision in the nature of an international contract which would be in disagreement with the present declarations exists or will be concluded by her.

I may add that — save as concerns the interpretation of the Mediterranean interests of the two Powers, which has a final character — in conformity with the spirit of the correspondence exchanged between Your Excellency and Marquis Visconti-Venosta, on December 14 and 16, 1900, as the preceding declarations are in harmony with the present international engagements of Italy, the Royal Government understands that they shall retain their full validity so long as it has not notified the Government of the Republic that these engagements have been modified.

I should be obliged if Your Excellency would be kind enough to acknowledge receipt of the present communication, which must remain secret, and to take note thereof in the name of the Government of the Republic.

Prinetti.

(b)

M. Barrère, Ambassador of the French Republic at Rome, to
M. Prinetti, Minister of Foreign Affairs of Italy.[15]

Rome, le 1ᵉʳ novembre 1902.

Par sa lettre en date de ce jour, Votre Excellence a bien voulu me rappeler qu'à la suite de nos conversations relatives à la situation réciproque de la France et de l'Italie dans le bassin méditerranéen et plus spécialement aux intérêts respectifs des deux pays en Tripolitaine Cyrénaïque et au Maroc, il nous a paru opportun de préciser les engagements qui résultent des lettres échangées à ce sujet les 14 et 16 décembre 1900 entre le Marquis Visconti Venosta et moi, en ce sens que chacune des deux puissances pourra librement développer sa sphére d'influence dans les régions susmentionnées au moment qu'elle jugera opportun et sans que l'action de l'une d'elles soit nécessairement subordonnée à celle de l'autre.

Il a été expliqué à cette occasion que par la limite de l'expansion française en Afrique septentrionale visée dans ma lettre précitée du 14 décembre 1900, on entend bien la frontiére de la Tripolitaine indiquée par la carte annexée à la déclaration du 21 mars 1899, additionnelle à la convention anglaise du 14 juin 1898.

Cette interprétation ne laissant, ainsi que nous l'avons constaté, subsister actuellement entre nos Gouvernements aucune divergence sur leurs intérêts respectifs dans la Méditerranée, et dans le but d'éliminer d'une maniére définitive tout malentendu possible entre nos deux pays, vous avez été autorisé par le Gouvernement de Sa Majesté à formuler spontanément certaines déclarations destinées à préciser les rapports généraux de l'Italie vis-à-vis de la France.

J'ai l'honneur d'accuser réception à Votre Excellence et de Lui donner acte au nom de mon Gouvernement de ces déclarations.

Je suis autorisé, en retour, à formuler de la maniére suivante les conditions dans lesquelles la France entend, de son côté, dans le méme esprit amical, régler ses rapports généraux vis-à-vis de l'Italie.

[15] *Les accords franco-italiens de 1900–1902*, no. 7; *Accordi italo-francesi*, pp. 3 f., no. 5; *Accords secrets*, pp. 47 f.

(b)

*M. Barrère, Ambassador of the French Republic at Rome, to
M. Prinetti, Minister of Foreign Affairs of Italy.*[15]

Rome, November 1, 1902.

By your letter of today's date, Your Excellency has been kind enough to recall to me that in the continuation of our conversations relative to the reciprocal situation of France and of Italy in the Mediterranean basin, and more especially to the respective interests of the two countries in Tripolitania-Cyrenaica and in Morocco, it seemed to us opportune to define the engagements which result from the letters exchanged on this subject between Marquis Visconti-Venosta and myself on December 14 and 16, 1900, in this sense, that each of the two Powers can freely develop its sphere of influence in the abovementioned regions at the moment it deems it opportune, and without the action of one of them being necessarily subordinated to that of the other.

It was explained on that occasion that the limit of French expansion in Northern Africa contemplated in my abovementioned letter of December 14, 1900, was fully understood to be the frontier of Tripolitania indicated by the map attached to the Declaration of March 21, 1899, additional to the English Convention of June 14, 1898.

This interpretation leaving, as we have noted, no divergence as to their respective interests in the Mediterranean still existing between our Governments, and with the purpose of eliminating in a definitive manner any possible misunderstanding between our two countries, you have been authorized by the Government of His Majesty to formulate of your own accord certain declarations intended to define the general relations of Italy towards France.

I have the honor to acknowledge receipt thereof to Your Excellency and to give you note of these declarations in the name of my Government.

I am authorized, in return, to formulate in the following manner the conditions under which France on her side intends, in the same friendly spirit, to order her general relations towards Italy.

Au cas où l'Italie serait l'objet d'une agression directe ou indirecte de la part d'une ou de plusieurs puissances, la France gardera une stricte neutralité.

Il en sera de méme au cas où l'Italie, par suite d'une provocation directe, se trouverait réduite à prendre, pour là défense de son honneur ou de sa sécurité, l'initiative d'une déclaration de guerre. Dans cette éventualité, le Gouvernement royal devra communiquer préalablement son intention au Gouvernement de la République, mis ainsi à méme de constater qu'il s'agit bien d'un cas de provocation directe.

Je suis autorisé également à vous déclarer qu'il n'existe de la part de la France, et qu'il ne sera conclu par elle aucun protocole ou disposition militaire d'ordre contractuel international qui serait en désaccord avec les présentes déclarations.

Il est entendu enfin que, sauf en ce qui concerne l'interprétation des intérêts méditerranéens des deux puissances, laquelle a un caractére définitif, conformément à l'esprit de la correspondance échangée les 14 et 16 décembre 1900 entre le Marquis Visconti Venosta et moi, les déclarations qui précédent et qui doivent rester secrétes, étant en harmonie avec les engagements internationaux actuels de l'Italie, auront leur pleine valeur aussi longtemps que le Gouvernment royal n'aura pas fait connaître au Gouvernement de la République que ces engagements ont été modifiés.

Barrére.

(c)

Definition of the word "direct" in the preceding.

(*1*) *M. Barrère, Ambassador of the French Republic at Rome, to M. Prinetti, Minister of Foreign Affairs of Italy.*[16]

Rome, le 2 novembre 1902.

Au sujet des déclarations que nous avons échangées par nos lettres en date d'hier sur les rapports généraux de la France et de l'Italie, il me semblerait nécessaire, pour éviter toute possibilité de malentendu, de préciser le sens et la portée qui doivent étre

---

[16] *Les accords franco-italiens de 1900–1902*, no. 9.

In case Italy should be the object of a direct or indirect aggression on the part of one or more Powers, France will maintain a strict neutrality.

The same shall hold good in case Italy, as the result of a direct provocation, should find herself compelled, in defence of her honor or of her security, to take the initiative of a declaration of war. In that eventuality, the Royal Government shall previously communicate its intention to the Government of the Republic, which will thus be enabled to determine whether there is really a case of direct provocation.

I am authorized equally to declare to you that on the part of France no protocol or military provision in the nature of an in ternational contract which would be in disagreement with the present declarations exists or will be concluded by her.

It is fully understood finally that — save as concerns the interpretation of the Mediterranean interests of the two Powers, which has a final character — in conformity with the spirit of the correspondence exchanged between Marquis Visconti-Venosta and myself, on December 14 and 16, 1900, as the declarations which precede, and which must remain secret, are in harmony with the present international engagements of Italy, they shall retain their full validity so long as the Royal Government has not notified the Government of the Republic that these engagements have been modified.

Barrère.

(c)

Definition of the word "direct" in the preceding.

(*1*) *M. Barrère, Ambassador of the French Republic at Rome, to M. Prinetti, Minister of Foreign Affairs of Italy.*[16]

Rôme, November 2, 1902.

On the subject of the declarations which we have exchanged by our letters of yesterday's date respecting the general relations of France and Italy, it would seem to me necessary, in order to avoid every possibility of misunderstanding, to define the sense and the scope which ought to be attributed to the word "direct" in the

attribués au mot "directe" dans l'expression "provocation directe" employée dans lesdites déclarations.

Je vous serais reconnaissant de me confirmer l'interprétation que comporte, dans votre opinion, le terme dont il s'agit.

Barrére.

(2) *M. Prinetti, Minister of Foreign Affairs of Italy, to M. Barrère, Ambassador of the French Republic at Rome.*[17]

Rome, le 2 novembre 1902.

Vous avez bien voulu m'exprimer, par votre lettre d'aujourd'-hui, le désir de voir précisés par moi, afin d'éviter toute possibilité de malentendu, le sens et la portée qui doivent étre attribués au mot *directe* dans l'expression *provocation directe*, employée dans les déclarations que je vous ai faites par ma lettre en date d'hier.

Je m'empresse de vous confirmer à ce sujet ce que j'ai eu l'occasion de vous dire de vive voix. Le mot *directe* a ce sens et cette portée, à savoir que les faits pouvant étre éventuellement invoqués comme constituant la provocation doivent concerner les rapports directs entre la Puissance provocatrice et la puissance provoquée.

Jules Prinetti.

5. EXCHANGE OF NOTES RESPECTING LIBYA AND MOROCCO. PARIS, OCTOBER 28, 1912.[18]

Le gouvernement de la République française [gouvernement royal d'Italie] et le gouvernement royal d'Italie [gouvernement de la République française], désireux d'exécuter dans l'esprit le plus amical leurs accords de 1902, confirment leur mutuelle intention de n'apporter réciproquement aucun obstacle à la réalisation de toutes les mesures qu'ils jugeront opportun d'édicter, la

---

[17] *Les accords franco-italiens de 1900–1902*, no. 10.

[18] *Revue générale de droit international public*, xx, Docs., p. 9; *Rivista di diritto internazionale*, vii, pp. 425–426 (1913). Italy signed substantially the same text with Spain at Rome on May 4, 1913, with reference to "Italy in Libya and Spain in her

expression "direct provocation" employed in the said declarations.

I should be obliged to you if you would confirm to me the interpretation which, in your opinion, belongs to the term in question.

Barrère.

(2) *M. Prinetti, Minister of Foreign Affairs of Italy, to M. Barrère, Ambassador of the French Republic at Rome.*[17]

Rome, November 2, 1902.

You have been kind enough to express to me, by your letter of today, the desire to see defined by me, in order to avoid every possibility of misunderstanding, the sense and the scope which ought to be attributed to the word *direct* in the expression *direct provocation*, employed in the declarations which I made to you by my letter of yesterday.

I hasten to confirm to you on this subject what I had occasion to say to you by word of mouth. The word *direct* has this sense and this meaning, to wit, that the facts capable of being eventually invoked as constituting the provocation must concern the direct relations between the Power provoking and the Power provoked.

Giulio Prinetti.

5. EXCHANGE OF NOTES RESPECTING LIBYA AND MOROCCO. PARIS, OCTOBER 28, 1912.[18]

The Government of the French Republic [Royal Government of Italy] and the Royal Government of Italy [Government of the French Republic], desirous of executing in the most friendly spirit their agreements of 1902, confirm their mutual intention of reciprocally not putting any obstacle in the way of the realization of all measures they shall deem it opportune to enact, France in

zone of influence in Morocco," A. di San Giuliano signing for Italy and Ambassador Pina y Millet for Spain. The text of the latter declaration is to be found in the *Gazzetta ufficiale* of May 16, 1913, and the *Bollettino ufficiale del Ministero delle Colonie*, i, no. 6, p. 295, and in *Rivista di diritto internazionale*, vii, p. 425.

France au Maroc et l'Italie en Libye [l'Italie en Libye et la France au Maroc].

Ils conviennent de même que le traitement de la nation la plus favorisée sera réciproquement assuré à la France en Libye et à l'Italie au Maroc [l'Italie au Maroc et à la France en Libye]: ledit traitement devant s'appliquer de la maniére la plus large aux nationaux, aux produits, aux établissements et aux entreprises de l'un et l'autre États sans exception.

Signé: Poincaré,
Tittoni.

Paris, 28 octobre 1912.

Morocco and Italy in Libya [Italy in Libya and France in Morocco].

They agree likewise that the most-favored-nation treatment shall be reciprocally assured to France in Libya and Italy in Morocco [Italy in Morocco and to France in Libya]: said treatment to be applied in the largest sense to the nationals, the products, the establishments, and the enterprises of both states, without exception.

(Signed) Poincaré.
Tittoni.

Paris, October 28, 1912.

INDEX

INDEX

Abbazia, conference at, between Goluchowski and Tittoni (1904), 137; between Berchtold and San Giuliano
(April, 1914), 178.
Abyssinia, 104, 105, 106.
Accord à trois, 107 f.
Adriatic, the, 5, 9, 15, 42, 47, 53, 54, 55,
60, 73, 78, 98, 115, 118, 123, 124, 134,
144, 149, 152, 157, 162, 168 f., 170, 175,
176, 180.
Aegean Sea, the, 55, 60, 79, 98, 123, 144,
155, 158, 165, note.
Aehrenthal, Aloys, Baron Lexa von,
Austro-Hungarian minister of foreign
affairs (1906–12), 140 f., 143–149, 151–
160, 165.
Africa, partition of, 121, note, 240, note,
249, 253.
Albania, 6, 9, 47, 70, 80, 115, 117, 121,
123, 124, 126, 135, 160, 161, 163, 164,
170, 172, 176 ff., 191, 203.
Albertone, Cavalier M., Italian military
delegate, 85, note.
Albricci, Major A., Italian military at-
taché, 174, note, 175, note.
Alexander I, prince of Battenberg, prince
of Bulgaria (1879–86), 46.
Alexander II, tsar of Russia (1855–81),
183, 184, 186, 187.
Alexander III, tsar of Russia (1881–94),
95, 206, 211.
Algeciras, conference of (1906), 135, 136,
note, 138, 139, 149, 229.
Algeria, 157.
Alps, the, 175.
Alsace, 95.
Ambrózy, Baron, counsellor of the
Austro-Hungarian embassy at Rome,
150, note, 169, note.
Andrássy, Count Julius, Austro-Hun-
garian minister of foreign affairs (1871–

79), 5, 11, note, 21, 41, 43, 184, 188,
note, 193, 199, 201, 203; life of, by
Wertheimer, 3, note.
Andrássy note, the (December 30, 1875;
presented January 31, 1876), 183, 193.
Antwerp, 166.
Arabs, the, in conflict with the Italians,
168.
Arco, Count, German diplomat, 49, note.
Arms and munitions, importation of, 189.
Asia Minor, 139, 158.
Aubert, Vice-Admiral, chief of the gen-
eral staff of the French navy, 223,
225.
Austro-German alliance of 1879, the, 5,
24, 42, 205.
Austro-Hungary, a member of the Triple
Alliance, 3–180; concludes an informal
league with Germany and Russia
(1872), 183; agreements with Russia
(1873–76), 183–204; alliance with
Germany (1879), 5, 24, 42, 205; league
with Germany and Russia (1881), 68,
105, 136, 183, 205, 226; Balkan agree-
ment with Russia (1897), 227.
Autonomy, principle of, 126, 193, 195.
Avarna, Duke of, Italian ambassador at
Vienna, 150, note, 152, 153, 165, note,
171.
Avlona, *see* Valona.

Balkan nations, the, 33, 42, 115, 120, 123,
124.
Balkan question, the, 6, 46 f., 50–56, 59,
61–73, 78 f., 82, 84, 92, 99, 105, 114 f.,
123–129, 136, 137, 149, 157–162, 167–
172, 174, 176–180, 183–203, 227.
Bardo, treaty of the (1881), 10.
Barrère, Camille, French ambassador at
Rome (from 1897), 115, 118, 139, 162,
228, 231–243, 248–257.

Lightning Source UK Ltd.
Milton Keynes UK
UKOW06f1833190416

272579UK00014B/233/P